french
conversation
DeMYSTiFieD

Demystified Series

Accounting Demystified

Advanced Calculus Demystified

Advanced Physics Demystified

Advanced Statistics Demystified

Algebra Demystified

Alternative Energy Demystified

American Sign Language Demystified

Anatomy Demystified

Astronomy Demystified

Audio Demystified

Biochemistry Demystified

Biology Demystified

Biotechnology Demystified

Business Calculus Demystified

Business Math Demystified

Business Statistics Demystified

C++ Demystified

Calculus Demystified

Chemistry Demystified

Circuit Analysis Demystified

College Algebra Demystified

Corporate Finance Demystified

Databases Demystified

Diabetes Demystified

Differential Equations Demystified

Digital Electronics Demystified

Earth Science Demystified

Electricity Demystified

Electronics Demystified

Engineering Statistics Demystified

English Grammar Demystified

Environmental Science Demystified

Everyday Math Demystified

Fertility Demystified

Financial Planning Demystified

Forensics Demystified

French Demystified

Genetics Demystified

Geometry Demystified

German Conversation Demystified

German Demystified

Global Warming and Climate Change Demystified

Hedge Funds Demystified

Investing Demystified

Italian Demystified

Java Demystified

JavaScript Demystified

Lean Six Sigma Demystified

Linear Algebra Demystified

Macroeconomics Demystified

Management Accounting Demystified

Math Proofs Demystified

Math Word Problems Demystified

MATLAB ® Demystified

Medical Billing and Coding Demystified

Medical-Surgical Nursing Demystified

Medical Terminology Demystified

Meteorology Demystified

Microbiology Demystified

Microeconomics Demystified

Nanotechnology Demystified

Nurse Management Demystified

OOP Demystified

Options Demystified

Organic Chemistry Demystified

Pharmacology Demystified

Physics Demystified

Physiology Demystified

Pre-Algebra Demystified

Precalculus Demystified

Probability Demystified

Project Management Demystified

Psychology Demystified

Public Speaking and Presentations Demystified

Quantum Field Theory Demystified

Quantum Mechanics Demystified

Real Estate Math Demystified

Relativity Demystified

Robotics Demystified

Sales Management Demystified

Signals and Systems Demystified

Six Sigma Demystified

Spanish Conversation Demystified

Spanish Demystified

sql Demystified

Statics and Dynamics Demystified

Statistics Demystified

Technical Analysis Demystified

Technical Math Demystified

Trigonometry Demystified

Vitamins and Minerals Demystified

french conversation
DeMYSTiFieD

Eliane Kurbegov

New York   Chicago   San Francisco   Lisbon   London   Madrid   Mexico City
Milan   New Delhi   San Juan   Seoul   Singapore   Sydney   Toronto

The **McGraw·Hill** Companies

Copyright © 2010 by The McGraw-Hill Companies, Inc. All rights reserved. Printed in the United States of America. Except as permitted under the United States Copyright Act of 1976, no part of this publication may be reproduced or distributed in any form or by any means, or stored in a database or retrieval system, without the prior written permission of the publisher.

1 2 3 4 5 6 7 8 9 10 11 12 13 14 15   WFR/WFR   1 9 8 7 6 5 4 3 2 1 0

ISBN 978-0-07-163544-8 (book and CD set)
MHID   0-07-163544-0 (book and CD set)

ISBN 978-0-07-163545-5 (book for set)
MHID   0-07-163545-9 (book for set)

Library of Congress Control Number: 2009942861

Trademarks: McGraw-Hill, the McGraw-Hill Publishing logo, Demystified, and related trade dress are trademarks or registered trademarks of The McGraw-Hill Companies and/or its affiliates in the United States and other countries and may not be used without written permission. All other trademarks are the property of their respective owners. The McGraw-Hill Companies is not associated with any product or vendor mentioned in this book.

McGraw-Hill books are available at special quantity discounts to use as premiums and sales promotions or for use in corporate training programs. To contact a representative, please e-mail us at bulksales@mcgraw-hill.com.

This book is printed on acid-free paper.

CONTENTS

INTRODUCTION

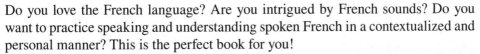

Do you love the French language? Are you intrigued by French sounds? Do you want to practice speaking and understanding spoken French in a contextualized and personal manner? This is the perfect book for you!

French Conversation Demystified is divided into three parts based on broad themes: "Meeting and Greeting," "Activities and Daily Life," and "Past and Future." Each of the three parts is subdivided into five or six chapters with more specific themes such as planning a trip in Québec or life in a French family. The first chapters focus on how to apply what you already know (French words used in English, such as *rendez-vous*, or cognates such as *nation*) in your quest to understand French and to get ready to pronounce natural French language. Subsequent chapters introduce new vocabulary driven by a theme as well as new structural and grammatical concepts. *French Conversation Demystified* is entertaining, with its myriad dialogues on practical and fun themes; it is also interactive and designed to help you speak with confidence.

The book aims to help the beginning-intermediate learner become familiar with French pronunciation and communicative vocabulary and structures. It stresses the speaking and listening skills necessary to engage in everyday conversation. To achieve this, the learner will listen to many short, sequential dialogues. The audio recordings on CD are complemented by written scripts in the book. The dialogues are based on everyday topics and take place mostly among friends and family members. However, we also introduce the formal register (**vous** forms) used for people outside this circle. Each dialogue is followed by a vocabulary list and a variety of written and oral exercises to practice specific vocabulary and skills. Grammatical structures embedded in dialogues are introduced as deemed necessary to support the overarching goal of oral communication. The ultimate goal is always natural conversation on a given theme. More advanced students may use this book to review oral communication skills on common everyday topics such as shopping, eating, traveling, studying, the daily routine, engaging in sports and entertainment activities. These practical communication skills, often overshadowed by the complex skills required in advanced French classes, deserve to be revisited and enjoyed at all levels of language acquisition.

In addition, the learner will find many explanations that aim to demystify cultural, lexical, and grammatical complexities or curiosities. For example, you will discover why there are two words for *bathroom* in French and how to use them. In every chapter you will meet interesting characters and become involved in their adventures. You will catch glimpses of francophone cultures in Europe and North America by traveling through Québec, France, and Switzerland.

How to Use This Book

French Conversation Demystified is sequential; it builds on knowledge acquired as you work through the book. So it makes sense to take a linear approach and start with Chapter 1. Those of you who have had some French before may prefer to focus on specific skills or vocabulary. Such learners may wish to use the Table of Contents to find specific sections for practice. However, since the book recycles learned language and skills, skipping to a later chapter may prove challenging, as it may be based on concepts you have not yet mastered. Thus it may be a good idea to skim briefly through the chapters and CD portions that precede it.

French Conversation Demystified is divided into three parts of five or six chapters each, for a total of sixteen chapters. Each chapter includes several conversations on a given topic; the recorded dialogues offer an opportunity to practice your listening skills while hearing native speakers interact. Follow-up to each conversation includes a variety of written and oral activities.

Oral exercises are accompanied by audio tracks linked to the companion CDs. They test speaking as well as listening skills: for example, you may be asked to listen and respond to questions, be an interlocutor in a conversation, listen to and demonstrate understanding of short dialogues, or translate from one language to the other. Even though the written exercises do not have an audio component, I urge you to say the answers out loud as much as possible. To provide visual support, some portions of the audio tracks that do not appear on the page and that may be challenging are found in the answer key in the back of the book. Audio materials appear primarily in the dialogues and oral practice exercises, as well as to present new language, as deemed appropriate. A single audio track may present a number of items in an exercise or a number of examples in a chapter. Don't forget to pause

between each excerpt to answer questions, repeat phrases and sentences, or role-play as directed.

Each chapter ends with a Chapter Practice section and a Chapter Quiz which will allow you to test your level of proficiency on this chapter's material. You may take the quiz open-book or closed-book style depending on your level of comfort. You should try to achieve a score of 80 percent or better before moving on to the next chapter.

Each part of the book ends with a 25-question Part Test that covers the content of that section as well as knowledge acquired in earlier chapters. You should try to get 75 percent of the questions correct before moving on to the next part. The Final Exam included in the book consists of 100 questions and covers everything in the book. The quizzes and tests will help you evaluate your progress and manage your own learning. The answers to the quizzes and tests are in the answer key in the back of the book.

CHAPTER 1

Using the French You Know

In this chapter you will learn:

Borrowed Words and Cognates
French Pronunciation: Vowels

Borrowed Words and Cognates

Looking at the dialogue below and the questions that follow, you can't help but notice they include many French words routinely used in everyday English, such as **cuisine**; these are called borrowed words. You'll also identify words such as **préférer** (*to prefer*) that share the same linguistic root in French and in English; these are called cognates.

MAKING PLANS FOR THE EVENING

In the following dialogue, Rémi and Sophie talk about what to do tonight. You will recognize many words borrowed from French. These will make the dialogue easy to understand.

 TRACK 1

SOPHIE: Dis, Rémi, on va à l'exposition d'art nouveau? — *Hey, Rémi, how about going to the art nouveau exhibit?*

RÉMI: Je préfère aller au restaurant. — *I prefer going to the restaurant.*

SOPHIE: J'ai lu une excellente critique du restaurant « Chez Antoine ». — *I read an excellent review of the restaurant "Chez Antoine."*

RÉMI: Ah oui! Leur chef a gagné le Prix du Cordon Bleu, tu sais. — *Oh yes! Their chef won the Cordon Bleu prize, you know.*

SOPHIE: On prend un apéritif avant de sortir? — *Should we have an aperitif before going out?*

RÉMI: Oui, je propose du champagne! — *Yes, I propose champagne!*

Oral Practice 1-1

 TRACK 2

Read and listen to the questions below, using the prompts in the right-hand column. After completing the answer, listen to the CD to see if it is correct.

1. Où est-ce que Rémi préfère aller aujourd'hui?   [*restaurant*]

   Where does Rémi prefer to go today?   [*restaurant*]

2. Comment est la critique du restaurant « Chez Antoine »?   [*excellente*]

   What is the review of the restaurant « Chez Antoine » like?   [*excellent*]

3. Qu'est-ce que Sophie propose avant de sortir?   [*un apéritif*]

   What does Sophie propose before going out?   [*an aperitif*]

CULTURE DEMYSTIFIED

French Words Used in English

The fact that numerous French words were incorporated into the English language is, in great part, the legacy of the Duke of Normandy, William the Conqueror, who invaded England and conquered the throne in 1066. At that time French became the dominant language imposed in England by the Normans.

---

4. Quel apéritif est-ce que Rémi propose?   [*champagne*]

   What apéritif does Rémi propose?   [*champagne*]

TALKING ABOUT FOOD

Some of the most frequently used French words and cognates in English pertain to food and eating. Look at the following examples and practice saying these words out loud:

café au lait	*coffee with milk*	omelette	*omelet*
crème brûlée	*custard dessert / flan*	pièce de résistance	*main dish / main course*
du jour	*of the day / today's*	quiche	*savory egg and cheese tart*
escargots	*snails*	sauté	*to fry lightly in a pan*
filet	*boneless cut of fish*	sorbet	*ice (fruit-flavored dessert)*
	or meat	soufflé	*puffed egg dish (dessert*
hors-d'œuvre	*appetizer*		*or savory)*

In the following dialogue, Rémi and Sophie dine at the restaurant "Chez Antoine." You will recognize many words, since English has borrowed them from French.

🔘 **TRACK 3**

SOPHIE: Regarde, Rémi, il y a toutes sortes de quiches et de salades sur la carte.

Look, Rémi, there are all sorts of quiches and salads on the menu.

RÉMI: Moi, je veux des escargots comme hors-d'œuvre et le bœuf bourguignon comme pièce de résistance.

I want snails for an appetizer and beef bourguignon for the main dish.

SOPHIE: Moi, je prends une salade et une quiche.

I am having a salad and a quiche.

RÉMI: Tu voudrais partager un soufflé au chocolat avec moi comme dessert?

Would you like to share a chocolate soufflé with me for dessert?

SOPHIE: Oui, mais j'adore aussi la crème brûlée.

Yes, but I also love crème brûlée.

Oral Practice 1-2

 TRACK 4

Read and listen to the questions below, using the prompts in the right-hand column. After answering, listen to the CD to see if your answer is correct.

1. Qu'est-ce que Rémi veut comme hors-d'œuvre?

   [des escargots]

   What does Rémi want as an appetizer? [snails]

2. Qu'est-ce que Sophie prend?

   [une salade et une quiche]

   What is Sophie having? [a salad and a quiche]

3. Qu'est-ce que Rémi veut comme dessert?

   [soufflé au chocolat]

   What does Rémi want for dessert? [chocolate soufflé]

4. Qu'est-ce que Sophie adore aussi comme dessert?

   [crème brûlée]

   What does Sophie also love for dessert? [crème brûlée]

SOCIAL LIFE

Many words borrowed from French and frequently used in English pertain to social life. Look at the following examples:

Le sujet de cette conversation est **banal**.

The subject of this conversation is banal.

Quelle idée **bizarre**!

What a bizarre/weird idea!

Un enfant gâté peut devenir **blasé**.

A spoiled child can become blasé.

Quelle veste **chic**!

What an elegant jacket!

Here are some additional borrowed words pertaining to social life. You may cover the translations on the right and later check to see whether you understood them. Practice repeating the words or expressions out loud.

blasé	*bored (due to indulgence)*	milieu	*class/circle of people*
cliché	*trite or common expression*	naïve	*gullible/naïve*
déjà vu	*previously seen or experienced*	petite	*small*
façade	*front / false front (of a building)*	rapport	*relation(s)/terms/rapport*
gauche	*awkward*	savoir-faire	*tact/know-how*

In the following dialogue, Rémi and Sophie have a tongue-in-cheek talk about a visit to Sophie's parents. You will recognize borrowed words related to social life.

 TRACK 5

RÉMI: Il faut rendre visite à tes parents ce soir.

We have to pay your parents a visit tonight.

SOPHIE: Oui, je veux garder de bons rapports avec eux.

Yes, I want to stay on good terms with them.

RÉMI: Oh, je serai suave avec ta mère et je porterai un costume chic pour ton père.

Oh, I'll be charming with your mother, and I'll wear an elegant suit for your father.

SOPHIE: Dans le milieu de mes parents, on observe l'étiquette sociale.

In my parents' circle, one respects social etiquette.

RÉMI: Ne t'inquiète pas. J'ai beaucoup de savoir-faire, ma petite Sophie.

Don't worry. I have a lot of savoir-faire, my little [dear] Sophie!

Written Practice 1-1

Complete each French sentence with the appropriate word or phrase.

1. Ce soir Rémi veut rendre _____ aux parents de Sophie.

2. Sophie veut garder de bons _____ avec ses parents.

3. Rémi va être _____ avec la maman de Sophie.

4. Les parents de Sophie observent _____ sociale.

COGNATES

In addition to actual French words and expressions incorporated into English, numerous French and English words share the same root and are therefore similar in spelling and meaning. Look at the following examples. You will easily make sense of them.

La **température** est quarante **degrés** F.   *The temperature is forty degrees F.*

Elle **adore l'automne**.   *She adores autumn.*

Look at the following cognates, cover the translations on the right, and check to see whether you understood them.

centre	*center*	long	*long*
concert	*concert*	musique	*music*
content	*content/happy*	théâtre	*theater*

Oral Practice 1-3

 TRACK 6

Repeat the following statements, covering the translations on the right. Then verify their meaning.

1. Rémi et Sophie aiment les concerts de jazz.   *Rémi and Sophie like jazz concerts.*

2. Ils adorent les expositions d'art.   *They love art exhibits.*

3. Sophie aime l'art moderne.   *Sophie likes modern art.*

French Pronunciation: Vowels

The many French words borrowed by English make up an arsenal of "free" vocabulary you may use as you learn and speak French. In addition, knowing these words allows English speakers to recognize certain pronunciation patterns and put them to use easily.

SIMPLE VOWELS

Simple vowel sounds in French make single sounds like the **a** in *father* or the **i** in *critique*. In this section you will practice those simple vowel sounds. Read each

VOCABULARY DEMYSTIFIED

False Cognates

False cognates are words that are written similarly in English and French but do not share a similar meaning. Beware of **faux amis** (literally, *false friends*) that do not mean what they appear to mean (in English). Here are a few common false cognates:

actuel(le)	*current/present-day*	librairie	*bookstore*
attendre	*to wait*	regarder	*to look*
caution	*deposit (money)*	travailler	*to work*
journée	*day*	vacances	*vacation*

word in your book, listen to its pronunciation on the CD, and repeat each word as you hear it.

 TRACK 7

a The phrase **faux pas** (*faux pas / awkward mistake*) and the word **cachet** (*cachet/prestige*) will remind you that the French vowel **a** is a single sound, as in the English word *father*. Repeat each of the following words containing this sound:

art	*art*	maman	*mom*
cachet	*cachet/prestige*	matin	*morning*

i The words **critique** and **mystique** will help remind you that the French vowel **i** as well as its homonym **y** represent the same sound as the *-ee-* in the English word *meet*. Repeat the following words that contain this sound:

bidet	*bidet*	mystère	*mystery*
boutique	*shop/boutique*	mystique	*mystique/mystic*

e and **eu** The expression **pas de deux** will help remind you that the French vowel **e** and the letter combination **eu** make a sound similar to the *e* sound in the English word *perk*. Note the softer **eu** sound before the French consonant **r**. Repeat the following words that contain these sounds:

demander	*to ask*	pas de deux	*pas de deux / dance for two*

But:

be**u**rre	*butter*	fle**u**r	*flower*

o The word **escargot** (*snail*) will remind you that the French vowel **o** makes a single, rather than a glided, sound. Repeat the following words that contain this sound:

loterie	*lottery*	sot	*silly*
mot	*word*	tôt	*early*

u The expression **déjà vu** will remind you that the French vowel **u** is a unique sound; it resembles an *ee* sound, but with the lips rounded. Repeat the following words that contain this sound:

obt**u**s	*obtuse/closed-minded*	t**u**nnel	*tunnel*
s**u**	*known*	v**u**	*seen*

ACCENTED VOWELS

Accented vowels in French make single sounds like the **é** in **cinéma**. In this section you will practice those accented vowel sounds. Read each word in your book, listen to its pronunciation on the CD, and repeat each word as you hear it.

 TRACK 7

é Words such as **café** or **cinéma** will help remind you that the vowel **e** with an **accent aigu** makes the vowel sound you hear in the English word *day*. Repeat the following words that contain this sound:

caf**é**	*coffee/café*	d**é**cembre	*December*
cin**é**ma	*cinema/movies*	th**é**	*tea*

è Words such as **crème** (*cream*) or **célèbre** (*famous*) will help remind you that the vowel **e** with an **accent grave** makes the vowel sound you hear in the English word *met*. Repeat the following words that contain this sound:

bi**è**re	*beer*	m**è**re	*mother*
c**é**l**è**bre	*famous*	p**è**re	*father*

ê Words such as **fête** (*party/holiday*) will help remind you that the vowel **e** with an **accent circonflexe** usually makes the vowel sound you hear in the English

word *met*, with the sound more drawn out. Repeat the following words that
contain this sound:

fenêtre	*window*	bête	*animal/beast*
fête	*feast/holiday/party*	prêtre	*priest*

ë and **ï**   Words such as **naïve** (*naive*) and **Noël** (*Christmas*) will help remind you
that a vowel with a **tréma** is pronounced as its own syllable, separately from the
vowel sound that precedes it. Repeat the following words that contain a vowel
accented with a **tréma**:

archaïque	*archaic*	naïve	*naïve/gullible*
maïs	*corn*	Noël	*Christmas*

When you see an **accent aigu**, an **accent grave**, or an **accent circonflexe** on vowels
other than **e**, don't worry about changing the pronunciation of that vowel. For example, in the expression **à la carte**, the accented vowel **à** is not pronounced differently
from the unaccented vowel **a** (as in **la**).

NASAL SOUNDS

Nasal sounds in French are special sounds that occur when a vowel is followed by
the letter **n** or **m** and the combination *vowel* + **n/m** is *not* followed by another vowel.
In this section you will practice those nasal sounds. Read each word in your book,
listen to its pronunciation on the CD, and repeat each word as you hear it.

 TRACK 7

i + **n** or **m**   The words **mer*in*gue** and **l*in*gerie** will remind you how to pronounce
this nasal sound, composed of the vowel **i** and the consonant **n** or **m**. Remember
not to pronounce the **n** or **m** in French. Repeat the following words that contain
the nasal sound **in/im**:

important	*important*	l**in**gerie	*lingerie*
impossible	*impossible*	mer**in**gue	*meringue*

e + **n** or **m**   The words **r*en*dez-vous** (*appointment/meeting/date*) and **double-
ent*en*dre** (*double meaning*) will remind you how to pronounce this nasal sound,
composed of the vowel **e** followed by the consonant **n** or **m**. Remember not to
pronounce the **n** or **m** in French. Repeat the following words that contain the nasal
sound **en/em**:

double-**en**ten**dre**	*double meaning*	long**temps**	*for a long time*
emporter	*to take away*	**ren**dez-vous	*appointment/meeting/date*

a + n or **m**   The words **mélange** and **champagne** will remind you how to pronounce this nasal sound, composed of the vowel **a** followed by the consonant **n** or **m**. Remember not to pronounce the **n** or **m** in French. Repeat the following words that contain the nasal sound **an/am**:

campagne	*countryside*	**pam**plemousse	*grapefruit*
manger	*to eat*	or**an**ge	*orange*

o + n or **m**   The words **sal**o**n** (*living room/salon*) and **cord**o**n** (*cord/sash*) will remind you how to pronounce this nasal sound, composed of the vowel **o** followed by the consonant **n.** Remember not to pronounce the **n** or **m** in French. Repeat the following words that contain the nasal sound **on/om**:

chans**on**	*song*	ball**on**	*balloon / volley- or soccerball*
l**on**g	*long*	t**on**	*tone*

u + n or **m**   There are unfortunately no common cognates, phrases, or words that contain the French nasal sound **un** or **um**. To remember how to pronounce this important sound, think of the English word *lung*, but do not pronounce the *n* or *g* sounds. In French, remember not to pronounce the **n** or **m**. Repeat the following words that contain the nasal sound **un/um**:

br**un**	*brown*	parf**um**	*perfume*
h**um**ble	*humble*	**un**	*one*

VOWEL DIPHTHONGS

In French, diphthongs are either the combination of a vowel and a consonant as in the nasal sounds you just practiced or the combination of two vowels treated as one sound. In this section, you will practice pronouncing some common vowel diphthongs.

 TRACK 7

au and **eau**   The words **rest**au**rant** and **nouv**eau (*new*) can help you remember that **au** or **eau** makes the same sound as the French sound **o**. Repeat the following words that contain this sound:

tabl**eau**	*painting/picture*	**au**tonome	*autonomous*
chât**eau**	*château/castle*	**au**berge	*inn*

ou The words **petit four** (*pastry*) and **du jour** (*today's / of the day*) can help you remember that the French diphthong **ou** makes the same, single sound as the English sound *oo*. Repeat the following words that contain this sound:

poupée	*doll*	route	*route*
soupe	*soup*	tour de force	*tour de force / feat*

ai The words **maître d'hôtel** (*maître d'*) and **chaise** (*chair*) help you remember that the diphthong **ai** followed by a pronounced consonant makes the same, single sound you hear in the English words *let* or *get*. Repeat the following words that contain this sound:

chaise	*chair*	maître d'hôtel	*maître d'*
anglaise	*English (feminine)*	spectaculaire	*spectacular*

The French diphthong **ai** followed by a silent consonant, as in the words **lait** (*milk*) and **mais** (*but*), makes the same sound as a French **é** (close to what you hear in the English word *day*). Important: Pronounce all French vowels as short and "clipped." The English word *day* is more drawn out and almost sounds like two syllables (*day-ee*).

oi The words **moi** (*myself*) and **voilà** (*there is/are*) will remind you how to pronounce this diphthong which sounds like the *wha* in the English word *what*. Repeat the following words that contain this sound:

moi	*me/myself*	savoir-faire	*savoir-faire/know-how*
patois	*patois/dialect*	voilà	*voilà / there is/are*

oy Similarly, the expression **bon voyage** (*have a good trip*) will remind you how to pronounce the diphthong **oy** which also sounds like *wha*. Repeat the following words and expressions that contain this sound:

Bon voyage.	*Have a good trip.*	royal	*royal/regal*

ui The words **cuisine** and **suite** will remind you how to pronounce this diphthong which makes the sound *wee*. Repeat the following words that contain this sound:

lui	*him*	oui	*yes*
nuit	*night*	tuile	*tile*

Remember that a final unaccented **e**, such as in the word **suite** or **tuile**, is not pronounced.

Chapter Practice 1

TRACK 8

Say each of the following words out loud before listening to its pronunciation on your CD.

1. les concerts de jazz
2. l'exposition
3. l'art moderne
4. la critique
5. le bon restaurant
6. le savoir-faire
7. les parents de Sophie
8. l'auberge

CHAPTER QUIZ 1

Say the following sentences out loud, and translate them into English. Then, listen to the answers on the CD.

TRACK 9

1. Sophie adore l'art nouveau et le jazz.
2. Rémi adore aller au restaurant.
3. Le restaurant s'appelle « Chez Antoine ».
4. Le chef a gagné le prix du Cordon Bleu.
5. Sophie propose un apéritif.
6. Rémi propose le champagne.
7. Au restaurant, Rémi veut le bœuf bourguignon.
8. Sophie veut la quiche et une salade.
9. Le maître d'hôtel est excellent.
10. Les parents de Sophie observent l'étiquette sociale.

CHAPTER 2

Meeting People

In this chapter you will learn:

Getting Acquainted
*French Pronunciation: Special Consonant Sounds and **liaisons***
Subject Pronouns and Stress Pronouns

Getting Acquainted

Laura is an exchange student meeting her host family for the first time. Listen to their greetings.

 TRACK 10

LAURA: Bonjour, Monsieur Lafange!   *Hello, Mr. Lafange!*

M. LAFANGE: Bonjour, Laura! Enchanté de faire ta connaissance. Comment ça va?	*Hello, Laura! Delighted to make your acquaintance. How are you?*
LAURA: Bien, merci, Monsieur.	*Fine, thank you, Sir.*
M. LAFANGE: Voici Josiane.	*This is Josiane.*
JOSIANE: Salut, Laura! Tu vas bien?	*Hi Laura! How are you?*
LAURA: Très bien, merci. Et toi?	*Very well, thank you. How about you?*
JOSIANE: Ça va. Je suis super contente de te rencontrer.	*I'm fine. I am super happy to meet you.*

FORMAL AND INFORMAL GREETINGS

In French, there are two ways people greet each other when they meet. When meeting adults for the first time or interacting with salespeople or restaurant or hotel personnel, it is customary to be formal. Therefore, with direct address, use a title such as **Madame** (*Mrs.*), **Mademoiselle** (*Miss*), or **Monsieur** (*Sir*) along with the formal **vous** (*you*). When meeting a child, a young person your age (if you are student age), someone you know well, or a relative, simply use the person's first name. In a familiar setting, when you say hello to someone, say either **Bonjour** or **Salut** (*Hi*) along with the person's first name. In a formal setting, say **Bonjour**, followed by the title, usually without the person's last name. In certain circumstances, the last name may also be used.

Oral Practice 2-1

 TRACK 11

In this exercise, look at each person's title or first name, then say hello to each of them appropriately. Use **Bonjour** (*Hello*) for a person with a title, but you may use **Salut** (*Hi*) or **Bonjour** with someone with whom you are on a first-name basis. Listen to the answers on the CD.

1. Monsieur   *Mr.*
2. Madame   *Mrs.*
3. Mademoiselle   *Miss*
4. Monsieur le professeur   *Professor* (*male*)
5. Madame le professeur   *Professor* (*female*)

CULTURE DEMYSTIFIED

Non-Verbal Greetings

In a formal situation, a verbal greeting is accompanied by a handshake. However, in an informal situation, people give each other two, three, or even four kisses on the cheek depending where in France you happen to be.

---

6. Laura	*Laura*
7. Josiane	*Josiane*
8. les copains	*male (or male and female) friends*
9. les copines	*female friends*

SAYING GOOD-BYE

Laura and Josiane are leaving the house to meet Josiane's friends.

 TRACK 12

JOSIANE: Laura et moi, on sort rencontrer des copains.	*Laura and I are going out to meet friends.*
M. LAFANGE: Oui, allez-y! Mais ne rentrez pas trop tard!	*Yes, go ahead! But don't come back too late!*
JOSIANE: À tout à l'heure, Papa!	*See you later, Dad!*
M. LAFANGE: Fais-moi un bisou avant de sortir, Josiane!	*Give me a kiss before you leave, Josiane!*

Oral Practice 2-2

There are many ways to say good-bye. Listen and repeat the following:

 TRACK 13

À bientôt, les copains.	*See you soon, guys.*
À ce soir, Monique.	*See you tonight, Monique.*

À cet après-midi, Lori.	*See you this afternoon, Lori.*
À demain, Madame.	*See you tomorrow, Madam.*
À lundi, Mireille.	*See you on Monday, Mireille.*
À tout à l'heure, Michel.	*See you in a while, Michel.*
À tout de suite, René.	*See you in a little bit, René.*
Au revoir, Monsieur.	*Good-bye, Sir.*
Salut, Maman.	*Bye, Mom.*

ASKING PEOPLE HOW THEY ARE

There are several ways to ask people how they are. Remember to speak to adults you have just met in a formal manner. Generally speaking, use the familiar forms to speak to friends and relatives.

Formal *How are you?*	Familiar *How are you?*
Comment allez-vous?	Comment ça va? *or* Ça va?

Here are typical responses to the question *How are you?* Notice the + signs that tell you how positive each response is.

Très bien, merci. + + + + +	*Very well, thank you.*
Bien, merci. + + + +	*Fine, thank you.*
Pas mal. + + +	*Not bad.*
Comme ci, comme ça. + +	*So so.*
Pas trop bien. +	*Not too good.*

VOCABULARY DEMYSTIFIED

Bonjour, bonsoir, bonne nuit, salut, **and** au revoir

The word **Bonjour** literally means *Good day.* It is the appropriate greeting to use all day until around six P.M. After that time, use the expression **Bonsoir** (*Good evening*). When it is quite late, and when you're leaving or going to bed, say **Bonne nuit** (*Good night*). As for *Good-bye*, you may say **Salut** or **Au revoir** in a familiar setting. Be sure to use **Au revoir** in a formal setting.

 Oral Practice 2-3

 TRACK 14

Ask each person listed how he or she is. Then, based on the number of +signs provided, give his or her likely response. Listen to the questions and answers on the CD.

Example: Éric + + + + +   Comment ça va, Éric? Très bien, merci.

1. Marc +
2. Isabelle + +
3. Gilles + + +
4. Christophe + +
5. Nathalie + + + +
6. Sophie +

French Pronunciation: Special Consonant Sounds and Liaisons

Although most consonants have the same sound in English and in French, a few French consonants show variations, exceptions, and special features. Here, you will also learn to link words by means of liaisons.

SPECIAL CONSONANT SOUNDS

 TRACK 15

c As in English, the consonant **c** can have both a soft and a hard sound. The French soft **c** sounds like the **c** in *citrus* and occurs before the vowels **e, i,** and **y.** The hard **c** sounds like the **c** in the English word *cool* and occurs before the vowels **a, o,** and **u,** as well as before another consonant. Repeat the following words with soft and hard **c** sounds:

Soft **c:**	mer**c**i	*thank you*	**c**ertain	*certain*
Hard **c:**	**c**as**c**ade	*cascade/waterfall*	**c**ontent	*content/happy*

ç The French consonant **c** with a *cedilla* (**ç**) appears before the vowels **a**, **o**, and **u**, and makes an **s** sound. Repeat the following words:

ça	*this/that*	garçon	*boy/waiter*
François	*Francis*	reçu	*receipt*

ch The French combination **ch** is a soft sound, like **sh** in *shoe*, when followed by a vowel. It is a hard sound and pronounced like English *k* when followed by a consonant. Repeat the following words:

Soft **ch**:	**ch**âteau	*castle*		**Ch**ine	*China*
Hard **ch**:	**ch**oriste	*chorister / choral singer*		te**ch**no	*techno*

g As in English, the French consonant **g** can have a soft and a hard sound. The soft **g** sounds like the *s* in the English word *pleasure* and occurs before the French vowel sounds **e**, **i**, and **y**. In all other cases, use the hard **g** as in the English word *egg*. Repeat the following words:

Soft **g**:	Geor**g**es	*George*	siè**g**e	*siege*
Hard **g**:	**g**oût	*taste*	**g**ris	*gray*

gn The French letter combination **gn** is pronounced like *ni* in the English word *onion*. Repeat the following words:

champa**gn**e	*champagne*	monta**gn**e	*mountain*	ga**gn**er	*to win / to earn*

h The letter **h** is *never* pronounced in French, regardless of where it appears. Repeat the following words:

Hélène	*Helen*	thé	*tea*	théorie	*theory*

j The French consonant **j** is the same sound as a soft **g**, like the *s* in the English word *pleasure*. Repeat the following words:

dé**j**à	*already*	**j**our	*day*	**j**oyeux	*joyous*

l The letter **l** is usually pronounced the same as in English. However, when it is part of a final **-il** or **-ille** syllable, it is pronounced like the *y* in the English word *yes*. Repeat the following words:

L sound:	fina**l**	*final*	**l**ac	*lake*
Y sound:	fami**ll**e	*family*	travai**l**	*work*

p and **ph**   The letter **p** is pronounced the same as in English. Be careful not to pronounce **p** with an "English" puff of air! The combination **ph** is pronounced like **f**. Repeat the following words:

phase *phase*	**Ph**ilippe *Philip*	télé**ph**one *telephone*

q and **qu**   The letter **q** and the combination **qu** make the same sound as *q* in English. Repeat the following words:

consé**qu**ence *consequence*	**qu**atre *four*	**qu**erelle *quarrel*

r   The consonant **r** has a very different sound in French than in English. It is pronounced at the back of the mouth or top of the throat. Repeat the following words:

amou**r** *love*	**r**esponsable *responsible*	**r**ouge *rouge/red*

s   This consonant sometimes sounds like the hard *s* found in the English word *soon*. However, between two vowels in French, it makes a soft **z** sound. Repeat the following words:

Hard **s**:	**s**age	*well behaved/wise*	**s**auci**ss**e	*sausage*
Soft **s**:	mai**s**on	*house*	u**s**é	*used / worn out*

t   The consonant **t** often sounds like the English *t*. Again, avoid the puff of air. When followed by **-ion**, **t-** makes a soft **s** sound. Repeat the following words:

composi**tion** *composition*	posi**tion** *position*	na**tion** *nation*

x   The French consonant **x** can have both a soft and a hard sound. The soft **x** sounds like the *x* in the English word *exam*, while the hard **x** sounds like the *x* in the English word *fax*. Repeat the following words:

Soft **x**:	e**x**ercice	*exercise*	e**x**amen	*exam*
Hard **x**:	e**x**tra	*extra*	ma**x**imum	*maximum*

LIAISONS

In French, final consonants such as **d**, **n**, **t**, **s**, and **x** are usually silent at the end of a word. However, they are often pronounced at the beginning of the next word when they precede a vowel sound. This is called a liaison. For example, the consonant **n** is silent in the word **un** (*one/a*) but pronounced before a word starting with a vowel sound (**un hôtel**). Repeat the following words and expressions:

TRACK 16

un canard	*a duck*	but	un-(n)-euro	*a euro*
un grand monument	*a big monument*	but	un grand-(d)-arc	*a big arch*
c'est moi	*it's me*	but	c'est-(t)-à moi	*it belongs to me*
des Français	*some French people*	but	des-(z)-omelettes	*some omelets*
aux champignons	*with mushrooms*	but	aux-(z)-asperges	*with asparagus*

The expression **Bon-(n)-appétit!** (*Enjoy your food!*) exemplifies the French **liaison** that links the final **n** sound of a word to the beginning vowel sound of the next word. Repeat the following words, and make the **liaison:**

Bon-(n)-appétit!	*Enjoy your food/meal!*	mon-(n)-amour	*my love*	un-(n)-hôtel	*a hotel*

The expression **un fait-(t)-accompli** (*a done deed*) exemplifies the French **liaison** that links the final **t** sound of a word to the beginning vowel sound of the next word. The final **d** sound of a word linked to the beginning vowel of the next word also makes the sound **t**. Repeat the following words, and make the **liaison.**

un fait-(t)-accompli	*a done deed*	tout-(t)-à fait *entirely*
un grand-(t)-amour	*a great love*	

The expression **vis-(z)-à-vis** (*face-to-face/opposite*) exemplifies the French **liaison** that links the final **s** sound of a word to the beginning vowel sound of the next word. This **s** sounds like the letter **z**. Repeat the following words, and make the **liaison.**

vis-(z)-à-vis	*face to face/ opposite*	des-(z)-amis	*some friends*	six-(z)-heures *six o'clock*

Remember that final consonants are usually not pronounced in a French word except for some words ending in **c**, **r**, **f**, and **l** (you can remember them as the consonants in the English word *CaReFuL*). Also, remember *never* to pronounce the silent letter **h** (as in **hôtel**).

Subject Pronouns and Stress Pronouns

Both subject pronouns and stress pronouns are important parts of speech in French. They are used to refer to people and things that have been previously mentioned. In addition, stress pronouns, as indicated by their name, help to emphasize a subject.

SUBJECT PRONOUNS

Subject pronouns are frequently used because they help conversations flow, avoiding the redundancy of naming people or things already mentioned. Once René has been named, he can be referred to as **il** (*he*). Similarly, once **le studio** has been mentioned, it can be referred to as **il** (*it*, replacing a masculine noun subject). Here are the French subject pronouns:

je/j'	*I*	nous	*we*
tu	*you* (singular, familiar)	vous	*you* (singular, formal and all plurals)
il	*he/it*	ils	*they* (masculine or masculine + feminine)
elle	*she/it*	elles	*they* (exclusively feminine)

The subject pronoun **on** takes on various meanings. It often means *one*, *they*, or *people* in a general sense, but it can also replace **nous** (*we*) in a familiar context.

On doit être honnête.	*One/They/People must be honest.*
On y va?	*Are we going?*

STRESS PRONOUNS

Stress pronouns serve various purposes in a French sentence. Here is the complete list:

moi	*I/me*	nous	*we/us*
toi	*you* (singular, familiar)	vous	*you* (singular, formal and all plurals)
lui	*he/him*	eux	*they/them* (masculine or masculine + feminine)
elle	*she/her*	elles	*they/them* (exclusively feminine)

Sometimes stress pronouns are used to emphasize a subject. In English, the stress is usually conveyed by voice only. Repeat the following French and English sentences. Note how the French sentence relies on the added stress pronoun at the beginning or at the end of the sentence rather than voice to convey the emphasis.

Moi, je parle français.	*I speak French.*	Tu parles français, **toi**?	*You speak French?*
Lui, il est gentil.	*He is nice.*	**Elle**, elle est charmante.	*She is charming.*
Nous, nous aimons la plage.	*We like the beach.*	**Vous**, vous aimez la musique.	*You like music.*
Eux, ils écoutent.	*They listen.*	Elles travaillent, **elles**.	*They work.*

Stress pronouns are also used after prepositions such as **pour** (*for*), **avec** (*with*), **devant** (*in front of*), **derrière** (*behind*), **chez** (*at/to someone's place*), **à** (*to*), etc. Look at the following examples:

Ariane travaille **pour moi**.	*Ariane works for me.*
Ce bracelet est **à toi**.	*This bracelet belongs to you / is yours.*
Je vais **chez lui**.	*I am going to his place.*
Elle est **devant eux**.	*She is in front of them.*
Il est **avec moi**.	*He is with me.*

VOCABULARY DEMYSTIFIED

Chez

There are two ways to say *home* or *to/at home* in French. One easy way is to simply say **à la maison**; another is to use the preposition **chez** followed by the name of the person or people or the appropriate stress pronoun. Look at the following examples:

Les Lafange sont **à la maison**. / Les Lafange sont **chez eux**.   *The Lafanges are at home.*

Laura arrive **à la maison** de Josiane. / Laura arrive **chez Josiane**.   *Laura arrives at Josiane's place.*

Josiane est **à la maison**. / Josiane est **chez elle**.   *Josiane is at home.*

In addition, many French restaurants have names such as **Chez Philippe** or **Chez Michel**. Such names traditionally identify the owner, giving the business a quaint feeling, as if you were to dine at Philippe's or at Michel's home.

Written Practice 2-1

Complete each sentence with the appropriate subject pronoun or stress pronoun.

1. Laura est la correspondante de Josiane. _____ arrive chez Josiane le 8 décembre.
2. Les parents de Josiane sont super! _____ permettent à Josiane de sortir.
3. Ils sont cool, _____ !
4. Les copains de Josiane! _____ sont contents de rencontrer Josiane.
5. Josiane rentre chez _____ à neuf heures.
6. Laura rentre avec _____ .

Chapter Practice 2

Use the appropriate word from the bank below to complete the sentences in each of the following dialogues.

Dialogue 1

bien / demain / pas / salut / toi / va

1. Laura: _____ , Jean-Luc. Ça _____ ?
2. Jean-Luc: Bonjour, Josiane. Ça va _____ , merci. Et _____ ?
3. Laura: _____ mal.
4. Jean-Luc: À _____ , Josiane.

Dialogue 2

bonjour / comme / comment / il / moi / oui

1. Mme Louis: _____ , Monsieur Rodas. _____ allez-vous?
2. M. Rodas: Ça va _____ ci comme ça, merci.

3. Mme Louis: Quel dommage! Venez chez _____ pour un café!

4. M. Rodas: Et M. Louis? _____ est à la maison?

5. Mme Louis: _____ , le voilà!

CHAPTER QUIZ 2

From the given choices select the appropriate greeting for the people shown.

Bonjour, Madame. / Bonjour, Maman! / Bonjour, Monsieur. / Bonjour, tout le monde! / Salut!

1. your friend Corinne _____

2. Mr. Charles, your professor at the university _____

3. a saleslady in a store _____

4. your mother _____

5. your friends _____

Complete the following dialogue.

6. Jean-Paul: _____ (*Hi*), Chantal. _____ (*How are you*)?

7. Chantal: _____ (*fine*), Jean-Paul, merci. Et _____ (*you*)?

8. Jean-Paul: _____ (*Not bad*) mais je suis pressé. _____ (*Bye*)

9. Chantal. _____ (*See you tomorrow*)!

CHAPTER 3

Who Is Who

In this chapter you will learn:

Describing People
Introducing People
Definite and Indefinite Articles

Describing People

In the following dialogue, Josiane and her friend Guy are leaving their class at the university. She sees a gentleman she does not recognize and asks questions about him. Listen to this conversation:

 TRACK 17

JOSIANE: Je suis curieuse, qui est le grand monsieur là-bas? Il a les cheveux gris; il n'est pas jeune.

I'm curious, who is the tall gentleman over there? He has gray hair; he is not young.

GUY: C'est le professeur d'anglais. — *That's the English teacher.*

JOSIANE: Il a l'air sérieux! Il est français? — *He looks serious! Is he French?*

GUY: Non, il est anglais! Dis, Josiane, viens au café rencontrer des copains! — *No, he is English. Say, Josiane, come to the café to meet some friends!*

JOSIANE: Je les connais? — *Do I know them?*

GUY: Non. Ils sont américains. — *No. They're American.*

JOSIANE: Super! Je veux les rencontrer. Comment s'appellent-ils? — *Great! I want to meet them. What are their names?*

GUY: Kevin et Nick. Ils sont vraiment sympathiques. — *Kevin and Nick. They're really nice.*

ASKING SOMEONE'S NAME

When talking about people, use **c'est** (*This is / It is*) to describe who the person is or what the person does for a living, but use **il/elle s'appelle** (*his/her name is*) to tell the person's name. Use **il est / elle est** (*he is / she is*) before any adjective that describes the person. Look at the following examples:

Qui est-ce? *or* Qui c'est? — *Who is this?*

C'est le professeur d'anglais. — *It's the English teacher.*

Comment s'appelle-t-il? — *What is his name?*

Il s'appelle M. Dupuis. — *His name is Mr. Dupuis.*

Qui est-ce? *or* Qui c'est? — *Who is this?*

C'est ma copine. — *She's/That's my friend.*

Comment s'appelle-t-elle? — *What's her name?*

Elle s'appelle Lisette. — *Her name is Lisette.*

When asking the names of several people, use one of the following expressions. Note that the written forms differ, but they are pronounced exactly the same as their equivalents in the singular:

Comment s'appellent-ils? — *What are their names?*

Ils s'appellent Marc et Nicolas. — *Their names are Marc and Nicolas.*

Comment s'appellent-elles?   *What are their names?*

Elles s'appellent Suzanne et Colette.   *Their names are Suzanne and Colette.*

In the following dialogue, Josiane is very curious, and Guy seems to know every-one. Listen and observe the changes that occur as they now talk about several people rather than one person.

 TRACK 18

JOSIANE: Qui sont les gars?   *Who are the guys?*

GUY: Ce sont mes copains américains.   *These are my American friends.*

JOSIANE: Comment s'appellent-ils et d'où sont-ils?   *What are their names, and where are they from?*

GUY: Ils s'appellent Nick et Kevin et ils sont de New York.   *Their names are Nick and Kevin, and they are from New York.*

JOSIANE: Qui sont les jolies filles?   *Who are the pretty girls?*

GUY: Ce sont des étudiantes espagnoles. Elles s'appellent Nina et Maria. Elles sont de Toledo.   *They are Spanish students. Their names are Nina and Maria. They are from Toledo.*

TALKING ABOUT NATIONALITIES

Adjectives of nationality follow the same rules as other French adjectives. They must agree in gender with the noun they describe, which means adding -**e** to the end of an adjective to make it feminine (unless the adjective already ends in -**e**). There is often a difference in pronunciation between the masculine and feminine forms of the adjective. Look at the following examples and repeat the French sentences:

 TRACK 19

Il est américain.	*He is American.*	Elle est américaine.	*She is American.*
Il est anglais.	*He is English.*	Elle est anglaise.	*She is English.*
Il est belge.	*He is Belgian.*	Elle est belge.	*She is Belgian.*
Il est canadien.	*He is Canadian.*	Elle est canadienne.	*She is Canadian.*
Il est espagnol.	*He is Spanish.*	Elle est espagnole.	*She is Spanish.*

Il est français.	*He is French.*	Elle est française.	*She is French.*
Il est haïtien.	*He is Haitian.*	Elle est haïtienne.	*She is Haitian.*
Il est marocain.	*He is Moroccan.*	Elle est marocaine.	*She is Moroccan.*
Il est suisse.	*He is Swiss.*	Elle est suisse.	*She is Swiss.*

In writing, do not capitalize the adjective of nationality in French. However, when it is used as a noun, the nationality is capitalized. Look at the following examples:

Le professeur est **anglais**.	*The teacher is English.*	C'est un **Anglais**.	*He is an Englishman.*
Josiane est **française**.	*Josiane is French.*	C'est une **Française**.	*She is a French person.*

Adjectives of nationality, like other adjectives, agree in number with the noun they describe, which means adding -**s** unless the adjective already ends in -**s**. Since a final -**s** is normally silent in French, the plural does not change the pronunciation of the adjective. Remember that a plural adjective remains in the masculine form when there is at least one male in the group described.

Kevin et Nick sont **américains**.	*Kevin and Nick are American.*
Josiane et Guy sont **français**.	*Josiane and Guy are French.*

Written Practice 3-1

Using the following cues, answer the question **Qui est-ce?** (*Who is this?*) for each person.

Example: Lisette / Josiane's friend / French: *C'est Lisette. C'est la copine de Josiane. Elle est française.*

1. Laura / Josiane's correspondent / American: _____
2. Guy / Josiane's friend / French: _____
3. Kevin / Guy's friend / American: _____
4. M. Dupuis / English teacher / English: _____

The French-Speaking World

There are many countries, regions, and island nations in the world where French is the official language or where it is one of the working languages. Some of these countries and regions are in North America (Québec, Louisiana), others are in Europe (Belgium, Luxembourg, Switzerland, and France), many are in Africa (Morocco, Tunisia, Algeria, Senegal, Côte d'Ivoire, etc.), some are in the Caribbean (Haïti, Martinique, and Guadeloupe), in addition to other places around the world. Feel free to use a bilingual dictionary to look up nationalities related to these Francophone regions.

CLARIFYING RELATIONSHIPS

In the following dialogue, Nick, an American student new in town, and his French friend Guy are at a party. Guy is trying to make Nick a part of his entourage by telling him about everyone.

 TRACK 20

GUY: Tu connais déjà Josiane. La voilà.

You already know Josiane. There she is.

NICK: Non, je ne connais pas Josiane, mais je sais que c'est ta copine. Mais qui est la fille brune avec elle?

No, I don't know Josiane, but I know she's your friend. But who is the brunette with her?

GUY: C'est Monica, la correspondante italienne de Josiane. Elle est en visite.

That's Monica, Josiane's Italian pen pal. She's visiting.

NICK: Et les deux filles rousses qui se ressemblent, c'est qui?

And how about the two red-haired girls who look alike, who are they?

GUY: Ce sont les inséparables jumelles Lili et Dara. Je ne sais jamais qui est Lili ou qui est Dara.

Those are the inseparable twins Lili and Dara. I never know who Lili is or who Dara is.

NICK: Je vois! Et le couple là-bas dans le coin? Tu sais qui c'est?

I see! And how about the couple over there in the corner? Do you know who they are?

GUY: Bien sûr! Ce sont Rémi et Sophie. Ils sont nouveaux mariés.

Of course! That's Rémi and Sophie. They are newlyweds.

NICK: Les deux jeunes qui dansent comme des fous, c'est qui?

The two young people who are dancing like crazy, who are they?

GUY: Tiens, je ne sais pas. Ce sont peut-être des copains de Bruno.

Well, I don't know. They may be friends of Bruno's.

NICK: C'est Bruno qui a organisé cette fête party, n'est-ce pas?

It's Bruno who's throwing this party, right?

GUY: Lui et son frère Nicolas.

He and his brother Nicolas.

NICK: Et où sont les parents de Bruno et de Nicolas?

And where are Bruno and Nicolas's parents?

GUY: Ah ça, je n'en sais rien!

That I don't know!

FAMILY AND FRIENDS

Describing a relationship often requires the use of the preposition **de**. Look at the following examples:

la correspondante de Josiane	*Josiane's pen pal*
la sœur jumelle de Dara	*Dara's twin sister*
le frère de Bruno	*Bruno's brother*
le mari de Sophie	*Sophie's husband*
la femme de Rémi	*Rémi's wife*
les copains de Bruno	*Bruno's friends*
les parents de Bruno et de Nicolas	*Bruno and Nicolas's parents*

Other useful nouns to describe relationships are as follows:

l'ami	*the friend (male)*	l'amie	*the friend (female)*
le collègue	*the colleague (male)*	la collègue	*the colleague (female)*
le patron	*the boss (male)*	la patronne	*the boss (female)*
le voisin	*the neighbor (male)*	la voisine	*the neighbor (female)*
le beau-père	*the stepfather/ father-in-law*	la belle-mère	*the stepmother/mother-in-law*

VOCABULARY DEMYSTIFIED

Connaître **and** savoir

Remember that the verb **savoir** is used to mean *knowing something for a fact* or *knowing how to do something*, while the verb **connaître** is used to mean *knowing or being familiar with a person or a place*. Look at the following examples:

C'est Josiane. —Je **sais**.	*This is Josiane. —I know.*
Tu **sais** parler français?	*Do you know how to speak French?*
Tu **connais** Josiane?	*Do you know Josiane?*
Moi, je **connais** bien Paris.	*I know Paris well.*

le cousin	*the cousin (male)*	la cousine	*the cousin (female)*
le fiancé	*the fiancé (male)*	la fiancée	*the fiancée (female)*
le grand-père	*the grandfather*	la grand-mère	*the grandmother*
l'oncle	*the uncle*	la tante	*the aunt*
le père	*the father*	la mère	*the mother*

DESCRIBING APPEARANCE AND PERSONALITY

In the previous dialogues, various people were described not only in terms of their nationality but also by their physical appearance and personality. Under each person or set of persons, study the adjectives that described them, and note how they agree in gender and number with the person they describe.

Le professeur	**Kevin et Nick**	**Josiane**	**Nina et Maria**
masculine singular	*masculine plural*	*feminine singular*	*feminine plural*
grand/anglais/sérieux	américains/sympathiques	curieuse	jolies/ espagnoles

PATTERNS OF MASCULINE AND FEMININE ADJECTIVES

For many adjectives, it suffices to add **-e** to the masculine form to make it feminine.

Il est grand./ Elle est grand**e**.	*He is tall. / She is tall.*	Il est énervé. / Elle est énervé**e**.	*He is / She is irritated.*

Il est petit. / Elle est petite.	*He is small. / She is small.*	Il est poli. / Elle est polie.	*He is / She is polite.*
Il est blond. / Elle est blonde.	*He is blond. / She is blonde.*	Il est brun. / Elle est brune.	*He is / She is brown-haired.*

However, there are a few exceptions to this pattern. Look at the following examples of adjectives that describe people in the masculine and feminine forms:

Adjectives Ending in -e

calme	*calm*
énergique	*energetic*
jeune	*young*
mince	*slim*

Adjectives Ending in -eux

ambitieux (-se)	*ambitious*
chanceux (-se)	*lucky*
heureux (-se)	*happy*
sérieux (-se)	*serious*

Adjectives Ending in -f

actif (-ve)	*active*
naïf (-ve)	*naïve*
sportif (-ve)	*athletic*
vif (-ve)	*lively*

Adjectives Ending in -l, -n, -s

cruel(le)	*cruel*
gentil(le	*nice*
gros(se)	*fat*
mignon(ne)	*cute*

There also are a few common adjectives with irregular feminine forms:

Il est **beau**. / Elle est **belle**.	*He is handsome. / She is beautiful.*
Il est **vieux**. / Elle est **vieille**.	*He is old. / She is old.*
Il est **fou**. / Elle est **folle**.	*He is crazy. / She is crazy.*

Written Practice 3-2

Describe each of the following people using the cues provided.

1. Josiane is tall, blond, and curious. _____
2. The lady is beautiful, calm, and nice. _____
3. Nick is young, athletic, and ambitious. _____
4. Bruno's brother is tall, blond, and nice. _____
5. Bruno's mother is short, intelligent, and lively. She has black hair. _____
6. Rémi, Sophie's husband, is handsome and lucky. _____

Describing Size and Hair Color in French

When describing someone's appearance, the most common features are size and hair color. With regard to size, remember that **petit** means *small* (not necessarily *petite* meaning *slim*), and **grand** means *tall* (not necessarily *big* meaning *heavy-set*).

When hair color is blond or brown, use **il/elle est** (*he/she is*) followed by the adjective **blond(e)** or **brun(e)**; if it is other than blond or brown, use the phrase **il/elle a les cheveux...** (*his/her hair is . . .*), followed by the appropriate color word in the plural form: **gris** (*gray*), **noirs** (*black*), **roux** (*red*).

Introducing People

In the following dialogue, Josiane meets Guy's American friends who are studying in France. Listen to their introductions:

TRACK 21

KEVIN: Bonjour. Je m'appelle Kevin et je viens de New York.

Hello. My name is Kevin, and I come from New York.

JOSIANE: Bonjour, Kevin. Moi, je suis parisienne, mais je parle anglais.

Hello, Kevin. I am from Paris, but I speak English.

KEVIN: Super! Mais moi, j'adore parler français, surtout avec une Française.

Great! But I love to speak French, especially with a French girl.

NICK: Bonjour, Josiane. Moi, je veux bien te parler en anglais.

Hello Josiane. I would be happy to speak to you in English.

JOSIANE: Et comment t'appelles-tu, toi?

And what's your name?

NICK: Moi, c'est Nick! Enchanté!

I'm Nick! Delighted [to meet you]!

ORIGINS AND NAMES

When asking someone *Where are you from?* use one of the following phrases, and be careful to use the correct register: familiar or formal. Don't forget that **vous** is *always* used when you address more than one person.

Familiar	**Formal or Plural**
Tu es d'où? *or* D'où es-tu?	Vous êtes d'où? *or* D'où êtes-vous?
Tu viens d'où? *or* D'où viens-tu?	Vous venez d'où? *or* D'où venez-vous?

When answering the question *Where are you from?* use **Je suis de...** (*I am from . . .*) or **Je viens de...** (*I come from . . .*), or simply state your citizenship. Look at this example:

Je suis de Miami. Je viens de Miami. Je suis américaine.	*I am from Miami. I come from Miami. I am American.*
Je suis parisienne. Je viens de Paris. Je suis française.	*I am Parisian. I come from Paris. I am French.*

Remember to use **tu** (*you,* familiar or informal) when speaking to a friend or relative but use **vous** (*you,* formal) with an adult you just met. Also, remember to use **vous** any time you speak to more than one person.

In French, there are several ways to ask the same question. For example, the subject may come *before* the verb (for a more familiar tone) or *after* the verb (in the so-called inverted form). Look at the following examples:

Familiar	**Formal or Plural**
Comment t'appelles-tu?	Comment vous appelez-vous?
What is your name?	*What is your name?* or *What are your names?*
Comment tu t'appelles?	Comment vous vous appelez?
What is your name?	*What is your name?* or *What are your names?*

People in service occupations, such as hotel, post office, or bank clerks will ask your name this way: **Votre nom, s'il vous plaît?** (*Your name please?*)

VOCABULARY DEMYSTIFIED

Adjectives of Nationality Derived from Names of Cities

When people come from major cities like Paris or Québec City, they can often be described with an adjective derived from the name of the city. These adjectives, like other adjectives of nationality, have a masculine, feminine, and two plural forms. A male from Paris is **parisien**, a female is **parisienne**, and together they are **parisiens**; two females are **parisiennes**. A male from Québec City is **québécois**, a female is **québécoise**, and together they are **québécois**; two females from Québec are **québécoises**.

Oral Practice 3-1

 TRACK 22

Consider the following scenarios where people meet. Repeat the question and the answer in each scenario. Note that in familiar settings, we will use the question structure with the subject before the verb.

Two Teenagers

NICOLAS: Comment tu t'appelles?

LUC: Je m'appelle Luc.

NICOLAS: Tu es d'où?

LUC: Je suis parisien.

Manager and New Employee

LE MANAGER: Comment vous appelez-vous?

L'EMPLOYÉE: Je m'appelle Madame Selat.

LE MANAGER: Vous êtes d'où?

L'EMPLOYÉE: Je suis de Cannes.

Hotel Receptionist and Guest

LA RÉCEPTIONNISTE: Votre nom, s'il vous plaît?

LE CLIENT: Monsieur Verre.

LA RÉCEPTIONNISTE: D'où êtes-vous, Monsieur?

LE CLIENT: Je suis québécois.

Two Women Introducing Themselves

MME SOUCI: Je suis Madame Souci. Et vous?

MME TONKA: Je suis Madame Tonka.

EXCHANGING CONTACT INFORMATION

To ask for a telephone number or an address, use the following questions. Remember to use **ton** (*your*) if you are on a familiar basis; use **votre** (*your*) if your relationship is formal.

Quel est ton/votre numéro de téléphone?	*What is your phone number?*
Quelle est ton/votre adresse (e-mail)?	*What is your (e-mail) address?*

To give a telephone number or an address, use the following expressions:

Mon numéro de téléphone / Mon adresse / Mon adresse e-mail est...	*My phone number / My address / My e-mail address is . . .*

Definite and Indefinite Articles

Definite articles (in English, *the*) as well as *indefinite* articles (in English, *a/an/some*) change according to the gender and number of the noun they accompany. In French, there are three different words for the English article *the* before a singular noun.

The definite article **le** precedes a masculine noun starting with a consonant: *le* **monsieur** (*the gentleman*). The article **la** precedes a feminine noun starting with a consonant: *la* **dame** (*the woman/lady*). The article **l'** precedes both masculine and feminine singular nouns starting with a vowel or vowel sound: *l'***orange** (*f.*), **l'appartement** (*m.*), **l'hôtel** (*m.*) (*the hotel*). In the plural, there is only one definite article (for both genders and preceding both consonant and vowel sounds): *les* **dames**, *les* **hôtels**.

There are two singular *indefinite* articles: *un* **monsieur** (*a gentleman*), *une* **dame** (*a lady*) and one plural indefinite article: *des* **dames** (*some ladies*).

For people, the gender of a noun depends on the sex of the person. Objects, by convention, also have either masculine or feminine gender. Look at the following examples:

le copain	*the friend (m.)*	**un** copain	*a friend (m.)*	**les/des** copains	*the/some friends*
la copine	*the friend (f.)*	**une** copine	*a friend (f.)*	**les/des** copines	*the/some friends*
l'hôtel (*m.*)	*the hotel*	**un** hôtel	*a hotel*	**les/des** hôtels	*the/some hotels*
l'eau (*f.*)	*the water*	**une** eau	*a water*	**les/des** eaux	*the/some waters*

To use the correct definite or indefinite singular article, you will always need to know the gender of the noun. Many nouns can be memorized along with their gender; for others, you may use a bilingual dictionary. There are also some useful rules of thumb to help you come up with the gender: (1) nouns are feminine if they end in -**tion** or -**sion** and they are usually feminine if they end in -**e** (But beware! There are many exceptions to the -**e** ending rule!); (2) nouns ending in -**al**, -**eau**, and -**eur** are usually masculine.

Chapter Practice 3

The following dialogue lines are out of sequence. Place a number from 1 to 10 on the line provided to show the correct order of the lines. Éric speaks first.

_____ Je suis québécois.

_____ Tu es d'où, Jean-Paul?

_____ Super. Et ton copain?

_____ Il est québécois aussi. Il vient de Montréal.

_____ Moi, je m'appelle Jean-Paul.

_____ C'est le 03-55-39-41.

_____ Quel est ton numéro de téléphone?

_____ Bonjour, je m'appelle Éric. Et toi, comment tu t'appelles?

_____ Salut, les gars. À bientôt.

_____ Au revoir, Éric!

CHAPTER QUIZ 3

Select the appropriate answer for each question.

1. _____ Comment ça va?

2. _____ Comment s'appelle-t-il?

3. _____ Il est américain?

4. _____ Comment allez-vous?

5. _____ Comment est Josiane?
Elle est...

6. _____ Comment s'appelle la
copine de Josiane?

7. _____ Il est du Maroc? Oui,
il est...

8. _____ Le monsieur est
sympathique?

9. _____ Vous venez d'où,
Madame? Je suis...

10. _____ Votre nom, s'il vous
plaît, Monsieur?

a. Au revoir. / Enchanté. / Bien, merci.

b. Pascal / Mademoiselle Célibat /
Josiane

c. Oui, de San Francisco. / Oui,
parisien. / Non, new-yorkais.

d. Merci, oui. / Pas très bien. / Salut.

e. blond/brune/petit.

f. Il/Elle/On s'appelle Lisette.

g. marocain/sympathique/gros.

h. Oui, il est sérieux. / Elle est gentille.
/ Ils sont sympathiques.

i. canadien/canadienne/canadiens.

j. C'est Dubois. / Je suis anglais. / Il
s'appelle Tatin.

CHAPTER 4

Getting to Know Someone

In this chapter you will learn:

Talking About What People Do

In this dialogue, Nick and Lili have just met. Note how both use the question **Qu'est-ce que tu fais?**

●► TRACK 23

LILI: Qu'est-ce que tu fais à Paris, Nick?	*What do you do in Paris, Nick?*
NICK: J'étudie le droit international.	*I am studying international law.*
LILI: Dara étudie le droit aussi, tu sais!	*Dara studies law too, you know!*
NICK: Quelle sorte de droit est-ce qu'elle préfère?	*What kind of law does she prefer?*
LILI: Pour l'instant, elle voudrait être notaire.	*For the moment, she would like to be a contract lawyer.*
NICK: Et toi, Lili, qu'est-ce que tu fais?	*And you, Lili, what do you do?*
LILI: Moi, je fais des études de commerce!	*I'm studying business!*
NICK: Et qu'est-ce que tu voudrais faire après tes études?	*And what would you like to do after your studies?*
LILI: En fait, mon rêve c'est d'ouvrir une boutique pour femmes.	*Actually, my dream is to open a boutique for women.*
NICK: Chouette! Tu vas vendre des vêtements?	*Great! Are you going to sell clothes?*
LILI: Pas seulement des vêtements, mais aussi des parfums, des bijoux et des accessoires.	*Not only clothes but also perfume, jewelry, and accessories.*
NICK: J'espère que ton rêve va se réaliser.	*I hope your dream comes true.*

ASKING WHAT PEOPLE STUDY

Even though **Qu'est-ce que tu fais?** may be used to ask *What are you doing?* in the literal sense, it is also used to ask what someone is studying or what his or her job is. To learn how to answer the question, look at the following examples:

J'étudie le droit. / Je fais des études de droit.	*I am studying law.*
J'étudie le commerce. / Je fais des études de commerce.	*I am studying business.*

J'étudie la médecine. / Je fais des études de médecine.	*I am studying medicine.*
J'étudie le journalisme. / Je fais des études de journalisme.	*I am studying journalism.*
J'étudie la littérature. / Je fais des études de littérature.	*I am studying literature.*

Oral Practice 4-1

After listening to the following French students say which higher education school (**faculté** or **fac**) they attend, pause the CD, and say what studies they pursue in two different ways, as previously illustrated. Then listen to your CD to verify your answer.

 TRACK 24

MARC: Je suis à la fac de droit	*I am in law school.*
OLIVIER: Je suis à la fac de médecine.	*I am in medical school.*
RENÉ: Je suis à la fac de sciences politiques.	*I am in political science.*
ANNE: Je suis à la fac de chimie.	*I am in chemistry.*
NICOLE: Je suis à la fac des lettres.	*I am in literature.*
MONIQUE: Je suis à l'École des Beaux Arts.	*I am in art school.*

ASKING WHAT PEOPLE DO FOR A LIVING

As Nick and Lili continue their conversation, they tell each other what their family members do. Note how the question **Qu'est-ce qu'il/elle fait?** is used to ask what a person does for a living.

 TRACK 25

LILI: Ma mère travaille dans un salon de beauté.	*My mother works in a beauty salon.*
NICK: Qu'est-ce qu'elle fait?	*What does she do?*
LILI: Elle est esthéticienne.	*She is a beautician.*

NICK: Et ton père, qu'est-ce qu'il fait?

And your father, what does he do?

LILI: Mon père est représentant. Il travaille pour une société de télécommunication.

My father is a salesman. He works for a telecommunications firm.

NICK: Moi, mon père est employé de banque et ma mère est professeur.

My father is a bank employee, and my mother is a teacher.

LILI: Qu'est-ce que les professeurs gagnent aux États-Unis?

What do teachers earn in the United States?

NICK: Ça dépend de beaucoup de choses comme l'ancienneté et ça varie d'état en état.

It depends on a lot of things like seniority, and it varies from state to state.

Occupations and Professions

l'acteur / l'actrice	*actor/actress*	l'infirmier / l'infirmière	*nurse*
l'avocat / l'avocate	*lawyer*	l'instituteur / l'institutrice	*teacher*
le caissier / la caissière	*cashier*	le/la journaliste	*journalist*
le chanteur / la chanteuse	*singer*	le médecin, le docteur	*doctor*
le coiffeur / la coiffeuse	*hairstylist*	le professeur	*teacher*
le cuisinier / la cuisinière	*cook*	le serveur / la serveuse	*waiter/waitress*
l'employé(e) de banque	*bank clerk*	le vendeur / la vendeuse	*salesman/ saleswoman*
le/la fonctionnaire	*government worker*	le viticulteur / la viticultrice	*wine grower/ vintner*

CULTURE DEMYSTIFIED

Earnings

Use your good judgment if you are tempted to ask what someone earns. This is considered to be a very personal matter in France.

VOCABULARY DEMYSTIFIED

Occupations and Professions

There are many words for *teacher* in French: **l'instituteur / l'institutrice** is used for *elementary school teachers*, while **le professeur** is used for *secondary and higher education teachers*. In addition, a music or dance teacher may be referred to as **un maître** or **une maîtresse de musique / de danse**. Some professions, such as **professeur,** were traditionally dominated by men and therefore only existed in the masculine form. But nowadays, it has become more common to refer to a female teacher as **la professeur** or, more familiarly, as **la prof**.

Written Practice 4-1

Read the following sentences describing various people's jobs, and name each person's occupation.

1. Alain travaille pour le gouvernement. _____
2. Fabienne cultive des vignes et fait de bons vins. _____
3. André fait la cuisine dans un restaurant. _____
4. Audrey Tautou joue dans des films. _____
5. MC Solar chante des chansons rap. _____
6. Françoise défend des clients en cour de justice. _____

Planning an Outing

In the following dialogue, Mireille invites Kevin to join her and a group of friends for a weekend outing.

 TRACK 26

MIREILLE: Salut, Kevin. Qu'est-ce que tu fais ce week-end?	*Hi, Kevin. What are you doing this weekend?*
KEVIN: Je ne sais pas. Il paraît qu'il va faire beau.	*I don't know. It looks like the weather is going to be nice.*

MIREILLE: Tu veux venir à Giverny avec une bande de copains?

Do you want to come to Giverny with a bunch of friends?

KEVIN: C'est sympa. Vous allez faire la visite des jardins de Monet?

That's nice. Are you going to visit Monet's gardens?

MIREILLE: Oui, et puisqu'il va faire beau, nous comptons faire un pique-nique dans le village.

Yes, and since the weather is going to be nice, we plan to have a picnic in the village.

TALKING ABOUT ACTIVITIES AND THE WEATHER WITH THE VERB FAIRE

The irregular present tense forms of the verb **faire** are as follows:

je **fais**	*I do / am doing*	nous **faisons**	*we do / are doing*
tu **fais**	*you do / are doing*	vous **faites**	*you do / are doing*
il/elle **fait**	*he/she does / is doing*	ils/elles **font**	*they do / are doing*
on **fait**	*one does, we do / are doing, people do / are doing*		

Just as in English, the verb **faire** is used to mean *to do* or *to make*, as well as *doing something for a living or as a job.*

Qu'est-ce que tu fais ce soir?	*What are you doing tonight?*
Je regarde la télé.	*I am watching TV.*
Qu'est-ce que tu fais, Étienne?	*What do you do (in life)?*
Je suis coiffeur.	*I am a hairstylist.*

However, the verb **faire** is also in many idiomatic expressions (that is, expressions that do not translate well literally from one language to the other). Look at the following examples:

Weather Expressions

Quel temps fait-il?	*What is the weather like?*
Il fait beau.	*It's nice.*
Il fait chaud.	*It's hot.*
Il fait frais.	*It's cool.*
Il fait froid.	*It's cold.*
Il fait mauvais.	*It's bad (out).*

Il fait du soleil.   *It's sunny.*
Il fait du vent.   *It's windy.*

Activities

faire du foot	*to play soccer*	faire un pique-nique	*to have a picnic*
faire du ski	*to go skiing*	faire un voyage	*to go on a trip*
faire du vélo / de la bicyclette	*to go biking*	faire une promenade	*to take a walk*
		faire une visite	*to pay a visit*
faire les courses / les achats	*to do the shopping*		

The following expressions usually mean *to go for a stroll/walk*. However, they also mean *to go for a ride*. In that case, they are usually followed by the mode of transportation. Look at the following examples:

On fait un tour en ville?   *Shall we go for a stroll in town?*

On fait un tour à pied?   *Shall we go for a walk?*

On fait un tour en vélo?   *Shall we go for a bike ride?*

On fait une promenade en voiture?   *Shall we go for a ride in the car?*

Oral Practice 4-2

 TRACK 27

Listen to the following questions. Pause and answer each question according to the cues in parentheses. Then listen to each answer on your CD.

1. Qu'est-ce que tu fais ce soir?   (je / faire une visite à des copains)
   What are you doing tonight?

2. Qu'est-ce que vous faites aujourd'hui? (nous / faire des courses)
   What are you doing today?

3. Qu'est-ce qu'on fait demain?   (on / faire un tour en ville)
   What are we doing tomorrow?

4. Qu'est-ce qu'ils font ce week-end?   (ils / faire du ski)
   What are they doing this weekend?

5. Quel temps fait-il?   (il / faire mauvais)
   What is the weather like?

Getting Personal

In the following dialogue, a group of young people are on the way to Claude Monet's garden located in the little Normandy town of Giverny. Kevin is riding with Mireille, and they talk about Lili.

 TRACK 28

KEVIN: Je suis ravi de revoir Lili.	*I'm delighted to see Lili again.*
MIREILLE: Ah oui? Elle te plaît?	*Yes? Do you like her?*
KEVIN: Oui. Elle me plaît beaucoup. Elle est ravissante.	*Yes. I like her a lot. She's delightful.*
MIREILLE: Tu aimes les rousses aux yeux bleus?	*You like redheads with blue eyes?*
KEVIN: Ce n'est pas son physique, c'est sa personnalité qui me plaît surtout.	*It's not her physical appearance, it's her personality that I especially like.*
MIREILLE: Bien sûr, Kevin! Je te crois.	*Sure, Kevin! I believe you.*
KEVIN: Mais c'est vrai. Je trouve Lili très naturelle et franche, tu vois.	*But it's true. I find Lili very natural and frank, you see.*
MIREILLE: Tu veux que je demande à Lili si tu lui plais?	*Do you want me to ask Lili if she likes you?*
KEVIN: Ah non, surtout pas! Je préfère me faire une idée moi-même.	*Oh no, not at all! I prefer to find out myself.*
MIREILLE: C'est comme tu veux!	*As you wish!*

EXPRESSING OPINIONS WITH THE VERB PLAIRE

To ask a *yes* or *no* question about a like, dislike, or opinion, the verb **plaire** (*to please*) is frequently used instead of the verb **aimer** (*to like/love*). Pay close attention to the structure required by this verb (something or someone is pleasing *to* a person). Look at the following examples:

Lili te plaît? —Oui, elle me plaît.	*Do you like Lili? —Yes, I like her.*
Le jardin de Giverny vous plaît? —Oui, il nous plaît.	*Do you like the Giverny garden? —Yes, we like it.*
L'idée de pique-nique plaît à Kevin? —Oui, l'idée lui plaît.	*Does Kevin like the idea of a picnic? —Yes, he likes the idea.*

Kevin plaît à Lili? —Oui, il lui plaît. | *Does Lili like Kevin? —Yes, she likes him.*

Kevin plaît aux copains de Mireille? —Oui, il leur plaît. | *Do Mireille's friends like Kevin? —Yes, they like him.*

When you are asked a question with the verb **plaire** (**Cela vous plaît?**), first identify the indirect object pronoun (**vous**) and translate it as the subject of the English equivalent sentence (*Do you like that?*). French indirect object pronouns (which become the subjects in the English equivalent) are as follows (these will be treated again in Chapter 10):

me = *I*	nous = *we*
te = *you*	vous = *you*
lui = *he/she*	leur = *they*

Look at the following sentences, and note how the subject in the French sentence is the *what* or the *who* that is *liked*:

Ce film **me** plaît. | *I like this movie.* | Ce film **lui** plaît. | *He/She likes this movie.*

La chanteuse **nous** plaît. | *We like the singer.* | L'acteur **vous** plaît. | *You like the actor.*

EXPRESSING THOUGHTS AND PREFERENCES

In the following dialogue, Kevin and Lili are walking through the gardens at Giverny. Kevin is happy to be alone with her and wants to find out if she likes him as much as he likes her.

 TRACK 29

KEVIN: Je suis vraiment content de te revoir, Lili. | *I'm really happy to see you again, Lili.*

LILI: Moi aussi. Ça me fait plaisir de te voir. | *Me too. I'm pleased to see you.*

KEVIN: Tu es bien jolie. Le bleu te va très bien. | *You're very pretty. Blue looks very good on you.*

LILI: Tu trouves? | *You think so?*

KEVIN: Oui, je t'assure. | *Yes, I assure you.*

LILI: Je crois qu'on va être meilleurs amis.   *I think we're going to be best friends.*

KEVIN: J'espère bien!   *I do hope so!*

LILI: On retrouve les autres?   *Should we find the others?*

KEVIN: Je préfère rester avec toi.   *I prefer to stay with you.*

Here are some common verbs to express an opinion or appreciation:

Verbs of Opinion		**Verbs of Appreciation**	
assurer	*to assure*	aimer	*to like/love*
croire	*to think/believe*	admirer	*to admire*
douter	*to doubt*	adorer	*to adore*
espérer	*to hope*	apprécier	*to appreciate*
penser	*to think*	désirer	*to desire*
trouver	*to think/find*	préférer	*to prefer*

Conjugating Regular Verbs in the Present Tense

Most French verbs fall into the category of regular **-er** verbs. In the previous list of verbs, only **croire** (*to believe*) is irregular. Remember that all regular **-er** verbs follow the same pattern of conjugation: stem + ending. The stem is obtained by dropping the ending (**-er**) from the infinitive form of the verb. The ending for each conjugated form is determined by the subject of the verb. Look at the conjugation of the verb **penser**, and note the ending for each form, highlighted in boldface:

je pense	*I think*	nous pens**ons**	*we think*
tu pens**es**	*you think*	vous pens**ez**	*you think*
il/elle pense	*he/she thinks*	ils/elles pens**ent**	*they think*
on pense	*one thinks* or *we/people think*		

Written Practice 4-2

Complete the sentences with words from the vocabulary bank to reconstitute what took place among Mireille, Kevin, and Lili.

assure / espère / fait un tour / font une promenade / pense / plaît

Kevin (1) _____ en voiture avec Mireille. Il dit à Mireille que Lili lui (2) _____. À Giverny, Kevin et Lili (3) _____ dans le jardin. Kevin (4) _____ Lili que le bleu lui va bien. Lili (5) _____ qu'ils vont être amis. Kevin (6) _____ cela aussi.

Planning a Future Date

In the following dialogue, Kevin and Lili, who had a great time in Giverny, make plans to see each other again.

TRACK 30

LILI: Quelle belle journée!	*What a beautiful day!*
KEVIN: Il faut vraiment rentrer?	*Do we really have to go back?*
LILI: Oui, mais on va rentrer ensemble avec Mireille.	*Yes, but we're going to go back with Mireille.*
KEVIN: Super! Dis, je peux te voir demain?	*Great! Say, may I see you tomorrow?*
LILI: Demain, non. Mais jeudi prochain peut-être.	*Tomorrow, no. But maybe next Thursday.*
KEVIN: D'accord. Tu voudrais dîner avec moi?	*OK. Would you like to have dinner with me?*
LILI: Oui, volontiers.	*Yes, gladly.*
KEVIN: À jeudi! Tu vas me manquer, tu sais.	*'Til Thursday! I'm going to miss you, you know.*

GRAMMAR DEMYSTIFIED

The Verb manquer

When the verb **manquer** is used to mean *to miss someone*, the sentence structure is the same as for the verb **plaire**. The person *who is being missed* is always the *subject* of the sentence. Look at the following examples:

Kevin aime Lili. **Elle** lui manque.   *Kevin likes Lili. He misses **her**.*

Je t'aime, et **tu** me manques.   *I love you, and I miss **you**.*

TALKING ABOUT THE FUTURE

Just as in English, there are several ways to talk about the future. Look at some examples:

Demain, je **dînerai** avec toi.	*Tomorrow, I will eat with you.*
Demain, je **vais dîner** avec toi.	*Tomorrow, I am going to eat with you.*
Demain, je **dîne** avec toi.	*Tomorrow, I am eating with you.*

In French, to express the future, we can use the simple future (**le futur simple**) as in the first example above (**je dînerai**). We may also use the near future (**le futur proche: je vais dîner**), a form of the verb **aller** + *infinitive*; we can even use the present tense (**je dîne**). In conversation, the near future and the present are increasingly favored. Look at these examples of the near future in French and in English:

Je **vais manger**.	*I am going to eat.*	Nous **allons partir**.	*We're going to leave.*
Tu **vas sortir**.	*You're going to go out.*	Vous **allez rentrer**.	*You're going to go back.*
Il/Elle **va voir**.	*He/She is going to see.*	Ils/Elles **vont rester**.	*They're going to stay.*
On **va regarder** un film.	*We are going to watch a movie.*		

Adverbs and Adverbial Phrases to Use When Planning for the Near Future

cet après-midi	*this afternoon*	le week-end prochain	*next weekend*
ce soir	*tonight*	dimanche prochain	*next Sunday*
demain	*tomorrow*	l'été prochain	*next summer*
après-demain	*the day after tomorrow*	l'hiver prochain	*next winter*
		la semaine prochaine	*next week*
bientôt	*soon*	le mois prochain	*next month*
plus tard	*later*	l'année prochaine	*next year*
tout de suite	*right away*		

Oral Practice 4-3

Listen to each question, pause your CD, and answer the question using the cue in parentheses. Then listen to the answer on your CD.

 TRACK 31

1. Qu'est-ce que tu vas faire ce soir? (sortir avec des copains)
2. Qu'est-ce que les copains vont faire demain? (faire la visite de Giverny)

3. Qu'est-ce que Mireille va faire bientôt? (rentrer à Paris)

4. Qu'est-ce que Lili et Kevin vont faire jeudi prochain? (dîner au restaurant)

5. Qu'est-ce que nous allons faire plus tard ce soir? (regarder un film)

Chapter Practice 4

Listen to each of the following mini-dialogues. You may cover the translations on the right and check your comprehension later. Then, tell whether the statements that follow are true (**vrai, V**) or false (**faux, F**). Check your answers in the Answer Key.

TRACK 32

Dialogue 1

ANDRÉ: Est-ce que tu fais des études, Gabrielle?	*[Are you a student, Gabrielle?]*
GABRIELLE: Oui, je suis en faculté de sciences politiques.	*[Yes, I am in political science.]*
ANDRÉ: Ça te plaît?	*[Do you like it?]*
GABRIELLE: Oui, beaucoup.	*[Yes, a lot.]*
ANDRÉ: Qu'est-ce que tu comptes faire plus tard?	*[What do you plan to do later (in life)?]*
GABRIELLE: Je voudrais être fonctionnaire.	*[I would like to work for the government.]*
ANDRÉ: Tu penses faire de la politique?	*[Are you thinking about going into politics?]*
GABRIELLE: Non, je préfère un travail tranquille.	*[No, I prefer a quiet job.]*

GABRIELLE...

1. ... va être médecin. _____

2. ... aime étudier les sciences politiques. _____

3. ... voudrait être fonctionnaire. _____

4. ... pense faire de la politique. _____

Dialogue 2

GABRIELLE: Et toi, André, qu'est-ce que tu fais?   *[How about you, André, what do you do?]*

ANDRÉ: Moi, je termine mes études de lettres.   *[I'm finishing my literature program.]*

GABRIELLE: Qu'est-ce que tu comptes faire plus tard?   *[What do you intend to do later?]*

ANDRÉ: Je veux être instituteur.   *[I want to be a teacher (elementary school).]*

GABRIELLE: Tu dois aimer les enfants.   *[You must like children.]*

ANDRÉ: Tu sais, j'ai cinq petits frères et sœurs.   *[You know, I have five little brothers and sisters.]*

GABRIELLE: Ils te manquent?   *[Do you miss them?]*

ANDRÉ: Oui, beaucoup.   *[Yes, a lot.]*

GABRIELLE: Tu as déjà un poste?   *[Do you already have a position?]*

ANDRÉ: Oui, je vais commencer en septembre prochain.   *[Yes, I'm going to start next September.]*

GABRIELLE: Super. Bonne chance!   *[Super. Good luck!]*

ANDRÉ...

1. ... est professeur. _____

2. ... fait des études de lettres. _____

3. ... aime beaucoup les enfants. _____

4. ... va bientôt travailler. _____

Dialogue 3

MARIE-LAURE: Salut, Jean-Paul. Qu'est-ce qu'on fait?   *[Hi, Jean-Paul. What should we do?]*

JEAN-PAUL: On va faire une promenade en vélo?   *[Shall we go for a bike ride?]*

MARIE-LAURE: Moi, je voudrais faire des achats en ville.   *[I'd like to go shopping in town.]*

JEAN-PAUL: Alors, allons en ville en vélo et faisons des achats!   *[So, let's go to town on our bikes and shop!]*

MARIE-LAURE: Volontiers! Il fait beau aujourd'hui.

[Gladly! The weather is nice today.]

JEAN-PAUL: Oui, on va profiter du beau temps et faire un tour au parc.

[Yes, we'll enjoy the nice weather and ride around the park.]

MARIE-LAURE: Très bien. On va partir tout de suite?

[Very well. Are we leaving right away?]

JEAN-PAUL: Oui, allons-y!

[Yes, let's go!]

JEAN-PAUL: ...

1. ...voudrait faire un tour en voiture. _____

2. ...voudrait surtout faire des achats. _____

3. ...va aller en ville en vélo. _____

4. ...va aussi faire une promenade au parc. _____

CHAPTER QUIZ 4

Complete the sentences with the appropriate word or expression from the list to find out what Hélène and Jean-Luc do and something about their friendship.

demain / faire un tour / fait / pense / serveur / travailler / serveuse / un pique-nique / vont / voudrait

1. Il _____ vraiment beau aujourd'hui.

2. Hélène voudrait faire _____ ou une promenade.

3. Mais Hélène va _____ .

4. Elle est _____ dans un café.

5. Hélène aime bien Luc. Il est _____ aussi.

6. _____ Hélène va travailler plus tard que Jean-Luc.

7. Alors Jean-Luc va _____ en ville.

8. Après ils _____ aller au cinéma ensemble.

9. Est-ce que Luc _____ qu'Hélène est mignonne?

10. Certainement! Il _____ plaire à Hélène!

CHAPTER 5

Getting Around Town

In this chapter you will learn:

Asking for and Giving Directions
Making a Date
Time, Place, and Date

Asking for and Giving Directions

In the following dialogue, Kevin is supposed to meet Nick in the courtyard of the Louvre. He is not yet familiar with Paris and needs help from passersby.

TRACK 33

KEVIN: Pardon, Monsieur. Où est la station de métro Passy?	*Excuse me, Sir. Where is the Passy subway station?*
LE MONSIEUR: C'est tout droit devant vous, jeune homme.	*It's straight ahead of you, young man.*
KEVIN: C'est près d'ici?	*Is it near here?*
LE MONSIEUR: Oui, à cinq minutes.	*Yes, five minutes away.*
KEVIN: Merci beaucoup, Monsieur.	*Thanks a lot, Sir.*
LE MONSIEUR: De rien, mais dans quelle direction allez-vous?	*Don't mention it. What direction are you going?*
KEVIN: En direction du Louvre.	*Toward the Louvre.*
LE MONSIEUR: Bon, restez à gauche.	*Good, stay on your left.*
KEVIN: Je vous remercie, Monsieur.	*Thank you, Sir.*

USING POLITE EXPRESSIONS

When you stop someone to ask for help, especially in big cities where people are usually in a hurry, be sure to use expressions like **Pardon, excusez-moi** and **S'il vous plaît**. Also use the appropriate title **Monsieur**, **Madame**, or **Mademoiselle** with people you meet, especially those older than you.

Pardon, Monsieur/Madame/Mademoiselle.	*Pardon me, Sir/Madam/Miss.*
Excusez-moi, Monsieur/Madame/Mademoiselle.	*Excuse me, Sir/Madam/Miss.*

VOCABULARY DEMYSTIFIED

Directions

As you make your way around Paris, you will surely use the **métro** (*subway*), by far the most efficient way to get from one place to another. The word **Direction** is of the utmost importance because it helps you find the correct track and train. You will follow signs labeled **Direction** plus the name of a Paris landmark; this indicates the end point of the line you need to take. In every metro station there are maps to locate a station near your destination. Often the station is named after a prominent site in that area, such as the **station Opéra** or the **station du Louvre**.

When people help you, use one of the following expressions to thank them.

Merci. / Merci beaucoup. / Je vous remercie.   *Thanks. / Thanks a lot. / Thank you.*

In the following dialogue, Kevin is in the **Quartier Latin** (*Latin Quarter*) to explore student-friendly bookstores and cafés. He is now looking for the **Café de Flore**, which used to be home to existentialist writers such as Jean-Paul Sartre and Simone de Beauvoir.

 TRACK 34

KEVIN: Excusez-moi, Mademoiselle, la rue Saint-Benoît, c'est encore loin d'ici?

Excuse me, Miss, rue Saint-Benoît, is that still far from here?

LA DEMOISELLE: D'abord, il faut trouver le boulevard Saint-Germain. Tournez ici à gauche et prenez la première rue à droite.

First, you have to find boulevard Saint-Germain. Turn left here and take the first street on the right.

KEVIN: Alors, je tourne à gauche ici et à droite c'est le boulevard Saint-Germain?

So, I turn left over here and on the right is the boulevard Saint-Germain?

LA DEMOISELLE: Non, c'est la rue qui va au boulevard Saint-Germain.

No, that's the street that goes to boulevard Saint-Germain.

KEVIN: Je vois. Après c'est encore loin?

I see. Afterward is it still far?

LA DEMOISELLE: Continuez sur le boulevard Saint-Germain et c'est dix minutes de marche.

Continue on boulevard Saint-Germain and it's a ten-minute walk.

KEVIN: C'est au coin du boulevard Saint-Germain et de la rue Saint-Benoît, n'est-ce pas?

It's on the corner of boulevard Saint-Germain and rue Saint-Benoît, right?

LA DEMOISELLE: Oui, oui, c'est ça!

Yes, that's it!

KEVIN: Et je suis bien sur la Rive gauche?

And I'm on the Left Bank?

LA DEMOISELLE: Mais oui, vous êtes sur la Rive gauche, dans le Quartier Latin!

Certainly, you're on the Left Bank, in the Latin Quarter!

KEVIN: Merci, Mademoiselle. Vous êtes bien aimable.

Thank you, Miss. You're very kind.

CULTURE DEMYSTIFIED

Le Quartier Latin

In French towns and cities, just as in North America, there are streets (**les rues**), boulevards (**les boulevards**), and avenues (**les avenues**). Street signs are often attached to the wall of a corner building rather than on freestanding posts; streets are often named for famous people or landmarks. The Latin Quarter is a neighborhood on the Left Bank (south side of the river Seine in Paris) where the famous university, the Sorbonne, was founded as a school of theology during the Middle Ages. The area is home to educational institutions and bookstores and is the center of student life. Many streets there are named after saints.

USING C'EST AND IL FAUT TO VERIFY DIRECTIONS AND LOCATIONS

To verify whether you know where you are going, use **c'est** and an expression such as **à droite**. Look at the the following statements and questions and practice saying them aloud:

Statement		Question	
C'est à droite.	*It's on the right.*	C'est à droite?	*Is it on the right?*
C'est à gauche.	*It's on the left.*	C'est à gauche?	*Is it on the left?*
C'est tout droit.	*It's straight ahead.*	C'est tout droit?	*Is it straight ahead?*
C'est au coin.	*It's on the corner.*	C'est au coin?	*Is it on the corner?*
C'est loin.	*It's far. / It will be far.*	C'est loin?	*Is it / Will it be far?*
C'est près.	*It's near. / It will be near.*	C'est près?	*Is it / Will it be near?*

Another way to verify where you are going is to use **Il faut** + *infinitive* as in the following examples:

Il faut traverser la rue?	*Must I/we cross the street?*
Il faut tourner au coin?	*Must I/we turn at the corner?*
Il faut aller de l'autre côté?	*Must I/we go to the other side?*
Il faut continuer dans ce sens?	*Must I/we continue in this direction?*
Il faut retourner en arrière?	*Must I/we go back?*

The impersonal expression **Il faut** (literally: *It is necessary*) can be translated by *you*, *we*, or *people* (in general) *must*. Use your judgment and context clues to deter-

mine what seems most logical. **Il faut** is always followed by an infinitive; when talking about directions, use verbs like **traverser** (*to pass/cross*) or **aller** (*to go*).

Il faut traverser ce pont. Vas-y!	*You have to cross this bridge. Go ahead!*
Il faut aller tout droit!	*You/We must go straight!*
Il ne faut pas tourner ici. Continuons!	*We must not turn here. Let's continue!*

USING OÙ EST **OR** OÙ SONT **TO ASK ABOUT LOCATIONS**

In the following dialogue, Kevin and Nick are trying to find the Cluny Museum, but neither one knows exactly where it is located.

 TRACK 35

KEVIN: Où est le musée de Cluny, Nick, tu le sais?	*Where is the Cluny Museum, do you know?*
NICK: Je sais que c'est dans le Quartier Latin près du Panthéon.	*I know that it's in the Latin Quarter near the Pantheon.*
KEVIN: Regardons sur la carte!	*Let's look at the map!*
NICK: Voici le Panthéon et voilà le musée de Cluny!	*Here's the Pantheon and there's the Cluny Museum!*
KEVIN: On tourne à droite sur le boulevard Saint-Michel?	*Do we turn right on the boulevard Saint-Michel?*
NICK: Oui, et regarde, voilà le Café des deux Magots!	*Yes, and look, there's the Café des Deux Magots!*
KEVIN: Et les librairies, où sont-elles?	*And the bookstores, where are they?*
NICK: Un peu partout. Allons par là!	*Scattered / A little bit everywhere. Let's go that way!*

To ask where something is, use **Où est / Où sont** as in the following examples:

Où est... (*Where is . . .*)
l'arrêt d'autobus? (*the bus stop*)
la banque? (*the bank*)
l'hôpital? (*the hospital*)
la librairie? (*the bookstore*)
la pharmacie? (*the pharmacy*)

Où sont... (*Where are . . .*)
les annonces? (*the ads*)
les distributeurs? (*the ATMs*)
les escaliers? (*the stairs*)
les guichets? (*the ticket windows*)
les horaires? (*the schedules*)

la piscine municipale? (*the public pool*) les prix? (*the prices*)
la poste? (*the post office*) les toilettes? (*the restrooms*)

To indicate that something is right *here* or *there*, use **voici** and **voilà**. Look at the following examples:

Voici l'ascenseur. *Here's the elevator.*

Voilà l'entrée. *There's the entrance.*

Oral Practice 5-1

TRACK 36

Ask for directions according to the cues. Turn on your CD to check the accuracy of your questions. Then listen to answers you might receive. You'll also find the dialogue text in the Answer Key.

1. Stop a young lady and ask her politely where the Saint-Michel subway station is.

2. Stop a gentleman, and ask him politely if the rue de Rivoli is straight ahead.

3. Stop a lady, and ask her if the Jardin du Luxembourg is near here.

4. Stop another lady, and ask where the department store Le Printemps is.

5. Stop a male employee in a store, and ask where the restrooms are.

VOCABULARY DEMYSTIFIED

Les toilettes

In a public place, always ask for **les toilettes** (*restrooms*), not for a **salle de bains** (*bathroom with shower and bathtub*). Another frequently used word for *restroom* is **les W.C.** (from the English term *water closet*). Notice that both words are used in the plural. The word **la toilette** in the singular is used in the expression **faire la/sa toilette** (*to groom oneself / to get ready*) or **l'eau de toilette** (*a light perfume*).

Making a Date

In this dialogue Kevin calls Lili and asks her out on a date for the next day. Will she accept?

 TRACK 37

KEVIN: Allô, Lili. C'est moi, Kevin.	*Hello, Lili. It's me, Kevin.*
LILI: Bonjour, Kevin. Ça va?	*Hello, Kevin. How are you?*
KEVIN: Ça va, mais tu me manques.	*Fine, but I miss you.*
LILI: Tu veux faire quelque chose demain?	*Do you want to do something tomorrow?*
KEVIN: Bien sûr. Qu'est-ce que tu as envie de faire?	*Of course. What do you feel like doing?*
LILI: Si on allait au musée d'Art moderne?	*How about going to the Museum of Modern Art?*
KEVIN: Si tu veux. Et après le musée?	*If you like. And after the museum?*
LILI: Si on allait à un concert de jazz?	*How about going to a jazz concert?*
KEVIN: Volontiers!	*Gladly!*
LILI: D'accord. Tu viens me chercher?	*OK. Will you come pick me up?*
KEVIN: Je veux bien, mais tu sais que je ne connais pas bien la ville.	*I don't mind, but you know I don't know the city well.*
LILI: Ah oui, c'est vrai. Tu veux m'attendre devant le musée?	*Oh yes, that's true. Do you want to wait for me in front of the museum?*
KEVIN: Si ça ne te dérange pas.	*If it's no bother to you.*
LILI: À demain alors, à trois heures devant le musée.	*See you tomorrow then, at three o'clock in front of the museum.*

ASKING AND SUGGESTING WHAT TO DO

Use one of the following expressions to ask a friend what he/she wants to do.

Qu'est-ce que tu **veux** faire?	*What do you want to do?*
Qu'est-ce que tu **voudrais** faire?	*What would you like to do?*
Qu'est-ce que tu **as envie de** faire?	*What do you feel like doing?*

To suggest what to do on a date, it is customary to use the word **si** and the **imparfait** tense in French. The **imparfait** will be reviewed in Chapter 11. Look at the following examples:

Si on...	How about . . .
allait danser?	*going dancing?*
dînait au restaurant?	*having dinner at a restaurant?*
faisait un pique-nique?	*going on a picnic?*
sortait ce soir?	*going out tonight?*
visitait Giverny?	*visiting Giverny?*

A **si**-clause (*if*-clause) including the **imparfait** tense is often used in French to make a suggestion. To obtain the stem of a verb in the **imparfait**, remember to drop the ending **-ons** from the **nous** form of the present tense of the verb. Look at the following examples of **imparfait** stems:

Infinitive	**Nous** Form of Present Tense	**Imparfait** Stem
aller (*to go*)	nous allons	**all-**
avoir (*to have*)	nous avons	**av-**
connaître (*to know*)	nous connaissons	**connaiss-**
faire (*to do*)	nous faisons	**fais-**
savoir (*to know a fact*)	nous savons	**sav-**
trouver (*to find*)	nous trouvons	**trouv-**

Then add the appropriate ending for that subject pronoun:

je **-ais**	nous **-ions**
tu **-ais**	vous **-iez**
il/elle/on **-ait**	ils/elles **-aient**

Note that the only French verb with an irregular stem in the **imparfait** is **être: ét-, j'étais** (*I was*).

Written Practice 5-1

Someone asks you **Qu'est-ce que tu voudrais faire?** (*What would you like to do?*) Answer by making a suggestion using **si** plus the **imparfait** of the verb provided in the cue.

1. on / aller au cinéma _____

2. on / danser _____

3. nous / visiter un monument historique _____

4. tu / chercher les copains _____

5. nous / faire une promenade en ville _____

6. nous / déjeuner au café _____

ACCEPTING AND DECLINING INVITATIONS

Look at the following frequently used expressions to accept an invitation:

Avec plaisir,	*With pleasure.*	Je veux bien.	*Sure. I don't mind.*
Bien sûr.	*Of course.*	Si tu veux.	*If you want/wish.*
D'accord.	*OK.*	Volontiers.	*Gladly.*

Look at the following expressions frequently used to decline an invitation:

Je suis désolé(e) / Je regrette mais...		*I'm sorry but . . .*	
Je voudrais bien mais...		*I would like to but . . .*	

Je suis occupé(e).	*I'm busy.*	Je ne peux pas...	*I can't . . .*
J'ai des projets.	*I have plans.*	Je n'ai pas le temps.	*I don't have time.*

Time, Place, and Date

When planning a date or get-together, you always have to agree on the time, place, and date. Look at the following examples of time:

Setting Time	
à midi / à minuit	*at noon / at midnight*
à deux heures dix.	*at two-ten*
à trois heures quinze / et quart	*at three-fifteen / quarter past three*

CULTURE DEMYSTIFIED

The Twenty-Four-Hour Clock

In a familiar setting, when it is clear you're referring to the A.M. or P.M. hours, it isn't necessary to use the twenty-four-hour clock. However, in Europe, schedules and timetables of any kind (movies, flights, buses, etc.) are based on the twenty-four-hour clock. Thus, P.M. hours will start at **treize heures** (*one P.M.*) and end at **vingt-quatre heures** (*midnight*).

Setting Time (continued)

à quatre heures trente / et demie	*at four-thirty / half past four*
vers vingt heures	*around ten P.M.*
vers dix-huit heures	*around six P.M.*

Setting the Place

à la place Charles de Gaulle	*at the Place Charles de Gaulle*
à l'entrée de l'hôtel	*at the entrance of the hotel*
au premier étage	*on the first floor (U.S. second floor)*
au rez-de-chaussée	*on the ground floor*
dans le foyer de l'immeuble	*in the lobby of the building*
devant l'Arc de Triomphe	*in front of the Arch of Triumph*

DAYS AND MONTHS

The names of the days and months will turn out to be very useful! Say them out loud while listening to your CD.

 TRACK 38

Stating the Day

lundi	*Monday*
mardi	*Tuesday*
mercredi	*Wednesday*
jeudi	*Thursday*
vendredi	*Friday*
samedi	*Saturday*
dimanche	*Sunday*

Stating the Month

janvier	*January*
février	*February*
mars	*March*
avril	*April*
mai	*May*
juin	*June*
juillet	*July*
août	*August*
septembre	*September*
octobre	*October*
novembre	*November*
décembre	*December*

ORDINAL NUMBERS 1–60

Here are the numbers you need to know in order to say or understand a date. Repeat them with your CD.

Numbering of Floors

In France, the street-level floor of any building is called **le rez-de-chaussée**, while in the United States, it is usually called *the first floor*. So an American *second floor* would actually be *the first floor* (**le premier étage**) in France, and so on.

🔘 **TRACK 39**

1	un	11	onze	21	vingt et un
2	deux	12	douze	22	vingt-deux
3	trois	13	treize	23	vingt-trois
4	quatre	14	quatorze	24	vingt-quatre
5	cinq	15	quinze	25	vingt-cinq
6	six	16	seize	26	vingt-six
7	sept	17	dix-sept	27	vingt-sept
8	huit	18	dix-huit	28	vingt-huit
9	neuf	19	dix-neuf	29	vingt-neuf
10	dix	20	vingt	30	trente

Here are the rest of the numbers you need to tell time:

40	quarante	50	cinquante	60	soixante

CARDINAL NUMBERS

Cardinal numbers (**deux**, **trois**, **quatre**...) are used to express dates, except for the first of the month. Look at the following examples:

dimanche, le **premier** janvier / le **1er** janvier	*Sunday, the first of January / January 1(st)*
samedi, le **deux** avril / le 2 avril	*Saturday, the second of April / April 2(nd)*
mercredi, le **trente** mai / le 30 mai	*Wednesday, the thirtieth of May / May 30(th)*

Oral Practice 5-2

TRACK 40

Someone wants to set up a date with you. Listen carefully, then pause, and accept or decline the invitation based on the cues provided. Play your CD to verify your answer. You can also find the answer in the Answer Key.

1. Answer: *Yes, with pleasure. See you on Monday.*

2. Answer: *Sorry, I can't.*

3. Answer: *OK. See you Saturday.*

Chapter Practice 5

A. Match each of Alain's questions or statements with Denise's most logical reply in order to reconstitute the dialogue.

Alain		**Denise**
1. _____ Où est la place Vendôme?		a. Mais non, je sais où c'est.
2. _____ Près d'ici?		b. Oui, au coin, à gauche.
3. _____ Si on demandait?		c. C'est le grand magasin à gauche.
4. _____ Bon, mais où est Chez Fauchon?		d. Oui, très près, à deux minutes d'ici.
5. _____ Ah oui, voici Chez Fauchon.		e. La place Vendôme est tout droit devant nous.

B. Alain and Denise are trying to figure out what to do for the rest of the day. Complete each of Alain's suggestions with the correct form of the verb in parentheses in the **imparfait** tense.

Denise	**Alain**
1. Je voudrais manger quelque chose.	—Si on _____ au Café de Flore? (déjeuner)
2. Je voudrais faire une promenade.	—Si on _____ un tour au parc du Luxembourg? (faire)
3. J'adore faire des achats.	—Si on _____ au Printemps? (aller)

4. J'ai envie de voir un bon film.   —Si on _____ le nouveau
                                     Star Trek? (regarder)

5. J'aime bien les musées.   —Si on _____ le Louvre?
                                     (visiter)

C. Write the following times, days, and dates using the correct French format. Do not spell out the number if it is part of a date, but spell it out if it is part of a time expression.

1. Friday, June 1 _____

2. Thursday, August 19 _____

3. Tuesday at four-fifteen P.M. _____

4. Saturday around eight A.M. _____

5. Monday, May 5 _____

CHAPTER QUIZ 5

◉ TRACK 41

Use the vocabulary bank to complete the following dialogue between Denise, her friend Alain, and a passerby (**un passant**) of whom Denise asks directions. Then listen to the entire dialogue on your CD.

c'est / faut / heure / merci / pardon / où / si / tout / vers / veux

DENISE: (1) _____ , Monsieur. (2) _____ est le musée d'Orsay?

PASSANT: Tournez ici à droite! Allez (3) _____ droit et c'est dix minutes de marche.

DENISE: Et le Louvre, (4) _____ par là?

PASSANT: Ah non! Il (5) _____ retourner en arrière et traverser le pont.

DENISE: (6) _____ , Monsieur. Alain, qu'est-ce que tu (7) _____ faire?

ALAIN: (8) _____ on allait au musée d'Orsay?

DENISE: D'accord. Allons-y!

ALAIN: À quelle (9) _____ il faut rentrer à l'hôtel?

DENISE: (10) _____ dix-huit heures.

PART ONE TEST

A. Savez-vous parler français? Say each sentence aloud; then check your pronunciation on the CD.

TRACK 42

1. Bonjour, Johnny. Comment ça va?
2. Le chef est excellent dans ce restaurant français.
3. Il fait des plats superbes.
4. Le plat du jour est succulent aujourd'hui.
5. Tu voudrais les escargots comme hors-d'œuvre?
6. Moi, j'adore les salades exotiques.
7. Toi, tu aimes le poulet et le bœuf.
8. On va au concert de musique classique?
9. Tu adores le jazz, je sais.
10. Le parking est un problème à Paris.
11. Les touristes sont nombreux.
12. Bon, nous rentrons chez nous.
13. Voilà le taxi!

B. Comprenez-vous le français? Using your knowledge of borrowed words and cognates, translate each of the sentences in Part A into English. Check your comprehension in the Answer Key at the back of the book.

14. _____
15. _____
16. _____
17. _____
18. _____
19. _____
20. _____
21. _____
22. _____

23. _____

24. _____

25. _____

26. _____

ACTIVITIES AND
DAILY LIFE

CHAPTER 6

Planning a Trip

In this chapter you will learn:

Budgeting for a Trip

Giving Commands

Expressing Restrictions

Planning Itineraries

Budgeting for a Trip

In the following dialogue, Rachel and Jean discuss their plans to go to Québec this summer. They are anticipating how much money they will need.

 TRACK 43

RACHEL: Tu sais, Jean, un voyage au Québec est une grosse dépense.

You know, Jean, a trip to Québec is a big expense.

JEAN: Oui, je sais mais, on parle de ça depuis longtemps.

Yes, I know, but we've been talking about it for a long time.

RACHEL: Oui, depuis l'année de notre mariage.

Yes, since we were married [the year of our wedding].

JEAN: Ça fait déjà trois ans!

It's already been three years!

RACHEL: Si on faisait un budget pour estimer ce que ça va coûter?

How about making a budget to estimate what it is going to cost?

JEAN: Excellente idée!

An excellent idea!

RACHEL: Un billet d'avion à partir de Paris, ça coûte combien?

A plane ticket from Paris, how much does that cost?

JEAN: Environ huit cents euros, je pense.

Approximately eight hundred euros, I think.

RACHEL: Bon, seize cents euros pour nous deux.

OK, sixteen hundred euros for both of us.

JEAN: Une chambre d'hôtel pour sept jours... , il faut compter environ sept cents euros.

A hotel room for seven days . . . , we have to count approximately seven hundred euros.

RACHEL: Et les repas, environ huit cents euros pour la semaine.

And for meals, approximately eight hundred euros for the week.

JEAN: Mille six cents, sept cents et huit cents, ça fait trois mille cent euros.

Sixteen hundred, seven hundred, and eight hundred, that makes three thousand one hundred euros.

RACHEL: Ajoutons trois cents euros pour des sorties et des excursions.

Let's add three hundred euros for outings and side trips.

JEAN: Ça fait trois mille quatre cents euros.

That's three thousand four hundred euros.

RACHEL: Bon, disons trois mille cinq cents euros!

OK, let's say three thousand five hundred euros!

CARDINAL NUMBERS 70 AND ABOVE

You have already learned to use numbers to tell time. Adding the numbers 70 and above will let you talk about prices and other matters.

70	soixante-dix	80	quatre-vingts	90	quatre-vingt-dix
71	soixante et onze	81	quatre-vingt-un	91	quatre-vingt-onze
72	soixante-douze	82	quatre-vingt-deux	92	quatre-vingt-douze
73	soixante-treize	83	quatre-vingt-trois	93	quatre-vingt-treize

74	soixante-quatorze	84	quatre-vingt-quatre	94	quatre-vingt-quatorze
75	soixante-quinze	85	quatre-vingt-cinq	95	quatre-vingt-quinze
76	soixante-seize	86	quatre-vingt-six	96	quatre-vingt-seize
77	soixante-dix-sept	87	quatre-vingt-sept	97	quatre-vingt-dix-sept
78	soixante-dix-huit	88	quatre-vingt-huit	98	quatre-vingt-dix-huit
79	soixante-dix-neuf	89	quatre-vingt-neuf	99	quatre-vingt-dix-neuf
100	cent	500	cinq cents	1000	mille

For *one hundred* and *one thousand*, the word *one* is omitted and implied in French.

cent	*one hundred*	mille	*one thousand*

The word **cent** takes the plural **-s** ending for *hundreds* (except when followed by another number), but the word **mille** is invariable and never takes an **-s**.

200	deux cents	5000	cinq mille
350	trois cent cinquante	6700	six mille sept cents

Oral Practice 6-1

Say each of the following French numbers. Then listen to the answer on your CD. Remember not to pronounce the final **q** in **cinq**, the final **t** in **huit** and **vingt**, or

---

GRAMMAR DEMYSTIFIED

Depuis **and the Present Tense**

The adverb **depuis** is used to express *for* (a length of time) or *since* (starting at a point in time). It is used with a verb in the present tense, because it describes an action that is still going on in the present. While the focus in the English sentence is on the fact that the action started in the past, in the French sentence the focus is on the present. Look at these examples:

J'étudie le français **depuis** deux ans.	*I've been studying French for two years.*
Nous **habitons** ici **depuis** l'an 2002.	*We've been living here since [the year] 2002.*
Il **pleut depuis** hier.	*It's been raining since yesterday.*

the final **x** in **six** and **dix** when these numbers appear before another word, even though these letters are pronounced when they are used in counting.

 TRACK 44

1. 100	6. 78
2. 500	7. 85
3. 600	8. 92
4. 4000	9. 76
5. 10 000	10. 93

EARNING MONEY

In the following dialogue, Rachel and Jean are discussing how they will earn and save the money necessary for their trip.

 TRACK 45

RACHEL: Nous avons deux mille euros dans notre compte d'épargne.

We have two thousand euros in our savings account.

JEAN: Oui, mais ne touchons pas ce compte!

Yes, but let's not touch that account!

RACHEL: Tu as raison, économisons plutôt une bonne somme d'argent!

You're right, instead, let's save a bunch of money!

JEAN: Moi, je vais faire des heures supplémentaires!

I'm going to work overtime!

RACHEL: Et moi, je vais mettre une annonce dans le journal pour faire du babysitting.

And I'm going to put an ad in the paper to do babysitting.

JEAN: Il me faut une vingtaine d'heures supplémentaires pour gagner mille euros!

I need about twenty overtime hours to earn a thousand euros!

RACHEL: Vas-y! Fais-le! Tu crois que c'est possible?

Go ahead! Do it! Do you think it's possible?

JEAN: Je pense que oui.

I think so.

RACHEL: Moi, j'ai peur de ne pas assez gagner au babysitting.

I'm afraid I won't earn enough at babysitting.

JEAN: Tes cours vont terminer fin avril. Travaille donc dans un café pour la saison!

Your classes are going to be over at the end of April. Work in a café for the season!

RACHEL: Quelle bonne idée! Donne-moi le journal!

What a good idea! Give me the newspaper!

SAVING MONEY

In the following dialogue, Rachel and Jean discuss how they will earn and save the money they need for their trip.

 TRACK 46

RACHEL: Mon premier chèque est à la banque.

My first check is in the bank.

JEAN: Bravo! On fête?

Bravo! Should we celebrate?

RACHEL: Arrête, Jean! On économise ou non?

Stop it, Jean! Are we saving or not?

VOCABULARY DEMYSTIFIED

Avoir **Idioms**

Many expressions that include the verb **avoir,** such as **avoir raison** (*to be right*) and **avoir tort** (*to be wrong*), do not translate literally from French to English. Look at these examples of idiomatic expressions that use **avoir**:

avoir besoin de	*to need*	avoir peur de	*to be afraid of*
avoir envie de	*to feel like / to want*	avoir raison	*to be right*
avoir faim	*to be hungry*	avoir soif	*to be thirsty*
avoir honte de	*to be ashamed of*	avoir sommeil	*to be sleepy*
avoir lieu	*to take place*	avoir tort	*to be wrong*

Remember that the irregular forms of the verb **avoir** in the present tense are as follows:

j'**ai**	*I have*	nous **avons**	*we have*
tu **as**	*you have*	vous **avez**	*you have*
il/elle **a**	*he/she has*	ils/elles **ont**	*they have*
on **a**	*one has / we have*		

JEAN: Ça fait quatre semaines qu'on ne va pas au restaurant!

We haven't been to a restaurant for four weeks!

RACHEL: Et ça fait quatre semaines que la carte de crédit reste dans le portefeuille, n'est-ce pas?

And the credit card has stayed in your wallet for four weeks, right?

JEAN: C'est vrai. Mais je voudrais sortir un peu.

It's true. But I'd like to go out a little.

RACHEL: Tu as tort de te plaindre, Jean.

You're wrong to complain, Jean.

JEAN: Allons au cinéma au moins!

Let's go to the movies at least!

RACHEL: D'accord, mais j'ai faim. Faisons-nous une omelette!

OK, but I'm hungry. Let's make ourselves an omelet!

Here are some useful words to talk about saving money:

la banque	*bank*	les dettes (*f.pl.*)	*debts*
le chèque	*check*	les économies (*f.pl.*)	*savings*
le compte en banque	*bank account*	l'intérêt (*m.*)	*interest*
le compte d'épargne	*savings account*	le portefeuille	*wallet*
le crédit	*credit*	le versement	*payment/installment*

Giving Commands

The imperative mood is used to give commands or instructions. Use the **tu** form of a verb in the present tense to give an instruction to a person you know; drop the **-s**

GRAMMAR DEMYSTIFIED

Ça fait... que **and the Present Tense**

The expression **Ça fait... que** followed by a time expression and the *present* tense are used to say that an action has gone on for a period of time and is continuing. Look at these examples:

Ça fait longtemps **que** j'étudie.

I've been studying for a long time.

Ça fait une heure **que** nous travaillons.

We've been working for one hour.

ending of the verb for regular **-er** verbs and for the verb **aller**. Compare the following statements and commands:

Statement		Order/Command	
tu arrêtes	*you stop*	Arrête!	*Stop!*
tu économises	*you save*	Économise!	*Save!*
tu vas	*you go*	Va!	*Go!*
tu le fais	*you do it*	Fais-le!	*Do it!*

Use the **nous** form when giving an order to a group that includes yourself. Use the **vous** form to give an order to others (or to one person in a formal context), without including yourself. Compare the following statements and commands:

nous partons	*we leave*	Partons!	*Let's leave!*
vous l'offrez	*you offer it*	Offrez-le!	*Offer it!*

Only a few verbs have irregular imperative forms. They are **avoir**, **être**, and **savoir**. Look at the following sentences:

Aie/Ayons/Ayez... patience!	*Have / Let's have / Have . . . patience!*
Sois/Soyons/Soyez... calme(s)!	*Be / Let's be / Be . . . calm!*
Sache/Sachons/Sachez... la vérité!	*Know / Let's know / Know . . . the truth!*

The adverb **donc** often follows the verb in command forms, adding emphasis to the command. It may show an emotion such as impatience, resignation, or irritation on the part of the speaker. In English, this would be conveyed by tone of voice. Look at these examples:

Va **donc** au travail! Tu vas être en retard.	*Go to work! You'll be late.* (Impatience)
Faites **donc** attention!	*Pay attention!* (Irritation or frustration)

Oral Practice 6-2

Change each of the following statements to a command, say the command out loud, and finally listen to it on the CD. For the final four commands, practice using the adverb **donc** to make the command more emphatic.

TRACK 47

1. Tu vas à la banque, Marie-Josée.

2. Tu termines l'exercice, Yasmin.

3. Nous allons au cinéma.

4. Nous travaillons.

5. Vous êtes polis, les enfants.

6. Vous proposez une idée, Monsieur.

7. Vous économisez de l'argent.

8. Nous utilisons la carte de crédit.

9. Tu ouvres un compte d'épargne.

10. Tu fais un versement.

Expressing Restrictions

In the following dialogue, Rachel and Jean realize that they are well on their way to having the money for their trip, but Jean, impatient and tired of economizing, is starting to get a bit negative.

 TRACK 48

RACHEL: Jean, regarde combien d'argent nous avons dans notre compte en banque!

Jean, look how much money we have in our bank account!

JEAN: Super! Plus d'omelettes au dîner! On sort au restaurant!

Great! No more omelets for dinner! We'll go out to a restaurant!

RACHEL: Pas de folies, Jean!

No excesses, Jean!

JEAN: Jamais de la vie, Rachel!

Not on your life, Rachel!

RACHEL: Pas de filet mignon!

No filet mignon!

JEAN: Pas de ça, plus de ça, jamais de ça! Tu n'es pas drôle, Rachel.

None of that, no more of that, never that! You're no fun, Rachel.

RACHEL: Je n'ai pas envie de dépenser
    l'argent de nos vacances.

*I don't feel like spending our vacation
    money.*

JEAN: Commande donc une pizza!

OK, so order a pizza!

USING NEGATIVE EXPRESSIONS

You can make verbs, nouns, and other words negative in a variety of ways. A conjugated verb is surrounded or "hugged" by two negative words, for example, **ne/n'…pas** (*not*), while a negative infinitive is *preceded* by both negative words. Look at the following examples:

Conjugated Verbs vs. Infinitive Verbs

Je **n**'ai **pas** envie.	*I do **not** feel like it.*
Je préfère **ne pas** sortir.	*I prefer **not** to go out.*
Je **n**'ai **plus** envie.	*I don't feel like it **anymore**.*
Je préfère **ne plus** sortir.	*I prefer **not** to go out **anymore**.*
Je **n**'ai **jamais** envie.	*I **never** feel like it.*
Je préfère **ne jamais** sortir.	*I prefer **never** to go out.*
Je **ne** dépense **rien**.	*I don't spend **anything**.*
Je préfère **ne rien** dépenser.	*I prefer **not** to spend **anything**.*

A noun can be preceded by **pas de/d'** (*not*), **plus de/d'** (*no more, no longer*), **jamais de/d'** (*never*). A single adverb is simply preceded by **pas**, **plus**, or **jamais**.

Nouns		Adverbs	
Pas de dettes.	*No debts.*	**Pas** maintenant.	*Not now.*
Plus de dépenses.	*No more expenses.*	**Plus** rien.	*Nothing left. / Nothing else.*
Jamais de crédit.	*Never any credit.*	**Jamais** rien.	*Never anything.*

CULTURE DEMYSTIFIED

Breakfast and Dinner in France

A typical breakfast in France consists of juice, coffee or hot chocolate, and bread, butter, and jam. The bread is occasionally replaced with **croissants**, **petits pains au chocolat** (*chocolate croissants*), or **brioches** (*buttery rolls*). Eggs are rarely served at breakfast (if they are, they are soft-boiled). However, lunch or dinner (often a lighter meal) may sometimes include an omelet.

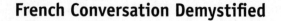

Look at these other frequently used negative expressions:

ne/n'... ni... ni	*neither . . . nor*	Pas du tout!	*Not at all!*
ne/n'... que	*only*	Certainement pas!	*Certainly not!*
ne/n'... personne	*nobody*	Absolument pas!	*Absolutely not!*

Je **n'**ai **ni** chèque **ni** carte de crédit.	*I have **neither** a check **nor** a credit card.*
Je **n'**ai **que** dix euros.	*I **only** have ten euros.*
Je **n'**invite **personne**.	*I invite **no one**. / I don't invite **anyone**.*

Written Practice 6-1

A. Au contraire. Change the affirmative sentences to negative sentences using the cues provided.

1. Elle est sympathique. (ne... pas) _____

2. Nous avons un compte d'épargne. (ne... plus) _____

3. Ils sont ici. (ne... jamais) _____

4. Je préfère aller au cinéma. (ne pas) _____

5. Il invite des amis. (ne... personne) _____

B. You are in a very negative mood. Show it in your answers to the following questions. Write the letter(s) of the correct response(s) on the line provided.

1. _____ Combien d'argent tu as dans ton portefeuille?   a. Rien.

2. _____ Tu as envie de faire des achats un de   b. Pas
ces jours?   maintenant.

3. _____ Il est sept heures. On va au restaurant?   c. Plus jamais.

4. _____ Tu as envie de quoi?   d. Ni l'une ni

5. _____ On retourne au Québec?   l'autre.

6. _____ Tu veux une omelette ou une pizza?   e. Pas
aujourd'hui.

       f. Plus rien.

Planning Itineraries

In the following dialogue, Rachel and Jean are ready to finalize plans for their Quebec trip. Where will they go? How will they get around? What do they want to see?

 TRACK 49

JEAN: J'achète ces billets d'avion, Rachel? Destination Montréal avec escale à Chicago.	*Should I buy these tickets, Rachel? Destination Montreal with a layover in Chicago.*
RACHEL: Oui, vas-y! Et fais aussi les réservations d'hôtel!	*Yes, go ahead! And make hotel reservations too!*
JEAN: Voilà, c'est fait!	*There, it's done!*
RACHEL: Pour aller à Québec, on prend l'avion ou on loue une voiture?	*To go to Québec City, are we taking a plane or renting a car?*
JEAN: Ni l'un ni l'autre. On va prendre le car; c'est moins cher.	*Neither. We're going to take the bus; it's less expensive.*
RACHEL: On a des réservations dans cette petite auberge sympa, Jean?	*Do we have reservations at that nice little inn, Jean?*
JEAN: Oui, le tarif de la chambre avec le petit déjeuner compris, c'est soixante-cinq dollars canadiens!	*Yes, the room rate with breakfast included is sixty-five Canadian dollars!*
RACHEL: Bon, Il ne reste que les excursions à organiser.	*Good. We only have side trips left to organize.*
JEAN: On va faire une longue promenade à vélo autour de la ville de Québec.	*We'll go on a long bike ride around Québec City.*
RACHEL: Pas trop longue, j'espère.	*Not too long, I hope.*
JEAN: Seize kilomètres, et c'est beau, tu vas voir.	*Sixteen kilometers, and it's beautiful, you'll see.*
RACHEL: Moi, je vais acheter un guide et faire une liste de sites à voir.	*I'm going to buy a guidebook and make a list of places to see.*

TALKING ABOUT TRAVEL AND ACTIVITIES
WITH FAIRE EXPRESSIONS

The verb **faire** usually means *to do* or *make* but it is also used in many idiomatic expressions. Look at the following examples:

faire appel à	*to call upon*	faire du vélo	*to go bicycling*
faire attention	*to pay attention*	faire du yoga	*to take yoga*
faire de l'arabe	*to take Arabic*	faire escale	*to have a layover*

faire des promenades à pied	*to go for walks*	faire les préparatifs	*to make preparations*
faire des réservations	*to make reservations*	faire un tour en voiture	*to go for a ride/drive*
faire du chinois	*to take Chinese*	faire un voyage	*to take a trip*
faire du ski	*to go skiing*	faire une croisière	*to go on a cruise*
faire du sport	*to do sports*	faire une visite guidée	*to take a guided tour*

Review the irregular conjugated forms of the verb **faire**:

je **fais**	*I do/make*	nous **faisons**	*we do/make*
tu **fais**	*you do/make*	vous **faites**	*you do/make*
il/elle **fait**	*he/she does/makes*	ils/elles **font**	*they do/make*
on **fait**	*one does/makes / we do/make*		

TALKING ABOUT TRANSPORTATION WITH PRENDRE **EXPRESSIONS**

The verb **prendre** (*to take*) is used with means of transportation, but also means *to have* with food and drink. Look at the following examples:

prendre...	*to take . . .*	**prendre...**	*to have . . .*
l'avion	*the/a plane*	le menu à dix euros	*the meal for ten euros*
le bateau	*the/a boat*	le petit déjeuner	*breakfast*
le bus / l'autobus	*the/a bus*	un pot	*a drink*
le car / l'autocar	*the/a bus/coach*	la quiche	*the quiche*
la voiture	*the car*	un verre de vin	*a glass of wine*

Remember that the irregular verb **prendre** has the following forms in the present tense:

je **prends**	*I take*	nous **prenons**	*we take*
tu **prends**	*you take*	vous **prenez**	*you take*
il/elle **prend**	*he/she takes*	ils/elles **prennent**	*they take*
on **prend**	*one takes / we take*		

Oral Practice 6-3

Answer each question using the cues in parentheses, and check the answer by listening to your CD. The answers are also in the Answer Key.

TRACK 50

1. Qu'est-ce que tu fais le soir? (faire du yoga)

2. Qu'est-ce que je fais vers six heures du matin? (prendre le petit déjeuner)

3. Qu'est ce-que tes amis font le week-end? (faire du sport)

4. Qu'est-ce que nous faisons en classe? (prendre des notes)

5. Qu'est-ce qu'on fait en cas d'accident? (faire appel à la police)

6. Comment tu vas au cours? (prendre le bus)

7. Tu prends un pot le matin? (Non / ne... jamais)

8. Elle prend le train pour aller à Avignon? (Non / ne... pas)

9. Tes amis font du ski dans les Alpes? (Non / ne... plus)

10. Tu fais du chinois et de l'arabe? (Non / ni... ni)

VACATION ACTIVITIES

In the following dialogue, Rachel and Jean talk about the activities they will engage in on their trip and what type of vacation they want to enjoy.

TRACK 51

JEAN: Moi, je voudrais des vacances actives dans la nature: faire de la nage, de la pêche, des promenades à pied et en vélo.

I would like an active vacation in nature: going swimming, fishing, walking, and bicycling.

RACHEL: J'adore la nature mais j'aime aussi les endroits historiques!

I love nature, but I also like historical sites!

JEAN: Descendre le Saint-Laurent en bateau, c'est une expérience historique!

To go down the St. Lawrence by boat, that's a historical experience!

RACHEL: Qu'est-ce que tu veux dire?

What do you mean?

JEAN: L'exploration du Canada par les Français a commencé le long du Saint-Laurent, non?

The exploration of Canada by the French started along the St. Lawrence, right?

RACHEL: Je vois. Tu parles des voyages de Jacques Cartier.

I see. You're talking about Jacques Cartier's voyages.

JEAN: Écoute, Rachel! Le vieux Québec est classé Patrimoine mondial et on va y passer tout le temps que tu veux.

Listen, Rachel! Old Québec is rated a World Patrimony site, and we'll spend all the time you want there.

RACHEL: Je t'assure qu'on va y marcher pendant des heures.

I assure you that we are going to walk there for hours.

Chapter Practice 6

A. Que font Rachel et Jean? Put Rachel and Jean's activities in chronological order from 1 to 5.

_____ Ils font des économies.

_____ Rachel travaille dans un café et Jean fait des heures supplémentaires.

_____ Ils pensent depuis longtemps à aller en vacances au Québec.

_____ Jean fait des réservations d'avion et d'hôtel.

_____ Ils décident d'aller au Québec en août.

B. Vrai ou faux? Are the following statements about Jean and Rachel true or false? Write **V** or **F** on the line provided.

1. _____ Ils ont cinq mille dollars à la banque en avril.

2. _____ Ils ne vont plus au restaurant d'avril à août.

3. _____ Ils font des économies.

4. _____ Ils ne mangent jamais d'omelette au dîner.

5. _____ Ils vont prendre l'avion de Montréal à Québec.

6. _____ Rachel aime les sites historiques depuis longtemps.

CULTURE DEMYSTIFIED

Le Patrimoine mondial

UNESCO (United Nations Educational, Scientific, and Cultural Organization) catalogues, names, and conserves world sites of outstanding cultural or natural importance to the common heritage of humanity. The Old City of Québec was classified a treasure of World Patrimony by this organization.

C. Answer the question **Qu'est-ce que Jean voudrait faire?** (*What would Jean like to do?*) using the cues provided. Then check the Answer Key.

1. He would like to go for walks. _____

2. He would like to take a cruise. _____

3. He would like to go bicycling. _____

4. He would like to go out to a restaurant. _____

5. He would like to take the bus. _____

CHAPTER QUIZ 6

Write the following sentences in French.

1. I would like to go bicycling. _____

2. You (**Tu**) never go on cruises. _____

3. We (**Nous**) take neither the train nor the bus. _____

4. I do not have breakfast. _____

5. No more soda! _____

6. Let's have a drink! _____

7. Go to the movies, John! _____

8. I prefer not to go out. _____

9. We have to save six hundred euros. (**Il faut**) _____

10. I have been working for two hours. _____

CHAPTER 7

Taking a Trip

In this chapter you will learn:

At the Airport
Talking About Possession
Going Through Customs
Staying in a Hotel
Asking About Tourist Information

At the Airport

In the following dialogue, Rachel and Jean get to the airport early, but Rachel seems a little nervous.

 TRACK 52

RACHEL: Dis, Jean, la queue est longue au comptoir d'Air France.   *Say, Jean, the line is long at the Air France counter.*

JEAN: Oui, mais nous sommes en avance. Il n'est que sept heures.

Yes, but we're early. It's only seven o'clock.

RACHEL: Il faut être à l'aéroport trois heures avant le départ pour un voyage international.

We have to be at the airport three hours before departure for an international flight.

JEAN: Oui, oui, je sais! Tu as l'itinéraire?

Yes, yes, I know! Do you have the itinerary?

RACHEL: Le voilà! Et voici nos passeports!

There it is! And here are our passports!

JEAN: Regarde! Le vol est à l'heure!

Look! The flight is on time!

RACHEL: Oui, pour l'instant!

Yes, for the moment!

JEAN: Cherchons nos cartes d'embarquement!

Let's get our boarding passes!

RACHEL: Quelle est notre porte d'embarquement?

What is our boarding gate?

JEAN: C'est la porte F37.

It's gate F37.

AIRPORT AND FLIGHT VOCABULARY

Here are some useful words to use when traveling by plane.

L'aéroport (*m.*)	*airport*	Le vol	*flight*
les bagages (*m.pl.*)	*baggage*	l'arrivée (*f.*)	*arrival*
la boutique hors taxe	*duty-free boutique*	le départ	*departure*
la douane	*customs*	la destination	*destination*
l'enregistrement (*m.*)	*check-in counter*	l'escale (*f.*)	*layover*
l'escalier (*m.*) roulant	*escalator*	le steward /	*flight attendant*
l'itinéraire (*m.*)	*itinerary*	l'hôtesse (*f.*)	
la porte d'embarquement	*boarding gate*	de l'air	
la salle d'attente	*waiting room*	en avance	*early / ahead of time*
la sécurité	*security*	à l'heure	*on time*
les toilettes (*f.pl.*)	*restroom*	en retard	*late*
la valise	*suitcase/bag*	remis	*postponed*
		annulé	*cancelled*
		direct	*direct*

Written Practice 7-1

Match one of the expressions on the left with a word on the right. Write the letter of the corresponding answer on the line provided.

1. _____ attendre le départ   a. la boutique
2. _____ descendre   b. l'enregistrement
3. _____ ouvrir les bagages   c. la porte d'embarquement
4. _____ se laver les mains   d. les toilettes
5. _____ acheter un souvenir   e. l'escalier roulant
6. _____ obtenir la carte d'embarquement f. la douane

VERB CONJUGATION: -RE VERBS IN THE PRESENT TENSE

A small group of **-re** verbs (*i.e.*, verbs with infinitives ending in **-re**) are regular in the present tense. Here are some frequently used **-re** verbs:

attendre	*to wait*	entendre	*to hear*
descendre	*to go down / to get off*	perdre	*to lose*
défendre	*to defend / to forbid*	répondre	*to answer*

Like regular **-er** verbs, the endings of these **-re** verbs change as a function of the subject. Look at the following sample conjugation. The stem is the infinitive form minus its **-re** ending. The endings are shown in boldface. (Note that the third-person singular form consists of the stem alone without any ending.)

j'attend**s**	*I wait / am waiting*	nous attend**ons**	*we wait / are waiting*
tu attend**s**	*you wait / are waiting*	vous attend**ez**	*you wait / are waiting*
il/elle attend	*he/she waits / is waiting*	ils/elles attend**ent**	*they wait / are waiting*
on attend	*one waits / is waiting* or *we wait / are waiting*		

Written Practice 7-2

Write the following sentences in French, using regular **-re** verbs on the lines provided.

1. We are waiting for the plane. _____
2. The passengers are getting off. _____

3. She hears the attendant. _____

4. You (**Vous**) are losing your boarding pass. _____

5. You (**Tu**) are answering. _____

6. They (*m.*) forbid smoking (**de fumer**). _____

GOING THROUGH SECURITY

In the following dialogue, Jean and Rachel, holding their boarding passes, are going through airport security.

🔘 TRACK 53

RACHEL: Attends, Jean. Je vais sortir mes produits de beauté de mon sac.

Wait, Jean. I'm going to take my toiletries out of my bag.

JEAN: Dépêche-toi, Rachel! Il y a des gens derrière nous.

Hurry, Rachel! There are people behind us.

RACHEL: Ne t'inquiète donc pas!

Don't worry!

JEAN: Ne te fâche pas, Rachel! Nous sommes en vacances!

Don't get mad, Rachel! We're on vacation!

RACHEL: D'accord, mais calme-toi, et ne sois pas si pressé!

OK, but calm down, and don't be in such a hurry!

JEAN: Ne perds pas ton passeport, Rachel! Et où est le mien?

Don't lose your passport, Rachel! And where's mine?

RACHEL: Voilà le mien et voilà le tien! Allons-y!

Here's mine and here's yours! Let's go!

REFLEXIVE VERBS

Verbs that take a direct object can be *reflexive* in French, meaning that each form is conjugated with a reflexive pronoun. Look at the conjugation of the reflexive verb **se fâcher** (*to get mad/angry*), and note the position of the reflexive pronoun before the conjugated verb:

Je **me** fâche.	*I get angry.*	Nous **nous** fâchons.	*We get angry.*
Tu **te** fâches.	*You get angry.*	Vous **vous** fâchez.	*You get angry.*
Il/Elle **se** fâche.	*He/She gets angry.*	Ils/Elles **se** fâchent.	*They get angry.*
On **se** fâche.	*One gets angry. / We get angry.*		

Reflexive (or *pronominal*) verbs convey that the subject is doing the action of the verb to itself. Compare the meanings of the following verbs when they are not reflexive and when they are reflexive.

Nonreflexive Structure

Jean fâche Rachel.	*Jean makes Rachel angry.*
Jean amuse Rachel.	*Jean amuses Rachel.*
Jean calme Rachel.	*Jean calms Rachel down.*

Reflexive Structure

Jean **se** fâche.	*Jean gets angry.*
Jean **s'**amuse.	*Jean is having fun.*
Jean **se** calme.	*Jean calms down.*

In the imperative form of a reflexive verb, the reflexive pronoun is placed *before* the verb when the command is *negative*, but it *follows* the verb when the command is *affirmative*. In addition, the pronoun **te** becomes **toi** in an affirmative command. Compare the following affirmative and negative commands:

Dépêche-**toi**!	*Hurry up!*	Ne **te** dépêche pas!	*Don't rush!*
Levez-**vous**!	*Get up!*	Ne **vous** levez pas!	*Don't get up!*
Couchons-**nous**!	*Let's lie down! / Let's go to bed!*	Ne **nous** couchons pas!	*Let's not lie down! / Let's not go to bed!*

Other common reflexive verbs are:

se dépêcher	*to hurry*	se réveiller	*to wake up*
se presser	*to hurry*	se lever	*to get up*
se promener	*to stroll / to take a walk*	se laver	*to wash*
se reposer	*to rest*	s'habiller	*to get dressed*
se coucher	*to go to bed / to lie down*	se brosser les dents	*to brush one's teeth*
s'endormir	*to fall asleep*	s'en aller	*to go away*

Oral Practice 7-1

Say each sentence out loud while completing it with the appropriate reflexive pronoun. Then listen to the answer on your CD. The pronouns are also listed in the Answer Key.

 TRACK 54

1. Nous sommes en retard. Dépêchons-_____ !

2. Nous avons le temps. Reposons-_____ !

3. C'est l'heure du départ, Michel. Réveille-_____ !

S'en aller

The conjugation of the idiomatic reflexive verb **s'en aller** (*to go away*) includes both the object pronoun **en** and the appropriate reflexive pronoun. Look at its present tense conjugation and its imperative forms:

Je m'en vais.	*I go away.*	Nous nous en allons.	*We go away.*
Tu t'en vas.	*You go away.*	Vous vous en allez.	*You go away.*
Il/Elle s'en va.	*He/She goes away.*	Ils/Elles s'en vont.	*They go away.*
On s'en va.	*One goes / We go away.*		
Va-t'en!	*Go away!*	Ne t'en va pas!	*Don't go away!*
Allez-vous-en!	*Go away!*	Ne vous en allez pas!	*Don't go away!*
Allons-nous-en!	*Let's go away!*	Ne nous en allons pas!	*Let's not go away!*

4. Tu es nerveux. Calme-_____ !

5. Je suis fatigué(e)! Je vais _____ reposer.

6. Regarde les passagers! Ils _____ pressent.

7. Si tu _____ fâches, je _____ en vais.

8. Tu n'es pas gentil! Va-_____ en!

Talking About Possession

In the following dialogue, Jean and Rachel are boarding the plane and looking for their seats.

TRACK 55

RACHEL: Nos places sont le 12 C et le 12 B. Tu veux ma place près de la fenêtre?

Our seats are 12 C and 12 B. Do you want my place near the window?

JEAN: C'est comme tu veux, Rachel!

As you wish, Rachel!

RACHEL: Avec ton ordinateur, c'est mieux pour toi!

With your computer, it will be better for you!

JEAN: C'est vrai! De plus, je ne me lève pas souvent pour aller aux toilettes.

That's true! Besides, I don't get up often to go to the bathroom.

RACHEL: Bon. Je prends ton siège au milieu.

OK. I'm taking your seat in the middle.

JEAN: Rachel, tu es assise sur ma ceinture de sécurité.

Rachel, you are sitting on my seat belt.

RACHEL: Désolée! Voilà ta ceinture, mais où est la mienne?

Sorry! There's your belt but where's mine?

JEAN: Oh zut! Je suis assis sur la tienne!

Oh darn! I am sitting on yours!

RACHEL: Attends, Jean. Tu peux mettre mon sac à main dans le coffre à bagages, s'il te plaît?

Wait, Jean. Can you put my handbag into the overhead, please?

POSSESSION WITH THE PREPOSITION DE

To express possession in French, use the following form: *what is owned* + **de/d'** + *the owner.* Look at these examples:

C'est la valise **de** Jean.   *This is Jean's suitcase.*

Voici le passeport **de** Rachel.   *Here is Rachel's passport.*

Quel est le numéro de siège **d'**Alice?   *What is Alice's seat number?*

POSSESSIVE ADJECTIVES AND PRONOUNS

In French, the possessive adjectives **mon, ma, mes** (*my*), **ton, ta, tes** (*your*, familiar) and **son, sa, ses** (*his/her*) show the gender and number of the noun that follows. Look at these examples:

Masculine		Feminine		Plural	
mon sac	*my purse/bag*	**ma** valise	*my suitcase*	**mes** bagages	*my luggage*
ton ticket	*your ticket*	**ta** place	*your seat*	**tes** voisins	*your neighbors*
son numéro	*his/her number*	**sa** carte	*his/her pass/ card*	**ses** papiers	*his/her papers*

However, the possessive adjectives **notre, nos** (*our*), **votre, vos** (*your*, plural/formal) and **leur, leurs** (*their*) reflect only the number (and not the gender) of the noun that follows. Look at these examples:

Masculine		Feminine		Plural	
notre portable	*our cell phone*	**notre** agence	*our agency*	**nos** affaires	*our belongings*
votre steward	*your flight attendant*	**votre** hôtesse	*your flight attendant*	**vos** pilotes	*your pilots*
leur itinéraire	*their itinerary*	**leur** piste	*their runway*	**leurs** escales	*their layovers*

Now look at the French possessive pronouns. Note how they show the gender and number of the noun they replace:

	Masculine	Feminine	Masculine	Feminine
	Singular		*Plural*	
mine	le mien	la mienne	les miens	les miennes
yours	le tien	la tienne	les tiens	les tiennes
his/hers	le sien	la sienne	les siens	les siennes
ours	le nôtre	la nôtre	les nôtres	les nôtres
yours	le vôtre	la vôtre	les vôtres	les vôtres
theirs	le leur	la leur	les leurs	les leurs

Le magazine, c'est **le mien**.   *The magazine, it's mine.*

La carte, c'est **la mienne**.   *The card, it's **mine***

Le vol 410, c'est **le sien**.   *Flight 410, it's **his/hers**.*

Ces places, ce sont **les nôtres**.   *These seats, they're **ours**.*

Written Practice 7-3

Rachel is very tired and can't find anything. Complete each of the following sentences with the appropriate possessive adjective or pronoun.

1. Où est (*my*) _____ valise, Jean?

2. (*Your*) _____ valise est ici devant moi, Rachel.

3. Ah oui, mais où est la (*yours*) _____ , Jean?

4. À côté de la (*yours*) _____ , Rachel.

5. Mais où sont (*our*) _____ passeports?

6. Ici, Rachel! Regarde! (*our*) _____ avion est arrivé!

7. Ce n'est pas le (*ours*) _____ , Jean. Ce n'est pas Air France!

8. Tu as raison. Prépare quand même (*your*) _____ documents. L'avion va arriver.

Going Through Customs

In the following dialogue, Rachel and Jean are going through customs after landing in Montréal. Listen to Rachel's interaction with the customs officer.

 TRACK 56

LE DOUANIER: Bonjour, Mademoiselle. Votre passeport et votre fiche de déclaration s'il vous plaît.

Hello, Miss. Your passport and your declaration form please.

RACHEL: Les voici, Monsieur. Je n'ai rien à déclarer.

Here they are, Sir. I have nothing to declare.

LE DOUANIER: Vous n'apportez rien de grande valeur?

You aren't bringing in anything valuable?

RACHEL: Non, non. Mon mari et moi sommes en visite pour quelques semaines.

No, no. My husband and I are visiting for a few weeks.

LE DOUANIER: Passez, Mademoiselle. Bienvenue au Canada. Je vous souhaite un bon séjour dans la belle province du Québec!

Pass through, Miss. Welcome to Canada. I wish you a pleasant stay in the beautiful province of Quebec!

Oral Practice 7-2

You will hear Rachel ask the flight attendant for various items. Play the role of the flight attendant pointing to or handing over the things mentioned by Rachel. After listening to each question, pause your CD, answer according to the cues; then play the CD, and check your answer. The answers are also in the Answer Key.

 TRACK 57

1. Rachel: Où sont les magazines, s'il vous plaît?

   Where are the magazines, please?

   Vous: _____ !

   Say: Here they are!

2. Rachel: J'ai soif.

   I'm thirsty.

   Vous: _____

   Say: Here's a soda!

3. Rachel: Où sont les toilettes, s'il vous plaît?

   Where is the restroom please?

   Vous: _____ derrière vous!

   Say: There they are . . .

VOCABULARY DEMYSTIFIED

Voici **and** voilà

Voici (*here is/are*) and **voilà** (*there is/are*) are frequently used in French when pointing to things or handing things over to someone. They may be used before a noun or after the object pronouns **le**, **la**, or **les**. Look at these examples:

Voici mon passeport. **Le voici**.	*Here is my passport. Here it is.*
Voilà ma fiche. **La voilà**.	*There is my form. There it is.*
Voici mes valises. **Les voici**.	*Here are my suitcases. Here they are.*

---

4. Rachel: J'ai besoin d'une serviette.   *I need a napkin.*

   Vous: _____ en papier!   *Say: There's (Here's) a . . . napkin!*

5. Rachel: J'ai besoin d'écouteurs.   *I need earphones.*

   Vous: _____ !   *Say: Here are your earphones!*

6. Rachel: Où est ma couverture?   *Where is my blanket?*

   Vous: _____ !   *Say: There it is!*

Staying in a Hotel

In the following dialogue, Jean and Rachel have arrived at their hotel and are checking in.

TRACK 58

JEAN: Bonjour, Mademoiselle. Ma femme et moi, nous avons une réservation pour huit jours.	*Hello, Miss. My wife and I have a reservation for eight days.*
LA RÉCEPTIONNISTE: Bonjour, Monsieur. Bonjour, Madame. Votre nom s'il vous plaît, Monsieur?	*Hello, Sir. Hello, Madam. Your name, please, Sir?*
JEAN: Jean Chevalier.	*Jean Chevalier.*

LA RÉCEPTIONNISTE: Oui, voilà vos clefs. C'est la chambre 612 au sixième étage. Vous avez une vue sur la ville.

Yes, here are your keys. It's room number 612 on the sixth floor. You have a view of the city.

JEAN: Il y a bien un grand lit et une salle de bains dans la chambre, n'est-ce pas?

There is a double bed and a bathroom in the room, right?

LA RÉCEPTIONNISTE: Oui, tout à fait! Si vous avez besoin de quoi que ce soit d'autre, n'hésitez pas à nous le faire savoir.

Yes, certainly! If you need anything else, don't hesitate to let us know.

JEAN: Et la chambre est climatisée!

And the room has air-conditioning!

LA RÉCEPTIONNISTE: Oui, Monsieur.

Yes, Sir.

JEAN: Parfait! Où et quand sert-on le petit déjeuner?

Perfect! Where and when do you serve breakfast?

LA RÉCEPTIONNISTE: De six heures à neuf heures dans la salle à manger à votre droite.

From six to nine o'clock in the dining room to your right.

JEAN: Merci beaucoup, Mademoiselle.

Thanks a lot, Miss.

ASKING FOR SERVICE

Here are some useful expressions for asking for help at a hotel:

	Je voudrais parler...	*I would like to speak . . .*
Pour les valises:	au garçon	*to the bellboy*
Pour la réservation:	au / à la réceptionniste	*to the receptionist*
Pour des problèmes:	au gérant / à la gérante	*to the manager*
Pour la chambre:	à la femme de chambre	*to the chambermaid*
Pour le service restaurant:	au serveur / à la serveuse	*to the waiter/waitress*

VOCABULARY DEMYSTIFIED

Le petit lit et le grand lit

There is no literal equivalent for *twin*, *queen*, and *king-size* beds in French. Therefore the phrases **un petit lit** and **un grand lit** are used to designate a *small* or *big* bed.

Pouvez-vous...	*Can you . . .*	**Pourriez-vous...**	*Could you . . .*
appeler un taxi?	*call a cab?*	mettre le chauffage?	*turn on the heat?*
changer les draps?	*change the sheets?*	monter mes bagages?	*bring my luggage up?*
descendre ma valise?	*take down my suitcase?*	préparer ma note?	*prepare my bill?*
faire une réservation?	*make a reservation?*	régler la climatisation?	*regulate the air-conditioning?*
me réveiller demain matin?	*wake me tomorrow morning?*	servir le petit déjeuner dans la chambre?	*serve breakfast in the room?*

Pouvez-vous m'apporter...	*Can you bring me . . .*
des serviettes?	*towels?*
un séchoir à cheveux?	*a hair dryer?*
une couverture?	*a blanket?*

Oral Practice 7-3

Pouvez-vous... ? Pretend you are at a hotel and you need the things indicated. How would you ask for them using the phrase **Pouvez-vous?** Cover the questions

GRAMMAR DEMYSTIFIED

French Contractions

The preposition **à** (*to, at, in*) contracts with the article **le** to produce **au** (**à + le = au**) and with the article **les** to produce **aux** (**à + les = aux**). Look at the following examples:

Je voudrais parler **au** serveur.   *I would like to talk **to the** waiter.*

Il faut parler **aux** agents de police.   *You have to talk **to the** policemen.*

Similarly, the preposition **de** (*from, of*) contracts with the article **le** to produce **du** (**de + le = du**) and with the article **les** to produce **des** (**de + les = des**). Remember that **de** must be used to express possession in French. Look at the following examples:

C'est le bouton **du** radiateur.   *It is the knob of the radiator [the radiator knob].*

C'est le poste **du** réceptionniste.   *It is the receptionist's extension.*

C'est l'arrêt **des** taxis.   *It is the taxi stop.*

on the right, and ask for the items out loud. You may then uncover the questions
while listening to the answers on your CD.

 TRACK 59

1. a sheet and a blanket *Pouvez-vous m'apporter un drap et une couverture?*

2. a hair dryer *Pouvez-vous m'apporter un séchoir à cheveux?*

3. breakfast in the room *Pouvez-vous me servir le petit déjeuner dans la chambre?*

4. a cab *Pouvez-vous m'appeler un taxi?*

5. more heat *Pouvez-vous augmenter le chauffage?*

6. a wake-up call at six *Pouvez-vous me réveiller à six heures?*

7. a restaurant reservation *Pouvez-vous me faire une réservation au restaurant?*

8. bags brought down *Pouvez-vous descendre mes valises?*

Asking About Tourist Information

In the following dialogue, Jean and Rachel are at the **Office du Tourisme** in Québec City.

 TRACK 60

JEAN: Bonjour, Monsieur. Je voudrais des renseignements sur la ville de Québec et ses environs.

Hello, Sir. I would like some information on the city of Québec and its surroundings.

L'EMPLOYÉ: Bonjour, Monsieur. Je peux vous renseigner sur les hôtels, les restaurants, les concerts. Que désirez-vous?

Hello, Sir. I can give you information about hotels, restaurants, concerts. What would you like?

RACHEL: Les tours guidés de la vieille ville, par exemple.

Guided tours of the Old Town, for example.

L'EMPLOYÉ: D'accord. Voilà une brochure avec les horaires des visites guidées de la vieille ville.

OK. Here's a brochure with the times for guided visits of the Old Town.

RACHEL: Il faut probablement faire une réservation, n'est-ce pas?

We probably have to make a reservation, don't we?

L'EMPLOYÉ: Ah oui, c'est recommandé, surtout en pleine saison.

Yes, it is recommended, especially in high season.

JEAN: J'ai entendu parler de très belles chutes dans la région.

I've heard about some very beautiful waterfalls in the region.

L'EMPLOYÉ: Oui, Monsieur. Il y a le parc de la Chute de Montmorency près d'ici.

Yes, Sir. There's the Park Montmorency waterfall near here.

JEAN: Et comment y accède-t-on?

And how do we get to it?

L'EMPLOYÉ: En car ou à bicyclette. Que préférez-vous?

By bus or by bicycle. Which do you prefer?

RACHEL: Ça dépend! C'est à quelle distance?

That depends! What's the distance?

L'EMPLOYÉ: C'est à environ douze kilomètres du centre-ville.

It's about twelve kilometers from the center of town.

JEAN: Super! Allons-y à bicyclette, Rachel! Merci beaucoup, Monsieur.

Great! Let's go by bike, Rachel! Thanks a lot, Sir.

ASKING QUESTIONS IN FRENCH

There are several ways to ask a *yes/no* question in French.

First, you can use the sentence structure of a statement, simply raising the pitch of your voice at the end. This is very often done in conversation. Start your CD, listen, and repeat each statement and question.

CULTURE DEMYSTIFIED

The Metric System

Remember that French-speaking countries around the world use the metric system. This is particularly important when figuring out distances measured in kilometers. It helps to know that one kilometer is .62 miles. The abbreviation for **kilomètre** is **km**.

 TRACK 61

Statement		Question	
C'est la bonne route.	*It's the right road.*	C'est la bonne route?	*Is this the right road?*
Vous avez un plan de la ville.	*You have a city map.*	Vous avez un plan de la ville?	*Do you have a city map?*
Il y a des visites.	*There are visits.*	Il y a des visites?	*Are there visits?*

Second, you may add **est-ce que / est-ce qu'** to the beginning of any statement to turn it into a question. This is also frequently done in conversation. Start your CD, listen, and repeat each question.

Est-ce que c'est la bonne route?   *Is it the right road?*

Est-ce que vous avez un plan de la ville?   *Do you have a city map?*

Est-ce qu'il y a des visites?   *Are there visits?*

Third, you may use inversion, with an inverted verb-subject pronoun. This structure is more formal. Note that with one or two exceptions inversion is not used when the subject-pronoun is **je**. Start your CD, listen, and repeat each question.

Est-ce la bonne route?   *Is this the right road?*

Avez-vous un plan de la ville?   *Do you have a city map?*

Y a-t-il des visites?   *Are there visits?*

Chapter Practice 7

 TRACK 62

A. Posons des questions! Change the following statements into questions by using the pitch of your voice. You may check your answers on the CD.

1. La chambre n'est pas climatisée.

2. Il y a une couverture sur le lit.

3. Rachel s'habille.

4. Le garçon apporte les bagages.

5. La serveuse va servir le petit déjeuner.

6. Ils se reposent.

Inserting -t- in Third-Person Inversions

Remember to insert a hyphenated **-t-** between the verb and the subject pronoun when the verb form in the present tense ends in a vowel. This happens in the third-person singular of all **-er** verbs and with some irregular verbs. Look at these examples:

Porte-**t**-elle un sac à main?	*Does she carry a purse?*
Parle-**t**-on français?	*Do we/they speak French?*
Va-**t**-il en ville?	*Does he go / Is he going to town?*

B. Encore des questions! Now change the same statements into questions using **est-ce que/qu'**. You may check your answers on the CD.

C. Toujours des questions! Change each of the following statements into a question using the inverted subject pronoun. You may check your answers on your CD.

1. Nous allons à l'office du tourisme.
2. C'est mon siège.
3. Il s'en va.
4. Vous pouvez appeler un taxi.

D. Des réponses! Answer the following questions affirmatively using reflexive and possessive pronouns. You may check your answers on the CD and in the Answer Key.

1. Est-ce que Rachel se fâche quand elle ne trouve pas son passeport? —Oui, elle _____ .

2. Est-ce que tu te dépêches quand tu es en retard? —Oui, je _____ .

3. Est-ce que vous vous lavez le soir? —Oui, nous _____ .

4. C'est le plan de Jean? —Oui, c'est le _____ .

5. Ce sont vos bagages? —Oui, ce sont les _____ .

6. C'est la place de Rachel? —Oui, c'est la _____ .

CHAPTER QUIZ 7

Match the following questions and answers. Write the letter of the appropriate
response on the line provided.

_____   1. Votre carte d'embarquement, s'il vous
             plaît?

_____   2. Votre numéro de vol est le 743?

_____   3. C'est un vol direct?

_____   4. Allez-vous au Canada?

_____   5. C'est votre valise?

_____   6. Qui est ce monsieur?

_____   7. Avez-vous des brochures de Québec?

_____   8. Pouvez-vous me réveiller?

_____   9. On peut régler le chauffage?

_____ 10. Va-t'en, s'il te plaît. Je vais me reposer.

a. Oui, à quelle
   heure?

b. Oui, les voilà.

c. Non, c'est la
   sienne.

d. Oui, il fait froid
   ici.

e. Non, je fais escale à
   Chicago.

f. La voici.

g. Non, c'est le 515.

h. D'accord. Je vais
   faire un tour
   en ville.

i. Oui, à Montréal.

j. C'est mon mari.

CHAPTER 8

French Family Life

In this chapter you will learn:

Morning Routines
Around the House
Daily Schedules
Television and Movies
Using Adjectives

Morning Routines

Christina is spending the summer with a host family in France. In the following dialogue, Nicole, the eldest of the family's children, is explaining the morning routine to her.

 TRACK 63

NICOLE: Il te faut combien de temps dans la salle de bains, Christina?

How much time do you need in the bathroom, Christina?

CHRISTINA: Environ une demi-heure.	*About half an hour.*
NICOLE: D'accord. À toi d'abord et ensuite à moi.	*OK. You first and then me.*
CHRISTINA: Et ta sœur et ton frère?	*What about your brother and sister?*
NICOLE: Jacques utilise la salle de bains de maman et de papa. Danielle fait sa toilette très tôt le matin.	*Jacques uses mom and dad's bathroom. Danielle gets ready very early in the morning.*
CHRISTINA: C'est ma serviette?	*Is this my towel?*
NICOLE: Oui, et voilà du savon, du shampooing, de l'adoucissant et un gant de toilette.	*Yes, and here's some soap, some shampoo, some conditioner, and a washcloth.*
CHRISTINA: Merci, je prends ma trousse de maquillage et ça y est.	*Thank you, I'll get my make-up kit, and that's it.*
NICOLE: Attends! Je te montre comment fonctionne la douche.	*Wait! I'll show you how the shower works.*
CHRISTINA: Ah bon!?	*Really!?*

EATING BREAKFAST

In the following dialogue, Christina is having breakfast with her host family.

 TRACK 64

NICOLE: Tu veux du café, du thé ou du chocolat chaud, Christina?	*Do you want coffee, tea, or hot chocolate, Christina?*
CHRISTINA: Du chocolat chaud, s'il te plaît.	*Some hot chocolate, please.*
NICOLE: Un croissant, une brioche, un petit pain au chocolat, une tartine au beurre?	*A croissant, a brioche, a chocolate croissant, bread and butter?*
CHRISTINA: Je prends un croissant et un peu de confiture aux fraises.	*I'll have a croissant and a little strawberry jam.*
NICOLE: Tu sais, d'habitude, le matin, nous mangeons du pain et de la confiture.	*You know, usually, in the morning, we eat bread and jam.*
CHRISTINA: Ça ne me dérange pas du tout. Le pain français est si bon!	*That doesn't bother me at all. French bread is so good!*

CULTURE DEMYSTIFIED

French Bathrooms

In many French houses or apartments, there is a full bathroom with toilet, bathtub, and sink; there may be a clothes washer and dryer in that room as well. In addition, there is usually another room with a toilet and a sink—a "half-bath." It is quite common for family members to share bathrooms; this requires coordinating bath and shower time. French showers are different from American showers: The showerhead is often attached to a handheld flexible cord which may be clipped onto a bar in the bathtub. The bathtub usually has no curtain.

NICOLE: C'est vrai et il y a beaucoup de variétés de pain, tu vas voir.

It's true, and there are many kinds of bread, you'll see.

CHRISTINA: Super!

Great!

USING THE PARTITIVE ARTICLE TO ASK FOR FOOD

To express *some*, use **du** before a masculine singular noun, **de la** before a feminine singular noun, **de l'** before a singular noun that starts with a vowel sound, and **des** before any plural noun. In English, the adverb *some* is often omitted and implied, as in the sentences below. In French, it must be expressed. Look at the following examples:

Je prends **du** lait dans mon café.   *I'll have (some) milk in my coffee.*

Je voudrais **de la** confiture.   *I would like (some) jam.*

De l'eau s'il vous plaît.   *Some water, please.*

J'aimerais **des** serviettes.   *I would like some napkins.*

Before Masculine Nouns

du jus	*some juice*
du lait	*some milk*
du pain	*some bread*
du sucre	*some sugar*

Before Feminine Nouns

de la baguette	*some baguette*
de la confiture	*some jam*
de la marmelade	*some marmelade*
de la tarte	*some tart/pie*

Before Vowel Sounds

de l'abricot	*some apricot*
de l'eau	*some water*
de l'huile	*some oil*

Before Plural Nouns

des céréales	*some cereal*
des œufs	*some eggs*
des petits pains	*some rolls*

To be more specific with amounts of food, use the following expressions. Note that in each expression the preposition **de/d'** is immediately followed by the noun and is not affected by the gender and number of the noun.

Je voudrais **un peu de** lait.   *I would like a little milk.*

Je mange **beaucoup d'œufs.**   *I eat a lot of eggs.*

C'est **assez de** lait.   *This is enough milk.*

C'est **trop de** sucre.   *This is too much sugar.*

Written Practice 8-1

Complete the following dialogue lines with the French equivalents of the words in parentheses.

1. Papa: Est-ce qu'il y a (*some*) _____ petits pains au chocolat aujourd'hui?

2. Maman: Non, mais il y a (*some*) _____ croissants et tu adores ça.

3. Nicole: Et voilà (*some*) _____ confiture, papa.

4. Papa: Merci, Nicole. Il me faut aussi (*a little*) _____ beurre.

5. Nicole: Voilà. C'est (*enough*) _____ beurre, papa?

6. Maman: C'est (*too much*) _____ beurre pour papa. Attention au cholestérol!

7. Jacques: Je peux avoir encore (*some*) _____ chocolat chaud?

8. Maman: Bien sûr, Jacques! Mais mange aussi (*some*) _____ pain!

9. Jacques: Oui, oui, ne t'inquiète pas! J'ai (*a lot of*) _____ choses à faire aujourd'hui et je vais manger un bon petit déjeuner.

Around the House

In the following dialogue, Nicole is showing Christina around the house.

 TRACK 65

NICOLE: Tout d'abord, je vais te faire faire un tour de la maison, Christina.

First of all, I am going to give you a tour of the house, Christina.

CHRISTINA: D'accord, c'est gentil.

OK, that's nice of you.

NICOLE: Alors, ici c'est la cuisine où on prend le petit déjeuner. La salle à manger, c'est où on mange le dîner en famille.

So here is the kitchen where we have breakfast. The dining room, that's where we eat dinner as a family.

CHRISTINA: Alors le matin, c'est le petit déjeuner à la cuisine avec toi. Le soir, c'est le dîner avec toute la famille.

So in the morning, it's breakfast in the kitchen with you. In the evening, it's dinner with the whole family.

NICOLE: C'est ça! Par ici, c'est la salle de bains que nous partageons. Là-bas, au bout du couloir, c'est le petit W.C.

That's it! This way, this is the bathroom we share. Over there at the end of the hall is the little bathroom.

CHRISTINA: Et voilà la chambre à coucher que je partage avec toi.

And here's the bedroom I share with you.

NICOLE: Oui, et la chambre de Danielle et celle de Jacques sont à côté de la nôtre.

Yes, Danielle's and Jacques's rooms are next to ours.

CHRISTINA: Oui! Je suppose que la chambre de tes parents est en haut.

Yes! I assume your parents' room is upstairs.

NICOLE: En haut il y a leur chambre, leur salle de bains et le bureau de papa.

Upstairs, there's their room, their bathroom, and Dad's study.

CHRISTINA: En bas, j'ai vu une cave et un garage.

Downstairs, I saw a cellar and a garage.

NICOLE: Oui, dans le garage il y a des vélos que nous utilisons régulièrement.

Yes, in the garage there are bikes we use regularly.

VOCABULARY: THE HOUSE

Just as in North America, the architecture and layout of houses vary as you travel through French regions. An old Alsatian house may be recognized by its woodwork and multi-floor style, while a Provençal house may be a ranch style with French

The Verb être

Although the majority of verbs in the French language are regular **-er** verbs (that follow a set pattern of conjugation in the present tense), we have already seen some common verbs that have irregular conjugations. Review the forms of the verb **être** in the present tense:

je **suis**	*I am*	nous **sommes**	*we are*
tu **es**	*you are*	vous **êtes**	*you are (plural/formal)*
il/elle **est**	*he/she is*	ils/elles **sont**	*they are*
on **est**	*one is / we are*		

doors. The rooms in a French house are fairly standard, however. Look at the following room designations and what one does in various places in the house:

Où aller? (*Where to go?*)		**Que faire?** (*What to do?*)	
la salle de bains	*the bathroom*	faire sa toilette	*to groom oneself*
le(s) W.C.	*the bathroom / W.C.*	aller aux toilettes	*to go to the bathroom*
la cuisine	*the kitchen*	faire la cuisine	*to do the cooking*
la salle à manger	*the dining room*	déjeuner/dîner	*to have lunch/dinner*
la chambre (à coucher)	*the (bed)room*	dormir	*to sleep*
		travailler/étudier	*to work / to study*
le bureau	*the study*	mettre en dépôt / garder	*to store / to keep*
le grenier	*the attic*		
la cave	*the cellar*	entreposer/stocker	*to stock*
le garage	*the garage*	garder les vélos/ voitures	*to keep the bikes/cars*
le salon	*the living room*		
		regarder la télé(vision)	*to watch TV/television*

Oral Practice 8-1

TRACK 66

Complete each sentence by saying where one would most likely go to do the things mentioned. Listen to the answer on your CD after each item. Remember to use the contraction **au** before masculine singular nouns.

1. Pour dormir, on va _____
2. Pour étudier, on va _____
3. Pour regarder la télé, on va _____
4. Pour dîner, on va _____
5. Pour trouver de vieilles choses, on va _____
6. Pour trouver les vélos, on va _____
7. Pour prendre la voiture, on va _____
8. Pour se laver les mains, on va _____
9. Pour chercher un vieux vin, on va _____ .
10. Pour préparer le dîner, on va _____ .

Daily Schedules

In the following dialogue, Nicole explains to Christina what an ordinary day will look like during her stay.

 TRACK 67

NICOLE: Bon, Christina, planifions notre journée. Après le petit déjeuner, on va aux cours.

Good, Christina, let's plan our day. After breakfast, we'll go to class.

CHRISTINA: Comment y allons-nous?

How do we get there?

NICOLE: On va prendre le bus. L'arrêt est au coin de la rue.

We'll take the bus. The stop is on the corner [of the street].

CHRISTINA: On se retrouve où après les cours?

Where do we meet after class?

NICOLE: Je finis avant toi. Alors, on peut se rejoindre au café Chez Michel.

I finish before you. So we can meet at the café Chez Michel.

CHRISTINA: Et on déjeune là-bas?

Do we have lunch there?

NICOLE: Quelquefois oui; mais s'il fait beau, je prends juste une boisson et ensuite je vais manger un sandwich au parc.

Yes, sometimes; but if it's nice, I just have a drink and then I go eat a sandwich in the park.

CHRISTINA: Bonne idée!

Good idea!

NICOLE: L'après-midi, tu as généralement des activités et des excursions avec d'autres étudiants étrangers.

In the afternoon, you usually have activities and side trips with other foreign students.

CHRISTINA: C'est vrai. Aujourd'hui, je dois rejoindre mon groupe au centre d'étudiants à quatorze heures.

That's true. Today I have to meet my group at the student center at two P.M.

NICOLE: Oui, je vais te montrer où.

Yes, I'm going to show you where.

CHRISTINA: À l'heure du dîner, je dois être de retour chez toi pour manger en famille, n'est-ce pas?

At dinnertime, I have to be back at your house for a family dinner, right?

NICOLE: Oui, sauf les soirs où tu es occupée avec ton groupe, par exemple le samedi soir.

Yes, except for evenings when you are busy with your group, for example on Saturday nights.

DESCRIBING EVENTS IN THE PRESENT, PAST, AND FUTURE

There are many ways to situate events in the present, past, and future: by the clock, by specifying parts of the day such as *morning* or *evening*, by noting the days of the week, or with the use of adverbs that establish chronological sequences, such as **plus tard** (*later*).

CULTURE DEMYSTIFIED

Meals

In France, evenings start around six P.M. That is why people say **Bonjour** up until that time, and then **Bonsoir** starting around six. The evening meal, **le dîner**, is generally eaten later than in the United States, any time after seven P.M. When people go out to concerts or to the theater, they may have a late **souper** (*supper*) afterwards. In French-speaking Canada, people often refer to *lunch* as **le dîner** and to *dinner* as **le souper**.

Time of Day Although the twenty-four-hour clock is used to express P.M. time for official functions, it is usually not used in familiar conversations. In that case, you use the expressions **du matin** (*in the morning*), **de l'après-midi** (*in the afternoon*), and **du soir** (*in the evening*) to clarify which part of the day you mean. Look at the following examples. Note that in writing the time, the French abbreviation for **heure(s)** is **h**.

Je me réveille vers 6 h. **du matin**.	*I wake up around six A.M.*
Je vais rejoindre mes amis vers 2 h. **de l'après-midi**.	*I am going to join my friends around two P.M.*
J'ai rendez-vous à 8 h. **du soir**.	*I have a date at eight P.M.*

In French, do not try to translate the English preposition *in* when talking about *morning, afternoon, evening,* or *night*. Look at the following examples:

Parts of the Day

Le matin, je vais aux cours.	*In the morning I go to class.*
L'après-midi, je suis libre.	*In the afternoon I am free.*
Le soir, j'aime sortir.	*In the evening, I like to go out.*
La nuit, j'aime dormir.	*At night, I like to sleep.*

Days In French, do not try to translate the English preposition *on* when specifying on which day an activity takes place. But remember to use the article **le** before the day of the week to generalize the day. Look at the following examples:

On a Specific Day

Samedi, je vais au cinéma avec toi.
On Saturday, I'm going to the movies with you.
Dimanche, je vais étudier.
On Sunday, I'm going to study.

Generally on a Given Day

Le samedi, je sors avec des copains.
On Saturdays, I go out with friends.
Le dimanche, je me repose.
On Sundays, I rest.

Remember that on a French calendar, the week starts on **lundi** (*Monday*) and the days of the week are not capitalized.

lundi	*(on) Monday*	vendredi	*(on) Friday*
mardi	*(on)Tuesday*	samedi	*(on) Saturday*
mercredi	*(on) Wednesday*	dimanche	*(on) Sunday*
jeudi	*(on) Thursday*		

Adverbs of Time To narrate events in chronological order, you may use adverbs of time such as the following. Here are some frequently used adverbs. Look at the examples that follow:

(tout) d'abord	*first (of all)*	alors	*then/so*
avant	*before*	après	*after/afterwards*
ensuite	*then/afterwards*	finalement	*finally*
aujourd'hui	*today*	demain	*tomorrow*
en avance	*early*	à l'heure	*on time*
en retard	*late*	bientôt	*soon*

Oral Practice 8-2

🔘 TRACK 68

In which order will Christina most likely engage in the following activities? Match the activity with the time. Say the sentence out loud; then listen to the answer on your CD. You may also check the answers in the Answer Key.

1. À 7 h. du matin   a. elle va être aux cours.
2. Vers 8 h. du matin,   b. elle va étudier.
3. Vers 10 h. du matin,   c. elle va faire des excursions.
4. Vers midi,   d. elle va se coucher.
5. L'après-midi,   e. elle va prendre une douche.
6. Le soir vers 7 h.,   f. elle va déjeuner avec Nicole.
7. Après le dîner,   g. elle va prendre le petit déjeuner.
8. Vers 10 h. du soir,   h. elle va dîner en famille.

Television and Movies

In the following dialogue, Christina and Nicole are alone at home on a Friday night. They are discussing what to do.

🔘 TRACK 69

NICOLE: Qu'est-ce que tu as envie de faire, Christina?

What do you feel like doing, Christina?

CHRISTINA: Est-ce qu'il y a quelque chose d'intéressant à la télé?

Is there something interesting on TV?

NICOLE: Laisse-moi voir ce qu'il y a ce soir sur ARTE. Ils jouent de très bons films suivis de discussions.

Let me see what is on ARTE tonight. They show very good movies followed by discussions.

CHRISTINA: Est-ce que vous avez des émissions de télé réalité?

Do you have TV reality shows?

NICOLE: Oui, surtout sur TF1, mais je n'aime pas trop.

Yes, especially on TF1, but I do not like (them) too much.

CHRISTINA: C'est vrai qu'il y a beaucoup de films et de feuilletons américains à la télé française?

Is it true that there are many American movies and shows on French TV?

NICOLE: Oui, mais il y a aussi des films espagnols, italiens et allemands, par exemple.

Yes, but there are also Spanish, Italian, and German movies, for example.

CHRISTINA: Super, mais je ne comprendrais rien!

Great, but I wouldn't understand anything!

NICOLE: Mais si! N'oublie pas les sous-titres. Demain soir, il faut absolument qu'on regarde l'émission « Tout le monde en parle. »

Yes, you would. Don't forget the subtitles. Tomorrow night, we definitely have to watch the show "Everybody's Talking About It."

CHRISTINA: Pourquoi? Qu'est-ce que c'est?

Why? What is it?

NICOLE: Parce que c'est l'émission qui te renseigne sur les derniers scandales dans le monde du spectacle et en politique.

Because it is the show that brings you up to date on the latest scandals in the world of show business and politics.

CULTURE DEMYSTIFIED

French TV

There are six principal TV channels, privately or state-run, available across the country which attract over ninety percent of French viewers. Some channels offering news and current affairs, sports, reality shows, and foreign films with subtitles are TF1, France 2 and France 3. **La Cinq/ARTE** is a shared Franco-German channel showing many quality documentaries and movies. In addition, many French receive broadcasts from nearby European countries such as Belgium, Luxembourg, Switzerland, Italy, and Spain, as well as outside Europe.

GOING TO THE MOVIES

In the following dialogue, Christina and Nicole have decided to go to the movies. They are discussing what to see.

TRACK 70

NICOLE: Quel genre de films est-ce que tu préfères, Christina?

What type of movies do you prefer, Christina?

CHRISTINA: J'adore les films d'aventure et les films biographiques.

I love adventure and biographical movies.

NICOLE: Un grand nombre de films d'aventure sont américains.

A great number of adventure movies are American.

CHRISTINA: Je préfère voir quelque chose de très français.

I prefer seeing something very French.

NICOLE: Bon, je cherche sur Internet ce qu'on joue dans le quartier.

OK, I'm checking on the Internet for what's playing in the neighborhood.

CHRISTINA: Il paraît qu'il y a un film franco-belge qui raconte l'histoire d'une femme peintre.

There's supposed to be a Franco-Belgian movie that tells the story of a female painter.

NICOLE: Dis donc, tu es renseignée. Ah voilà. Il joue au Studio 1.

Say, you are well informed. Ah there it is! It's playing at Studio 1.

CHRISTINA: Oui, je m'intéresse beaucoup au cinéma français. Ce film va gagner des Césars.

Yes, I am very interested in French cinema. This movie is going to win Césars [French Oscars].

NICOLE: Il y a une séance à 19 h. et la suivante à 21 h.

There is a show at seven P.M. and the next one at nine P.M.

CHRISTINA: Si on se dépêche, on peut encore arriver à l'heure pour celle de 19 h.

If we hurry, we can still arrive on time for the seven P.M. one.

NICOLE: Sinon, on peut aller plus tard à la séance de 21 h.

If not, we can go later to the nine o'clock show.

DISCUSSING MOVIES

In the following dialogue, Christina and Nicole have seen the movie Christina had heard about. They are now exchanging opinions.

TRACK 71

CHRISTINA: Ce film est le meilleur film du monde!

This movie is the best movie in the world!

NICOLE: Je ne le trouve pas mauvais mais pas si brillant que ça non plus.

I don't find it bad but not that great either.

CHRISTINA: Oh! L'interprétation d'Isabelle est superbe!

Oh! Isabelle's performance is superb!

NICOLE: Je l'ai vu jouer mieux que ça.

I've seen her play better than that.

CHRISTINA: Vraiment! Eh bien, moi, je suis épatée!

Really! Well, (as for) me, I am in awe!

NICOLE: Pardonne-moi si je ne suis pas aussi épatée que toi.

Forgive me if I am not as awed as you.

CHRISTINA: Qu'est-ce que tu penses du sujet?

What do you think about the theme?

NICOLE: Le thème de la femme sous-estimée est moins excitant pour moi que pour toi.

The theme of the underestimated woman is less exciting for me than for you.

CHRISTINA: Tu n'es vraiment pas enchantée par ce film.

You are really not excited by this movie.

NICOLE: Si, si. C'est un bon film mais j'aime mieux la science-fiction que le drame, tu vois.

Yes, yes I am. It's a good movie, but I like science fiction better than drama, you see.

CULTURE DEMYSTIFIED

The César Awards

The **César** Award ceremony (the French counterpart of the American Oscars) has been held in Paris each February since 1975. The contestants are mostly French and Francophone films, but a foreign film category is also included. Winners are selected by the members of the **Académie des Arts et Techniques du Cinéma**. The award is named after the sculptor César Baldaccini (1921–1998); the trophies are sculptures by the artist.

Oui **and** si

The words **oui** and **si** both mean *yes*. However, **si** is used as an emphatic *yes* answer to a negative question. Look at the following examples:

Ce film te plaît? —**Oui**, il me plaît.	*Do you like this movie? —Yes, I like it.*
Ce film **ne** te plaît **pas**? —**Si**, il me plaît!	*Don't you like this movie? —Yes, I do like it!*

In addition, **si** can be used as an adverb before an adjective; in this case it means *so*. Look at the following examples:

Il est **si** aimable.	*He is **so** pleasant.*
Elle est **si** heureuse.	*She is **so** happy.*

Finally, **si** (**s'** before the letter **i**) can mean *if*, as in the following examples:

Si le film est bon, allons le voir!	*If the movie is good, let's go see it!*
S'il pleut, je vais rester à la maison.	*If it rains, I'm going to stay home.*

Using Adjectives

To describe a movie, you will need adjectives. Look at the following examples:

Le film est...	*The movie is . . .*		
bon	*good*	mauvais	*bad*
excellent	*superb*	horrible	*horrible*
génial	*amazing*	ennuyeux	*boring*
intéressant	*interesting*	déprimant	*depressing*
long	*long*	court	*short*

To compare movies, use the comparative structures **plus... que**, **moins... que**, and **aussi... que**.

Ce film est **plus** passionnant **que** l'autre.	*This movie is more inspiring than the other one.*
Ce dernier film est **moins** génial **que** le précédent.	*This last movie is less brilliant than the previous one.*

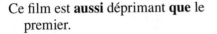

Ce film est **aussi** déprimant **que** le premier.	*This movie is as depressing as the first one.*

To single out one movie as *the most interesting* or *the most boring*, use the superlative structure as in the following examples:

Ce film est **le plus intéressant** de tous.	*This movie is the most interesting of them all.*
Ce film est **le plus ennuyeux** des trois.	*This movie is the most boring of the three.*

With comparatives and superlatives, the adjectives must agree in gender (masculine/feminine) and number (singular/plural) with the noun they describe.

Add -**e** to an adjective to make it feminine (unless the masculine singular form already ends in -**e**), and add -**es** to make an adjective feminine and plural.

Cette actrice est **plus** joli**e que** les autres.	*This actress is prettier than the others.*
Ces actrices sont **les plus** joli**es**.	*These actresses are the prettiest.*

Add -**s** to an adjective to make it plural (unless the masculine singular form already ends in -**s**).

Ces acteurs sont très doué**s**.	*These actors are very talented.*
Ces deux acteurs sont **les plus** doué**s** **de** tous.	*These actors are the most talented of them all.*

BON **AND** MEILLEUR

The irregular comparative/superlative form of the adjective **bon** (*good*) is **meilleur** (*better*) and **le meilleur** (*best*). Remember that **meilleur** must agree in gender and number with the noun it describes. Look at the following examples:

L'acteur est **bon**.	*The actor is good.*	L'actrice est **bonne**.	*The actress is good.*
Cet acteur est **meilleur**.	*This actor is better.*	Cette actrice est **meilleure**.	*This actress is better.*
Cet acteur est **le meilleur**.	*This actor is the best.*	Cette actrice est **la meilleure**.	*This actress is the best.*

MEILLEUR **AND** MIEUX

Although both these words are translated as *better* and *best*, they are not used inter-changeably. **Meilleur** is an *adjective* that describes a noun (person or thing), while **mieux** is an *adverb* that modifies a verb (showing how something is done). Look at the following examples:

Qui est **le meilleur** acteur français?	*Who is the best French actor?*
La meilleure version de *Cyrano* est la dernière.	*The best version of Cyrano is the last one.*
J'aime **mieux** les comédies.	*I like comedies better. / I prefer comedies.*
Qui joue le personnage de Cyrano **le mieux**?	*Who plays the character of Cyrano the best?*

Oral Practice 8-3

Using the following key to describe a movie, say sentences aloud based on the cues given. Then verify your response by listening to the answers on your CD. The first one has been done for you as an example.

🔘 TRACK 72

A: excellent / meilleur / le meilleur   B: bon   C: mauvais   D: horrible / pire / le pire

1. Ce film d'amour _____ . *Ce film d'amour est mauvais.*
2. Ce dernier film de *Star Trek* _____ de tous les *Star Trek.*
3. Tous les films de Truffaut _____ .
4. Ce film d'épouvante _____ que l'autre.
5. Je déteste les films longs et ennuyeux. Ce dernier _____ .
6. Quel film intéressant! _____ de tous les films actuels.

Chapter Practice 8

A. Qu'est-ce que tu voudrais ce matin? (*What would you like this morning?*) Starting your answers to the above question with **Je voudrais**, say out loud that you would like the following items. Be sure to use the appropriate partitive articles

to express the idea of *some* (**du / de l' / de la / des**) before each noun. Then check your answers by listening to the CD.

TRACK 73

1. *cereal*
2. *coffee*
3. *orange juice*
4. *bread*
5. *jam*
6. *water*

B. Quand et où? (*When and where?*) Reconstruct each sentence logically with one of the elements provided in each column. Write the corresponding letters on the line provided. You can find the answers in the Answer Key. The first one has been done for you as an example:

A. la nuit	a. à la cuisine
B. le soir	b. au restaurant
C. à 8 h. du matin	c. au parc
D. le samedi et le dimanche	d. à l'université
E. le matin et le soir	e. à la maison
F. le lundi et le mercredi	f. dans la chambre à coucher
G. après le dîner	g. au cinéma
H. après le concert	h. dans la salle de bains

  C / a   1. On prend le petit déjeuner
  _____   2. On dort
  _____   3. On prend le souper
  _____   4. On prend une douche
  _____   5. On regarde un film sur ARTE
  _____   6. On va au cours de français deux fois par semaine
  _____   7. On fait un tour en vélo le week-end
  _____   8. On va à la séance de 20 h.

C. Des comparaisons (*Comparisons*). Complete the following statements as appropriate, using one of the following choices.

meilleur / mieux / le mieux / moins / plus

1. Les USA sont _____ grands que la France.

2. Le vélo est _____ rapide que l'avion.

3. Le chocolat est _____ que la quiche (*better*).

4. J'aime _____ parler français en France (*better*).

5. Les Français mangent _____ à midi (*best*).

6. C'est le _____ film de l'année (*best*).

D. **Si** and **oui** (*Yes*). Write the appropriate *yes* answer in the space provided.

1. Le film est long? _____

2. Le cinéma n'est pas dans le quartier? _____

3. C'est ta chambre? _____

4. C'est aujourd'hui mardi? _____

5. Tu veux du thé? _____

6. Ce ne sont pas les toilettes? _____

CHAPTER QUIZ 8

Vrai ou faux? Read each statement out loud, and state **Vrai** or **Faux** accordingly. Then listen to the answers on your CD.

TRACK 74

_____ 1. Un film ennuyeux est meilleur qu'un film amusant.

_____ 2. On prend le déjeuner avant le dîner.

_____ 3. On gare la voiture dans le salon.

_____ 4. Les Français mangent beaucoup de pain.

_____ 5. Un César français est l'équivalent d'un Oscar américain.

_____ 6. On regarde un film au W.C.

_____ 7. Il faut arriver au cinéma en retard.

_____ 8. D'abord on dîne et ensuite on fait la cuisine.

_____ 9. Après le déjeuner, c'est l'après-midi.

_____ 10. On va généralement dormir le soir.

CHAPTER 9

Eating at Home

In this chapter you will learn:

Shopping for Food
Measurements and Foods
Preparing Dinner at Home

Shopping for Food

Christina and her host mother, Mme Duval, have gone shopping. Christina will soon discover that shopping for food in France can be quite an experience.

 TRACK 1

MME DUVAL: Allons d'abord au supermarché et ensuite au marché et à la boulangerie, Christina.

Let's first go to the supermarket and then to the market and the bakery, Christina.

CHRISTINA: Je voudrais acheter des fruits pour le pique-nique demain.

I would like to buy some fruit for the picnic tomorrow.

MME DUVAL: Ah oui, tu sors avec tes copains.

Oh yes, you're going out with your friends.

CHRISTINA: Oui, j'apporte aussi des serviettes.

Yes, I'm also bringing napkins.

MME DUVAL: Aucun problème! On va acheter des serviettes au supermarché.

No problem! We're going to buy the napkins at the supermarket.

CHRISTINA: Et des fruits aussi?

And fruit also?

MME DUVAL: Oh, Christina, des fruits, il vaut mieux en acheter au marché. Ils sont plus frais.

Oh, Christina, fruit, it's preferable to buy some at the market. It's fresher.

CHRISTINA: C'est où le marché?

Where is the market?

MME DUVAL: Aujourd'hui, c'est samedi. Il y en a plusieurs en ville.

Today is Saturday. There are several of them in town.

CHRISTINA: Ah bon!?

Really!?

MME DUVAL: Mais oui, j'achète toujours des fruits et des légumes frais le samedi.

Of course. I always buy fresh fruit and vegetables on Saturdays.

VOCABULARY: SUPERMARKETS AND OPEN MARKETS

Two essential places where a French person might shop for foods are the supermarket and the open market. Here are some foods one might find there:

Non-Countable Nouns

Fruit and *fish* are examples of non-countable nouns in English; they are not used in the plural. Even when the English word *fruit* refers to several pieces of fruit, it generally remains in the singular. However, a non-countable noun in English is not necessarily so in French, and vice-versa. *Fruit*, for example, is **les fruits** and *fish* is **les poissons** in French. **La charcuterie** (*cold cuts*) is an example of a noun which is non-countable in French, but is countable in English.

Au supermarché	*At the supermarket*	**Au marché**	*At the market*
le beurre	*butter*	la banane	*banana*
le café	*coffee*	le fruit	*fruit*
l'eau (*f.*)	*water*	le haricot vert	*green bean*
le jus	*juice*	la laitue	*lettuce*
le lait	*milk*	le légume	*vegetable*
la moutarde	*mustard*	l'orange (*f.*)	*orange*
le sucre	*sugar*	le poisson	*fish*
le vin	*wine*	la pomme	*apple*

Written Practice 9-1

Match the place and the food according to where you would be most likely to go to buy that food if you lived in a small French town, by writing **S** (**supermarché**) or **M** (**marché**) on the line provided. Write **S/M** if the food can be found in both places.

_____   1. le poisson

_____   2. le vin

_____   3. le café

_____   4. les bananes

_____   5. les légumes

_____   6. la moutarde

_____   7. la laitue

_____   8. le beurre

AT THE SUPERMARKET

In the following dialogue, Christina and Mme Duval are at the supermarket ready to shop.

 TRACK 2

CHRISTINA: Il y a vraiment beaucoup de sortes d'eau minérale: Vichy, Évian, Vittel.	*There really are many types of mineral water: Vichy, Evian, Vittel.*
MME DUVAL: Oui, nous aimons l'eau de Vichy. Prenons-en six bouteilles.	*Yes, we like Vichy water. Let's take six bottles [of it].*
CHRISTINA: Et les fromages, combien de sortes est-ce qu'il y a?	*How about cheeses, how many kinds are there?*

MME DUVAL: Oh! Il y en a trop pour les compter! — *Oh! There are too many (of them) to count!*

CHRISTINA: Ah bon!? — *Really!?*

MME DUVAL: Oui, et j'en achète toujours plusieurs sortes. — *Yes, and I always buy several kinds.*

CHRISTINA: Vous achetez du vin au supermarché? — *You buy wine at the supermarket?*

MME DUVAL: Généralement oui. On en trouve de très bons, tu sais. — *Usually, yes. You find some very good ones, you know.*

CHRISTINA: Mon père achète le vin dans un magasin de vins aux USA. — *In the U.S., my father buys wine in a wine store.*

MME DUVAL: Ici, nous achetons généralement les vins rares et chers au magasin de vins. — *Here we generally buy rare and expensive wines at the wine store.*

TALKING ABOUT FOOD WITH THE PRONOUN EN

We have previously seen how to use the partitive article (**du, de la, de l', des**) before foods when talking about *some* food. Once the food has been mentioned, it would be redundant to keep using the noun for it; therefore it is often replaced by the pronoun **en** in French. The pronoun **en** is placed before the verb except in affirmative commands. Look at the following examples:

Je veux **des fruits**. J'**en** veux trois ou quatre sortes. — *I want some fruit. I want three or four kinds [of them].*

Vous désirez **du jus de pomme**? —Oui, j'**en** désire un litre. — *Do you want some apple juice? —Yes, I'd like a liter [of it].*

The pronoun **en** is equivalent to *some* or *any* in English.

Cette limonade est délicieuse. J'**en** veux. — *This lemonade is delicious. I want some.*

Ce café est horrible. Je n'**en** veux pas. — *This coffee is horrible. I don't want any.*

Ces fruits sont délicieux. J'**en** achète un kilo. — *This fruit is delicious. I am buying a kilo [of it].*

The pronoun **en** is often used with the expression **Il y a** (*There is / There are*).

Il y a **des marchés** en ville? —Oui, il y **en** a.	*Are there any markets in town? —Yes, there are (some).*
Il y a **du sucre** dans ce thé? —Oui, il y **en** a.	*Is there sugar in this tea? —Yes, there is [some].*
Il y a trop **de sel** dans les légumes? —Non. Il n'y **en** a pas trop.	*Is there too much salt in the vegetables? —No, there is not too much [of it].*

The pronoun **en** is used with expressions of quantity such as **un peu** (*a little*) or **beaucoup** (*a lot*). Look at the following examples, noting how the equivalent of **en** is often omitted in English:

As-tu **de l'eau**? —Oui, j'**en** ai un peu.	*Do you have any water? —Yes, I have a little [of it].*
Tu achètes **des oranges**? —Oui, mais je n'**en** achète pas beaucoup.	*Are you buying oranges? —Yes, but I'm not buying a lot [of them].*
Tu voudrais **de la moutarde**? —Oui, j'**en** voudrais une cuillerée.	*Would you like some mustard? —Yes, I would like a spoonful [of it].*

In affirmative commands, the pronoun **en** is attached to the verb with a hyphen and follows it. Note that the verb preceding **en** in the affirmative command always ends in **-s** or **-z**. Don't forget to pronounce the **liaison** between the verb and **en** (*i.e.*, a **z** sound links verb and pronoun).

De la charcuterie? Prends-**en** une livre!	*Cold cuts? Take [familiar] a pound [of them]!*
Des baguettes? Prenons-**en** trois!	*Baguettes? Let's take three [of them]!*
De l'eau? Prenez-**en** une bouteille!	*Water? Take [formal or plural] a bottle [of it]!*

Oral Practice 9-1

Answer each of the following questions. Follow the cues, and remember to use the pronoun **en** to replace the food named. Verify your answers on the CD. The first one has been done for you.

 TRACK 3

1. Il y a de l'eau ici? (oui)   *Oui, il y en a.*
2. Il y a des légumes dans la soupe? (non)

3. Il y a du lait dans le café? (oui)

4. Tu prends de la glace? (oui, une livre)

5. Tu achètes de la charcuterie? (oui, un kilo)

6. Tu voudrais des fruits? (oui, mais pas trop)

7. Tu prends du sucre? (oui, une cuillerée)

8. Tu achètes des pommes? (oui, mais pas beaucoup)

9. Tu voudrais du beurre? (oui, un peu)

10. On prend de la limonade? (oui, une bouteille)

Now give the following affirmative commands. Remember to use the pronoun **en**, and place it after the verb.

11. Du pain? Oui, _____ ! (*Buy some!*)

12. Du poisson? Oui, _____ ! (*Let's buy some!*)

AT THE OUTDOOR MARKET

TRACK 4

MME DUVAL: Tu vois les beaux fruits et légumes, Christina?	*See the beautiful fruits and vegetables, Christina?*
CHRISTINA: Les melons sentent bon. Je peux en prendre un?	*The melons smell good. May I take one?*
MME DUVAL: N'en prends pas! Demande au marchand de t'en donner un.	*Don't take any! Ask the merchant to give you one.*
CHRISTINA: Pourquoi ça? Je voudrais en choisir un qui est mûr.	*Why? I'd like to choose one that is ripe.*
MME DUVAL: Alors, demande au monsieur de t'en donner un qui est mûr.	*So ask the gentleman to give you one that's ripe.*
CHRISTINA: Bon, d'accord. Je vais aussi prendre quelques pommes, peut-être un kilo.	*OK, fine. I am also going to take a few apples, maybe a kilo.*
MME DUVAL: Moi, je vais prendre deux kilos d'oranges. On en mange beaucoup.	*I am going to take two kilos of oranges. We eat a lot of them.*

Open Fruit and Vegetable Markets

When shopping for fruit and vegetables at open markets, including the stands in front of local **épiceries** (*small grocery stores*), you should refrain from touching any fruit or vegetables yourself. This is usually considered bad manners in France. Instead, tell the salesperson what you want: a ripe melon for tonight, bananas for the weekend, small peaches, etc.

USING DEFINITE ARTICLES FOR FOODS IN GENERAL

When talking about foods, you do not always use the partitive articles (**du**, etc.). To talk about foods *in general*, use the appropriate definite article: **le, la, l'**, and **les**. Look at the following examples of foods preceded by a definite article. Note that in the English sentence, the article is omitted in generalizations.

Le fromage est servi après le repas.	*Cheese is served after the meal.*
L'eau est bonne pour la santé.	*Water is good for your health.*
Nous achetons **la** glace au supermarché.	*We buy ice cream at the supermarket.*
Tu aimes **les** fruits?	*Do you like fruit?*

USING INDEFINITE AND DEMONSTRATIVE ARTICLES WITH COUNTABLE FOODS

To talk about a specific countable food, use the singular indefinite article **un** for a masculine noun or **une** for a feminine noun. To talk about *some* foods, use the plural indefinite article **des** (identical to the plural partitive article).

Je voudrais **un** melon, s'il vous plaît.	*I would like a melon, please.*
Je vais acheter **une** limonade.	*I am going to buy a lemonade.*
Prends **des** haricots verts!	*Take some green beans!*

When you single out specific foods and point to them, use the appropriate demonstrative adjective (**ce, cet, cette**, or **ces**, the equivalent of *this/that*). **Ce** is used before a masculine singular noun starting with a consonant, or before (one of the few) masculine singular nouns starting with an aspirate **h** (**le/ce haricot, le/ce héros**).

Donnez-moi **ce** melon, s'il vous plaît!   *Give me this melon, please!*

Regarde **ce** haricot vert! Il est pourri...   *Look at this green bean. It's rotten . . .*

Cet is used before a masculine singular noun starting with a vowel sound.

Cet appartement est bien situé.   *This/That apartment is well situated.*

Cette is used before all feminine singular nouns.

Je voudrais **cette** orange.   *I would like this orange.*

Ces is used before all plural nouns, masculine or feminine.

Je n'aime pas **ces** légumes.   *I don't like these vegetables.*

Measurements and Foods

You have already learned expressions of quantity, such as **assez** (*enough*), **un peu** (*a little*), **beaucoup** (*a lot / many*), and **trop** (*too much / many*). Note the addition of **quelques** (*a few*) and **plusieurs** (*several*) to the list below, as well as the nouns of quantity on the right.

Expressions of Quantity		**Nouns of Quantity**	
assez (de)	*enough (of)*	une bouteille (de)	*a bottle (of)*
beaucoup (de)	*a lot/many (of)*	une boîte (de)	*a can/box/package (of)*
quelques	*a few*	une douzaine (de)	*a dozen (of)*

GRAMMAR DEMYSTIFIED

-Ci and -là with Demonstrative Adjectives

The demonstrative adjectives **ce**, **cet**, and **cette** can mean *this* or *that*; the plural adjective **ces** can mean *these* or *those*. However, when comparing two items, it is sometimes necessary to underline the contrast between them: just add the elements **-ci** or **-là** to the noun. Look at the following example:

Je veux acheter un melon mais **ce** melon-**ci** est trop petit, **ce** melon-**là** est trop grand et les autres ne sont pas assez mûrs.   *I want to buy a melon, but **this** melon is too small, **that** melon is too big, and the others are not ripe enough.*

plusieurs	*several*	une livre (de)	*a pound (of)*
trop (de)	*too much / too many*	un kilo (de)	*a kilo(gram) (of)*
un peu (de)	*a little*	un litre (de)	*a liter (of)*

With the exception of **quelques** and **plusieurs**, which are always directly followed by plural nouns, all these expressions include the preposition **de/d'** (*of*).

Il y a **plusieurs** bananes mûres.	*There are several ripe bananes.*
Prends **quelques** oranges.	*Take a few oranges.*
J'achète **un peu de** laitue.	*I am buying a little lettuce.*
Je voudrais **une livre de** radis.	*I would like a pound of radishes.*
Achète **une douzaine d'**œufs!	*Buy a dozen eggs!*

Oral Practice 9-2

🔘 TRACK 5

Play the role of the shopper (**toi**) in the following dialogue. Give the correct definite article, indefinite article, or demonstrative adjective when answering the merchant (**le marchand**). You will find the answers in the Answer Key. Don't forget to listen to the entire dialogue on your CD.

LE MARCHAND: Vous désirez?

TOI: Je voudrais (1) (*some*) _____ pommes, s'il vous plaît.

LE MARCHAND: Des pommes rouges ou jaunes?

TOI: (2) (*These*) _____ pommes rouges!

CULTURE DEMYSTIFIED

Metric Weight System

In French-speaking regions around the world, you will get accustomed to the use of *grams* and *kilograms* when buying foods that are weighed. **Un kilogramme** or **un kilo** (*one kilogram*) has **mille grammes** (*1,000 grams*) and **un kilo** consists of **deux livres** (*two pounds*). Do not confuse **un livre** (*a book*) with **une livre** (*a pound*). Also remember that a U.S. pound is a little less than a pound in the metric system. Expect to see the abbreviations for **gramme** and **kilogramme**: **g** and **kg**.

LE MARCHAND: Voilà (3) (*a few*) _____ pommes rouges! Et avec ça?

TOI: Je prends aussi (4) (*a*) _____ melon bien mûr.

LE MARCHAND: (*This*) (5) _____ melon-ci est bon pour aujourd'hui!

TOI: D'accord. Et je voudrais trois de (6) (*these*) _____ oranges.

LE MARCHAND: Vous aimez (7) _____ légumes (*in general*)? Ils sont bien frais.

TOI: J'adore (8) _____ haricots verts (*in general*). Donnez-m'en un kilo.

AT THE BAKERY

 TRACK 6

MME DUVAL: Bonjour, Monsieur Jeanval, comment allez-vous aujourd'hui?	*Hello, Mr. Jeanval. How are you today?*
LE MARCHAND: Je sens un peu mes rhumatismes mais ça va, merci.	*I feel my rheumatism a little but I'm OK, thank you.*
MME DUVAL: Je vais prendre deux baguettes et un pain de campagne.	*I'm going to have two baguettes and a country bread.*
LE MARCHAND: Pas de croissants aujourd'hui?	*No croissants today?*
MME DUVAL: Si! Donnez-m'en six, s'il vous plaît!	*Yes, give me six of them, please!*
LE MARCHAND: Et avec ça?	*And with that?*
MME DUVAL: Donnez-moi aussi cette belle tarte!	*Give me this beautiful tart also!*
LE MARCHAND: Cette tarte-ci? La tarte aux fraises?	*This tart here? The strawberry tart?*
MME DUVAL: Oui, merci!	*Yes, thank you!*

VOCABULARY: SPECIALTY STORES

A French bakery is often both a bakery and a pastry shop; it is then called **une boulangerie-pâtisserie**. In addition to breads and pastries, they may offer a variety of sandwiches, quiches, and other lunch foods. Similarly, a butcher shop often includes a deli section and is then called **une boucherie-charcuterie**. Look at examples of foods you might find in these stores:

Greetings in Neighborhood Stores

In France, customers are expected to exhibit good manners when entering a store, especially a specialty or neighborhood store. This means saying **Bonjour** and using a title such as **Monsieur**, **Madame**, or **Mademoiselle** before asking for assistance. Regular customers, while remaining formal with the store clerk or merchant, will often show interest in the person's well-being by asking **Comment allez-vous?** and making small talk, if time and circumstances allow.

À la boulangerie-pâtisserie	At the bakery-pastry shop	À la boucherie-charcuterie	At the butcher-deli
la baguette	baguette	l'agneau (*m.*)	lamb
le croissant	croissant	le bifteck	steak
le gâteau / le petit gâteau	cake/cookie	la dinde	turkey
		le jambon	ham
le pain	bread	le poulet	chicken
la pâtisserie	pastry	le rosbif	roast beef
le petit pain	roll	le salami	salami
la tarte	tart		

Written Practice 9-2

Where would you logically find each food? Write **BP** (**boulangerie-pâtisserie**) or **BC** (**boucherie-charcuterie**) on the line provided.

_____ 1. de la pâtisserie

_____ 2. du poulet

_____ 3. du bifteck

_____ 4. du pain

_____ 5. des petits gâteaux

_____ 6. de la dinde

_____ 7. une tarte

_____ 8. du jambon

French Food Stores

In France, supermarkets (**supermarchés** or **hypermarchés**) are often found outside urban areas near highways. Although vastly popular for a once-a-week shopping trip, they are still an addition to, rather than a replacement for, smaller specialty stores like **boulangeries** and **boucheries**.

Preparing Dinner at Home

In the following dialogue, Nicole and Christina are helping Nicole's father prepare dinner.

 TRACK 7

NICOLE: Je veux bien nettoyer les haricots, papa.	*I'll gladly clean the green beans, Dad.*
CHRISTINA: Moi, je peux laver la salade.	*I can wash the salad.*
M. LAFANGE: D'accord. Tu peux aussi faire une vinaigrette, Nicole?	*Can you also make a vinaigrette, Nicole?*
NICOLE: Oui, bien sûr!	*Yes, of course!*
CHRISTINA: Tu fais la vinaigrette? Tu n'en achètes pas toute faite?	*You make the vinaigrette? You don't buy any ready-made?*
NICOLE: Non, nous en faisons avec de l'huile, du vinaigre et de la moutarde.	*No, we make some with oil, vinegar, and mustard.*
CHRISTINA: C'est si simple?	*Is it that simple?*
M. LAFANGE: Oui, Christina! Et ce soir, nous allons manger du bœuf bourguignon. Tu connais?	*Yes, Christina! And tonight we're going to eat beef bourguignon. Do you know [it]?*
CHRISTINA: Je sais que c'est du bœuf cuit dans du vin rouge.	*I know it's beef cooked in red wine.*
M. LAFANGE: Du vin de Bourgogne, naturellement. Pendant que tu finis de laver la salade, je vais faire rôtir le bœuf.	*Burgundy wine, naturally. While you finish washing the salad, I'll roast the beef.*

CHRISTINA: Voilà. La salade est prête. Je peux vous aider?

There! The salad is ready. Can I help you?

M. LAFANGE: Je vais ajouter un peu de farine, des oignons, des herbes, des épices et du vin. Passe-moi la bouteille de vin, veux-tu?

I'm going to add a little flour, some onions, herbs, spices, and wine. Pass me the bottle of wine, will you?

CHRISTINA: Super. Je vais bien regarder et apprendre!

Great. I'll watch carefully and learn!

VERB CONJUGATION: -IR VERBS IN THE PRESENT TENSE

There are three groups of regular verbs in French. You have already seen how to conjugate **-er** verbs (Part 1, Chapter 4) and **-re** verbs (Part 2, Chapter 7). Next, you will learn the conjugation of regular **-ir** verbs in the present tense. The endings corresponding to each subject, added to the stem (here, the infinitive minus the **-ir** ending), are in boldface. Remember *not* to pronounce the final **-s**, **-t**, **-z**, or **-ent** of these verbs.

rôtir	*to roast*		
je rôt**is**	*I roast*	nous rôt**issons**	*we roast*
tu rôt**is**	*you roast*	vous rôt**issez**	*you roast*
il/elle rôt**it**	*he/she roasts*	ils/elles rôt**issent**	*they roast*
on rôt**it**	*one roasts / we roast*		

Look at the following commonly used regular **-ir** verbs:

applaudir	*to applaud*	remplir	*to fill (up)*
choisir	*to choose*	réussir	*to succeed*
finir	*to finish*	rôtir	*to roast*

ASKING FOR THINGS USING THE VERBS VOULOIR AND POUVOIR

Vouloir (*to want*) and **pouvoir** (*to be able to / can*) are commonly used when asking for something. Look at the following examples, and note that these verb forms are often followed by an infinitive:

Tu **veux** du pain?	*Do you want some bread?*
Je **veux acheter** du jambon et du salami.	*I want to buy some ham and salami.*

Avec une bonne recette, on **peut réussir**.   *With a good recipe, you can succeed.*

Nous **pouvons faire** la cuisine ce soir.   *We can do the cooking tonight.*

These two important verbs have irregular but similar patterns of conjugation in the present tense. Remember *not* to pronounce the final **-x**, **-t**, **-z**, and **-ent** endings.

vouloir	*to want*	**pouvoir**	*to be able to*
je **veux**	*I want*	je **peux**	*I can*
tu **veux**	*you want*	tu **peux**	*you can*
il/elle **veut**	*he/she wants*	il/elle **peut**	*he/she can*
on **veut**	*one wants / we want*	on **peut**	*one/we can*
nous **voulons**	*we want*	nous **pouvons**	*we can*
vous **voulez**	*you want*	vous **pouvez**	*you can*
ils/elles **veulent**	*they want*	ils/elles **peuvent**	*they can*

Written Practice 9-3

Complete the following sentences with the correct form of the verbs in parentheses.

1. Nous _____ le dîner. (finir)

2. Elles _____ le poulet. (rôtir)

3. Tu _____ le vin. (choisir)

4. Paul _____ la bouteille. (remplir)

5. Ils _____ des pommes. (vouloir)

GRAMMAR DEMYSTIFIED

Je voudrais **and** je pourrais

Je voudrais and **je pourrais** are often used to ask for something. These are conditional forms of the verbs **vouloir** and **pouvoir**. Look at the following examples:

Je **voudrais** un peu plus de sel.   *I would like a little more salt.*

Est-ce que je **pourrais** me **resservir**?   *Could I help myself to another serving?*

6. Vous _____ choisir. (pouvoir)

7. Je _____ faire le steak. (vouloir)

8. On _____ manger? (pouvoir)

EATING DINNER

In the following dialogue, Nicole, her father, and Christina are having Dad's home-made **bœuf bourguignon** for dinner. Listen to the conversation.

 TRACK 8

M. LAFANGE: Nicole, la table est prête?	*Nicole, is the table ready?*
NICOLE: Oui, papa. Je sors les verres à vin?	*Yes, Dad. Shall I take out the wine glasses?*
M. LAFANGE: Oui, bien sûr. Je te sers, Christina. Passe ton assiette.	*Yes, of course. Let me serve you Christina. Pass your plate.*
CHRISTINA: Merci, Monsieur.	*Thank you, Sir.*
NICOLE: Le bœuf est délicieux, papa.	*The beef is delicious, Dad.*
M. LAFANGE: Oui, il est plutôt réussi.	*Yes, it is rather good.*
NICOLE: Passe le pain, Christina!	*Pass the bread, Christina!*
CHRISTINA: Voilà. Je te sers de l'eau?	*There. Can I serve you some water?*
NICOLE: Oui, remplis bien mon verre, s'il te plaît.	*Yes, fill my glass all the way, please.*
M. LAFANGE: Est-ce qu'il y a assez de sel?	*Is there enough salt?*
CHRISTINA: Pour moi, oui, c'est parfait.	*For me, yes, it's perfect.*
M. LAFANGE: Bon, moi, je me sers un verre de vin.	*Well, I will serve myself a glass of wine.*
NICOLE: Je peux en avoir un peu aussi, papa?	*May I have some too, Dad?*
M. LAFANGE: Bien sûr, Nicole. Et toi, Christina, tu en veux?	*Of course, Nicole. And you, Christina, do you want some?*
CHRISTINA: Oh non, merci, Monsieur. Pas pour moi.	*Oh no, thank you, Sir. Not for me.*

Bread, Wine, and Cheese

In France, bread, wine, and cheese are basic foods and traditional parts of many lunches and dinners. Bread is always on the table, and cheese is served after lunch and dinner. There are hundreds of cheeses in France. There are also many wines, and local wines are often good and inexpensive. Thus wine sometimes accompanies lunch and almost always accompanies dinner. It is not unusual for French adolescents to have an occasional glass of wine with dinner with their family at home or at a restaurant.

TALKING ABOUT FOOD USING THE VERBS SERVIR AND SORTIR

Look at the following examples of how **servir** (*to serve*) and **sortir** (*to take out / to go out*) may be used:

Tu **vas servir** la dinde?	*Are you going to serve the turkey?*
Jeanne, tu **vas sortir** le poulet du four?	*Jeanne, are you going to take the chicken out of the oven?*

Servir and **sortir** are not regular **-ir** verbs, but rather follow an irregular pattern of conjugation in the present tense. The verbs **partir** (*to leave*) and **dormir** (*to sleep*) are also in this group. Note that, for the singular persons of the conjugation (**je**, **tu**, **il/elle**), the stem shown in boldface is the infinitive minus its last three letters. In the plural conjugated forms, the stem is the infinitive minus its infinitive ending **-ir**. Remember *not* to pronounce the **-s**, **-t**, **-x**, and **-ent** endings of these verbs.

servir	to serve	sortir	to go out / to take out
je **ser**s	*I serve*	je **sor**s	*I go out / take out*
tu **ser**s	*you serve*	tu **sor**s	*you go out / take out*
il/elle **ser**t	*he/she serves*	il/elle **sor**t	*he/she goes out / takes out*
on **ser**t	*one serves / we serve*	on **sor**t	*one goes out / takes out*
nous **serv**ons	*we serve*	nous **sort**ons	*we go out / take out*
vous **serv**ez	*you serve*	vous **sort**ez	*you go out / take out*
ils/elles **serv**ent	*they serve*	ils/elles **sort**ent	*they go out / take out*

Written Practice 9-4

Which one makes sense? **Servir** or **sortir**? Complete each sentence with the correct present tense form of the appropriate verb.

1. Nous _____ du bœuf ce soir.

2. Les Durand _____ le samedi soir.

3. Marie _____ avec ses amis.

4. M. Durant _____ le vin au dîner.

5. Vous _____ ce week-end?

6. Tu _____ la salade, Jean?

Chapter Practice 9

A. Au marché. Listen to the following dialogue between a produce vendor and a shopper, and complete the sentences as appropriate. The answers are also in the Answer Key.

 TRACK 9

LE MARCHAND: Vous désirez _____ melon, Mademoiselle?

Would you like a melon, Miss?

LA CLIENTE: Oui, merci, pour _____ soir.

Yes, thank you, for tonight.

LE MARCHAND: Ce melon- _____ est bien mûr.

This melon here is quite ripe.

LA CLIENTE: Très bien. Donnez-moi aussi une livre _____ pommes.

Very good. Give me a pound of apples as well.

LE MARCHAND: _____ pommes-là?

Those apples there?

LA CLIENTE: Oui, merci, et _____ bananes.

Yes, thank you, and a few bananas.

LE MARCHAND: Vous en _____ deux ou trois?

Would you like two or three?

LA CLIENTE: Donnez-m' _____ quatre, s'il vous plaît.

Give me four (of them), please.

LE MARCHAND: Vous aimez _____ poires? Elles sont bien fraîches.

Do you like pears? They are quite fresh.

LA CLIENTE: Oui, un _____ s'il vous plaît.

Yes, one kilo please.

B. Le dîner. Complete each response in writing using the verb from the question in your answer.

1. Tu choisis le salami ou le jambon? —Je _____ le jambon.

2. Vous rôtissez le poulet? —Non, nous _____ le bœuf.

3. On sert la salade? —Non, je veux _____ la soupe d'abord.

4. Elles veulent de la tarte? —Oui, mais Marie _____ de la glace.

5. Tu peux faire la sauce? —Oui, je _____ faire la sauce.

6. Je remplis ton verre? —Oui merci, _____ mon verre, s'il te plaît!

CHAPTER QUIZ 9

Logique ou pas logique? Write **L** if the statement is logical; write **PL** if it is not logical.

_____ 1. Je remplis la livre.

_____ 2. Nous servons du bœuf.

_____ 3. Elle veut un kilo de vinaigrette.

_____ 4. Tu choisis la tarte aux pommes.

_____ 5. Vous voulez du vin.

_____ 6. Ils veulent une cuillerée de croissant.

_____ 7. Je voudrais ce pain-ci et ce pain-là.

_____ 8. Vous pouvez manger un peu d'eau.

_____ 9. Je peux finir cinq kilos d'agneau.

_____ 10. Du sel? Non, merci. Je n'en veux pas.

CHAPTER 10

Shopping for Clothes

In this chapter you will learn:

Shopping at a Department Store
Describing Colors
Paying for Clothes
Using Object Pronouns to Avoid Redundancy

Shopping at a Department Store

Today Christina and Nicole are going shopping in a department store. Christina is looking for a pair of shoes, and Nicole needs a dress for the upcoming wedding of a cousin.

TRACK 10

CHRISTINA: Tu veux bien m'accompagner au rayon de chaussures? Après, moi, je t'aide à choisir ta robe.

Do you mind accompanying me to the shoe department? Afterwards, I'll help you choose your dress.

NICOLE: Qu'est-ce que tu cherches exactement?

What exactly are you looking for?

CHRISTINA: Des chaussures d'été.

Summer shoes.

NICOLE: Des chaussures plates ou à talons, ouvertes, fermées? Quelle pointure?

Flat or high-heeled shoes, open, closed? What size?

CHRISTINA: Ma pointure aux États-Unis, c'est le huit mais je ne sais pas quelle pointure c'est en France.

My shoe size in the States is eight, but I don't know what size it is in France.

NICOLE: C'est du quarante chez nous, je pense.

That's a forty here, I think.

CHRISTINA: Tiens, regarde, quelles jolies chaussures rouges!

Hey, look, what pretty red shoes!

NICOLE: Et voilà les mêmes chaussures, mais elles sont bleues.

And there are the same shoes, but they're blue.

CHRISTINA: Elles sont jolies, mais les talons sont trop hauts.

They are pretty, but the heels are too high.

NICOLE: Je crois que je vais les essayer moi-même.

I think I'm going to try them on myself.

CHRISTINA: Oh! Comme elles te vont bien! Quelle jolie forme!

Oh! They look so good on you! What a pretty shape!

NICOLE: Écoute, Christina, je les paie, et je reviens.

Listen, Christina, I am going to pay for them, and I'll be back.

VOCABULARY: DEPARTMENT STORES

In a department store, look for a **panneau indicateur** (*directory*) that lists the **rayon** (*department*) you are interested in. Here are some **rayons** with items you would find there:

Using the Present Tense to Talk About the Future

In familiar conversation, the present tense is often used in place of the French future tense. This stresses the immediacy of the action that is about to happen. Look at the following examples:

J'arrive dans dix minutes.	*I'll arrive in ten minutes.*
Il joue dans une heure.	*He'll play in an hour.*
Je reviens tout de suite.	*I'll be back right away.*

Les chaussures	*shoes*	**Les accessoires**	*accessories*
le basket / le tennis	*sneaker*	la casquette	*(baseball) hat/cap*
la botte	*boot*	la ceinture	*belt*
la chaussure à talon	*high-heeled shoe*	le foulard	*scarf*
la sandale	*sandal*	le sac à main	*purse/handbag*

Les vêtements femmes	*women's clothing*	**Les vêtements hommes**	*men's clothing*
le bas	*stocking*	la chaussette	*sock*
le chemisier	*woman's shirt/blouse*	la chemise	*man's shirt*
la jupe	*skirt*	le costume	*man's suit*
le pull	*sweater*	la cravate	*tie*
la robe	*dress*	le pantalon	*pants/trousers*
le tailleur	*woman's suit*	le short	*shorts*

Oral Practice 10-1

 TRACK 11

If the item of clothing is most likely worn by a man, write **H** (**pour hommes**). If it is most likely worn by a woman, write **F** (**pour femmes**), and if it is worn by both men and women, write **HF** (**pour hommes et pour femmes**). Then listen to your CD.

1. le tailleur _____
2. la chaussette _____
3. le chemisier _____
4. la cravate _____
5. la chemise _____
6. la robe _____

7. la casquette _____
8. le pantalon _____
9. la jupe _____
10. le sac à main _____
11. la botte _____
12. la chaussure à talons _____

In the following dialogue, Nicole is back with her newly purchased shoes just as Christina has found a pair for herself.

 TRACK 12

CHRISTINA: Quelles chaussures adorables et confortables! Qu'est-ce que tu penses?	*What adorable and comfortable shoes! What do you think?*
NICOLE: Elles te vont très bien! Combien elles coûtent?	*They fit you very well! How much do they cost?*
CHRISTINA: Soixante euros. C'est un peu cher, mais je les adore.	*Sixty euros. It's a little expensive, but I love them.*
NICOLE: Alors, passe à la caisse!	*Then go to the cash register!*
CHRISTINA: Oui, et alors, allons chercher ta robe!	*Yes, and then let's go look for your dress!*
Au rayon des vêtements femmes.	*In the women's clothing department.*
NICOLE: Maman voudrait que je porte une robe violette au mariage de ma cousine, mais je préfère une couleur crème.	*Mom would like me to wear a purple dress to my cousin's wedding but I prefer a cream color.*
CHRISTINA: Tu préfères une robe ou un tailleur?	*Do you prefer a dress or a suit?*
NICOLE: Une robe sans manches. Le mariage est en août.	*A sleeveless dress. The wedding is in August.*
CHRISTINA: Et quelle est ta taille?	*And what's your size?*
NICOLE: C'est le trente-six. Chez vous, c'est le six, je crois.	*It's thirty-six. In your country, it's a six, I think.*
CHRISTINA: Tu veux une couleur claire alors?	*You want a light color then?*
NICOLE: Oui, rien de trop vif ou de foncé.	*Yes, nothing too bright or dark.*

CHRISTINA: Qu'est-ce que tu penses de cette robe mauve?

What do you think of that mauve dress?

NICOLE: Elle me plaît. Je l'essaie tout de suite.

I like it. I'll try it on right away.

CHRISTINA: Attends. Il y en a une autre ici; elle est crème.

Wait. There's another one here; it is cream-colored.

NICOLE: Je la prends aussi. Où est le salon d'essayage?

I'll take it too. Where is the fitting room?

CHRISTINA: Le voici à gauche!

Here it is on the left!

Quelques moments plus tard.

A few minutes later.

NICOLE: Christina, je ne peux pas décider laquelle des deux robes me va le mieux.

Christina, I can't decide which of the two dresses fits me best.

CHRISTINA: Laquelle coûte le moins cher?

Which one costs the least?

NICOLE: La mauve coûte le moins cher, et elle est vraiment jolie.

The mauve one costs the least, and it is really pretty.

CHRISTINA: Alors pourquoi n'achètes-tu pas la mauve?

So why don't you buy the mauve one?

Describing Colors

We have seen how to use adjectives such as **américain** and **français** to describe nationalities. Words for color are adjectives too. They generally follow the same rules as adjectives of nationality in placement as well as agreement.

PLACEMENT

When they are part of a noun phrase, color words follow the noun.

le pull **rouge**	*the red sweater*	l'ensemble **rose**	*the pink outfit*
le pantalon **noir**	*the black pants*	la robe **noire**	*the black dress*

FEMININE AGREEMENT

Adjectives of color usually agree in gender (masculine and feminine) with the noun they describe. Look at the following examples, and note that colors already ending in **-e** in the masculine will not change in the feminine, in spelling or speaking.

Sizes in Shoes and Clothes

European and American shoe and clothing sizes are different. You may check a conversion chart online or in a travel guide, or simply ask a salesperson to estimate what your size might be. Don't forget to try things on.

le bas **rose**	*the pink stocking*	**la** cravate **rose**	*the pink tie*
le foulard **jaune**	*the yellow scarf*	**la** veste **jaune**	*the yellow jacket*

Note that the color word **bleu**, ending in the vowel **-u** in the masculine, will add an **-e** in the feminine. Additionally, color words like **noir**, ending in a consonant, must add **-e** in the feminine. The masculine and feminine forms of these colors are pronounced the same.

le costume **bleu**	*the blue suit*	**la** robe **bleue**	*the blue dress*
le pantalon **noir**	*the black pants*	**la** jupe **noire**	*the black skirt*

Color words which end in the consonants **-s** or **-t** in the masculine add **-e** in the feminine. The added **-e** also influences pronunciation. The pronounced ending is highlighted in boldface in the following examples. Remember to pronounce the consonant sound only in the feminine form.

le basket gris	*the gray sneaker*	la chaussure gri**se**	*the gray shoe*
le tailleur vert	*the green suit*	la chaussette ver**te**	*the green sock*

The color word **violet** (*purple*) doubles the consonant **-t** before adding an **-e** in the feminine. Remember to pronounce the **t** sound only in the feminine.

le chemisier violet	*the purple shirt*	la jupe viole**tte**	*the purple skirt*

The color word **blanc** (*white*) adds **-he** in the feminine. Remember not to pronounce the consonant **-c** in the masculine, and to pronounce **-che** as a *sh* sound in the feminine.

le chemisier blanc	*the white shirt*	la botte blan**che**	*the white boot*

Some colors are *invariable* and do not change in the feminine. This is often when the color word is derived from a noun: the color word **orange** comes from the feminine noun **l'orange** (*the orange*), the color word **crème** comes from the feminine noun **la crème** (*the cream*), and the color word **marron** comes from the masculine noun **le marron** (*the chestnut*). Color words are also invariable when they are modified, for example, with **foncé** (*dark*), **clair** (*light*) or **vif** (*bright*).

le costume **marron**	*the brown suit*	**la** ceinture **marron**	*the brown belt*
la chaussure **vert clair**	*the light green shoe*	**la** botte **vert foncé**	*the dark green boot*

PLURAL AGREEMENT

Color words, like other adjectives, will end in a silent **-s** in the plural. Add the letter **-s** to make a color word plural in writing, but remember not to pronounce it in speaking.

le tailleur noir	*the black suit*	**les** tailleurs noirs	*the black suits*
la veste grise	*the gray jacket*	**les** vestes grise**s**	*the gray jackets*

The color word **gris** already ends in **-s** in the masculine singular. It will therefore remain the same in the masculine plural.

le basket **gris**	*the gray sneaker*	**les** baskets **gris**	*the gray sneakers*

Remember that color words like **orange** and **marron**, as well as modified colors such as **vert clair** are *invariable*: they do not change in the plural.

la ceinture **marron**	*the brown belt*	**les** ceintures **marron**	*the brown belts*

Oral Practice 10-2

TRACK 13

Listen to the questions of the salesman (**le vendeur**) in a clothing store, and answer as cued. After each answer, listen to the CD, and check your pronunciation.

1. Le vendeur: Vous désirez le pantalon gris ou vert? (vert)
2. Le vendeur: Vous désirez la chemise blanche ou marron? (blanche)
3. Le vendeur: Vous désirez la veste violette ou jaune? (violette)
4. Le vendeur: Vous désirez la ceinture marron ou grise? (grise)

5. Le vendeur: Vous désirez les chaussures bleues ou rouges? (bleues)

6. Le vendeur: Vous désirez les bas crème ou blancs? (blancs)

USING INTERROGATIVE ADJECTIVES AND PRONOUNS FOR CLARIFICATION

Interrogative adjectives (**Quel**, etc.) have a double function. They are used to ask which item(s) you are referring to and also in exclamations. They agree in gender and number with the noun they describe. Their spelling changes but their pronunciation is always the same.

Masculine Singular		Feminine Singular	
Quel chemisier?	*Which shirt?*	**Quelle** ceinture?	*Which belt?*
Quel joli chemisier!	*What a pretty shirt!*	**Quelle** jolie ceinture!	*What a pretty belt!*

Maculine Plural		Feminine Plural	
Quels foulards?	*Which scarves?*	**Quelles** vestes?	*Which jackets?*
Quels petits foulards!	*What small scarves!*	**Quelles** petites vestes!	*What small jackets!*

Interrogative pronouns (**Lequel**, etc.) are used in questions in lieu of interrogative adjectives when the noun referred to has already been mentioned. These pronouns are similar to interrogative adjectives and agree in gender and number with the nouns they replace.

Masculine

Il y a ce foulard-ci et ce foulard-là. **Lequel** désirez-vous?	*There is this scarf and that scarf. Which (one) would you like?*
Il y a beaucoup de baskets. **Lesquels** préférez-vous?	*There are many sneakers. Which (ones) do you prefer?*

Feminine

Il y a cette robe-ci et cette robe-là. **Laquelle** désirez-vous?	*There is this dress and that dress. Which one would you like?*
Il y a beaucoup de robes. **Lesquelles** préférez-vous?	*There are many dresses. Which ones do you prefer?*

Written Practice 10-1

A. Fill the blank in each sentence with an interrogative adjective: choose **quel**, **quelle**, **quels**, or **quelles** as appropriate. Look at the form of the descriptive adjective that describes each item (such as the color) and use it as a clue.

1. _____ joli tailleur!
2. _____ robe bleue?
3. _____ jolis tennis!
4. _____ bottes grises?
5. _____ jupe blanche?
6. _____ ceintures?

B. Fill the blank in each sentence with an interrogative pronoun: choose **lequel**, **laquelle**, **lesquels**, or **lesquelles** as appropriate.

1. Vous aimez cette cravate rouge et cette cravate bleue. _____ préférez-vous?
2. Vous aimez ce pantalon-ci et ce pantalon-là. _____ préférez-vous?
3. Vous voulez deux jolies cravates. _____ préférez-vous?
4. Vous voulez deux chemisiers blancs. _____ préférez-vous?

USING THE VERB ALLER (*TO FIT*) AND INDIRECT OBJECT PRONOUNS WITH CLOTHES AND COLORS

You may use the forms **va** (singular) and **vont** (plural), forms of the verb **aller**, to say that something *fits* or *looks good*. However, you must also use an *indirect object pronoun* to specify to whom it applies. Look at the following examples and note the object pronouns that precede the verb form:

Le bleu *me* **va** bien.	*Blue looks good on* **me**.
La robe *te* **va** bien.	*The dress looks good on* **you** (familiar).
Le pull ne *lui* **va** pas.	*The sweater does not fit* **him/her**.
Les pulls ne *lui* **vont** pas.	*The sweaters do not fit* **him/her**.
Le blanc *nous* **va**.	*White suits* **us** / *looks good* **on us**.

Le noir *vous* va.	Black suits **you** / looks good **on you** (formal or plural *you*).
Le rose *leur* **va** bien.	Pink looks good on **them**.

USING THE VERB PLAIRE (*TO PLEASE*) AND INDIRECT OBJECT PRONOUNS WITH CLOTHES AND COLORS

You may use **plaît** (singular) and **plaisent** (plural), forms of the verb **plaire** (*to please*), to say that something is agreeable to someone (or that he/she likes it). In this type of sentence, the *subject* is what is pleasing (or what is liked). As with the use of **va/vont** above, an indirect object pronoun must precede **plaît/plaisent** to specify who likes something. Look at the following examples. Note that the pronouns highlighted in boldface and italic are *object pronouns* in French but subject pronouns in English.

Le chemisier bleu *me* **plaît**.	*I* like the blue shirt.
La robe rouge *te* **plaît**?	*Do you* like the red dress (familiar *you*)?
Le costume ne *lui* **plaît** pas.	*He* does not like the suit.
Les jupes ne *lui* **plaisent** pas.	*She* does not like the skirts.
Le blanc *nous* **plaît**.	*We* like white.
Le noir *vous* **plaît**.	*You* like black (formal or plural *you*).
Le rose *leur* **plaît**.	*They* like pink.

Written Practice 10-2

Complete each French sentence so that it expresses the English equivalent.

1. La robe rouge _____ ! *The red dress fits me!*

2. Le pull bleu ne _____ pas. *The blue sweater does not fit him.*

3. Les sandales _____ ? *Do the sandals fit you (familiar)?*

4. Les bottes noires _____ . *The black boots fit her.*

5. Les baskets _____ . *The sneakers fit them.*

Paying for Clothes

Nicole ended up finding a mauve (*light purple*) dress. She is now at the cash register paying for it, while Christina keeps her company.

 TRACK 14

CHRISTINA: Ta mère va être contente. Tu vas avoir une robe mauve au mariage.

Your mother is going to be happy. You'll have a mauve dress at the wedding.

NICOLE: C'est vrai! Et de plus, mes nouvelles chaussures bleues vont bien avec la robe.

That's true! And also, my new blue shoes go well with the dress.

LE CAISSIER (*CASHIER*): Mademoiselle?

Miss?

NICOLE: Voilà, j'achète cette robe.

Here, I'm buying this dress.

LE CAISSIER: Je vous l'emballe et j'enlève l'étiquette. Pas de chaussures pour aller avec la robe?

I'll wrap it for you. And I'll take off the price tag. No shoes to go with the dress?

NICOLE: Non, merci. Je les ai déjà.

No, thanks. I already have them.

LE CAISSIER: Bon, cette robe est en solde. Ça fait soixante-dix euros!

OK, this dress is on sale. It's seventy euros!

NICOLE: C'est un bon prix. Voici ma carte de crédit.

That's a good price. Here's my credit card.

LE CAISSIER: Je vous remercie, Mademoiselle. Veuillez signer le reçu.

Thank you, Miss. Please sign the receipt.

NICOLE: Je voudrais un grand sac s'il vous plaît.

I'd like a big bag please.

LE CAISSIER: Bien sûr. Le voilà, Mademoiselle.

Of course. Here it is, Miss.

NICOLE: Merci, Monsieur.

Thank you, Sir.

LE CAISSIER: Je vous en prie, Mademoiselle.

You're welcome, Miss.

STEM-CHANGING -ER VERBS

Stem-changing verbs are conjugated just like regular **-er** verbs, but they have a slightly different stem in the present tense when the subjects are **je**, **tu**, **il/elle/on**, and **ils/elles**. These are spelling, rather than spoken, differences. There are several kinds of stem-changing verbs. Here are some common patterns:

In verbs like **payer** (*to pay*) and **essayer** (*to try / to try on*), the stem change converts the **-y-** from the stem to an **-i-** in all forms, except for **nous** and **vous**.

In verbs like **acheter** (*to buy*) and **enlever** (*to take off / to take away*), the stem change converts the **-e-** before the consonant (**t, v**) preceding the verb ending to **-è-** in all forms, except for **nous** and **vous**.

In verbs like **préférer** (*to prefer*) and **espérer** (*to hope*), the stem change converts the **-é-** before the consonant (the **r**) that precedes the verb ending to **-è-** in all forms, except for **nous** and **vous**. Here are examples of stem-change conjugations:

y→i	e→è	é→è
payer (*to pay*)	acheter (*to buy*)	préférer (*to prefer*)
je paie	j'achète	je préfère
tu paies	tu achètes	tu préfères
il/elle/on paie	il/elle/on achète	il/elle/on préfère
nous payons	nous achetons	nous préférons
vous payez	vous achetez	vous préférez
ils/elles paient	ils/elles achètent	ils/elles préfèrent

Useful Expressions for Shopping

Je voudrais l'essayer.	*I would like to try it on.*
Où est le salon d'essayage?	*Where is the fitting room?*
Ça fait combien?	*How much is it?*
Ça fait trente euros.	*It's thirty euros.*
C'est cher.	*It is expensive.*
C'est un bon prix.	*It's a good price.*
C'est en solde.	*It's on sale.*
Comment payez-vous?	*How are you going to pay?*
Voici ma carte de crédit.	*Here's my credit card.*
Je paie en espèces.	*I'm paying in cash.*
Je voudrais un reçu.	*I would like a receipt.*
Veuillez signer.	*Please sign.*
Je vous en prie.	*You're welcome. / Don't mention it.*

Using Object Pronouns to Avoid Redundancy

Using pronouns is necessary to avoid repetition and redundancy. There are several types of object pronouns that make speech flow more easily. Let's look at personal object pronouns, direct object pronouns, and indirect object pronouns.

The personal object pronouns **me** (*me / to* or *for me*), **te** (*you / to* or *for you, singular, familiar*), **nous** (*us / to* or *for us*), **vous** (*you / to* or *for you, plural* or *formal*) are always used to refer to people. Look at the following examples, and note that object pronouns are placed before the verb in a French sentence:

Ce pull **me** va.	*This sweater fits me.*
Cette robe ne **te** va pas.	*This dress does not fit you* (familiar *you*).
Le vendeur **nous** donne un reçu.	*The salesman gives us a receipt.*
La vendeuse **vous** emballe la robe.	*The saleslady wraps the dress for you* (formal or plural *you*).

The direct object pronouns **le** (*him/it*), **la** (*her/it*), **l'** (*him/her/it*) before a vowel sound, and **les** (*them*) are used to refer to *things* and *people*. Look at the following examples, and note again that object pronouns are placed before the verb in a French sentence:

Vous désirez ce sac? —Oui, je **le** désire.	*Would you like this bag? —Yes, I would like **it**.*
Vous cherchez le vendeur? —Oui, je **le** cherche.	*Are you looking for the salesman? —Yes, I'm looking for **him**.*
Vous désirez cette ceinture? —Oui, je **la** prends.	*Would you like this belt? —Yes, I'm taking **it**.*
Vous cherchez la vendeuse? —Oui, je **la** cherche.	*Are you looking for the saleslady? —Yes, I'm looking for **her**.*
Tu achètes ce foulard? —Oui, je **l'**achète.	*Are you buying this scarf? —Yes, I'm buying **it**.*
Tu achètes ces chaussures? —Oui, je **les** achète.	*Are you buying these shoes? —Yes, I'm buying **them**.*

The indirect object pronouns **lui** (*to him / to her* or *for him / for her*) and **leur** (*to them* or *for them*) are only used to refer to *people*. Look at the following examples, and note again that object pronouns are placed before the verb in a French sentence.

Nicole veut un sac.	*Nicole wants a bag.*
Le vendeur **lui** donne un sac.	*The salesman gives a bag **to her** / gives **her** a bag.*
Le vendeur veut une carte de crédit.	*The salesman wants a credit card.*

Nicole **lui** donne sa carte.   *Nicole gives her card **to him** / gives **him** her card.*

Nicole et Christina achètent des chaussures.   *Nicole and Christina buy shoes.*

La vendeuse **leur** emballe les chaussures.   *The saleslady packs up the shoes **for them**.*

Written Practice 10-3

A. Your friend is asking you questions. Complete each sentence in the dialogue with a personal object pronoun (**me**, **te**, **nous**).

1. Dis, est-ce que ce pantalon _____ va?   *Say, does this pair of pants fit me?*

2. Mais oui, il _____ va bien.   *Yes, it/they fit(s) you well.*

3. Est-ce qu'il _____ plaît?   *Do you like it/them?*

4. Oui, il _____ plaît beaucoup.   *Yes, I like it/them a lot.*

5. Le vendeur _____ emballe nos deux pantalons.   *The salesman packs up our two pairs of pants for us.*

B. Transaction between a client and a salesperson. Choose the correct direct or indirect object pronoun to complete each French sentence.

1. La cliente trouve une robe. Elle _____ essaie.   *The customer finds a dress. She tries it on.* (**la, l'**)

2. La robe _____ plaît.   *She likes the dress.* (**la, lui**)

3. La vendeuse _____ emballe.   *The saleslady packs it up.* (**l', la**)

4. Elle essaie aussi des sandales. Les sandales _____ vont.   *She also tries on sandals. The sandals fit her.* (**les, lui**)

5. La vendeuse _____ emballe.   *The saleslady packs them up.* (**les, l'**)

6. La cliente _____ donne sa carte de crédit.   *The customer gives her credit card to her / gives her her credit card.* (**lui, le**)

7. La vendeuse _____ donne un reçu.   *The saleslady gives a receipt to her / gives her a receipt.* (**la, lui**)

8. La cliente _____ signe.   *The client signs it.* (**la, le**)

Chapter Practice 10

A. Match the following phrases or sentences. Write the letter of the corresponding answer on the line provided.

_____	1. La jupe est jolie.	a.	*White looks good on you.*
_____	2. Quel bon prix!	b.	*You're welcome.*
_____	3. C'est en solde.	c.	*The skirt is pretty.*
_____	4. Je vous en prie.	d.	*This suit does not fit her.*
_____	5. Le blanc te va bien.	e.	*He gives them the receipt.*
_____	6. C'est cher?	f.	*It is on sale.*
_____	7. Ce tailleur ne lui va pas.	g.	*Would you like to try it on?*
_____	8. Quelle est ta pointure?	h.	*What a good price!*
_____	9. Tu voudrais l'essayer?	i.	*Is it expensive?*
_____	10. Il leur donne le reçu.	j.	*What is your shoe size?*

B. Interrogative adjective or pronoun? Select the correct answer from the choices given.

1. Voilà deux pantalons gris. _____ préférez-vous? (Quel, Lequel)

2. Il y a deux chemises blanches. _____ vous plaît? (Quelle, Laquelle)

3. _____ baskets achetez-vous? (Quels, Lesquels)

4. _____ est ta taille en France? (Quelle, Laquelle)

5. Voici deux jolis foulards bleus. _____ me va le mieux? (Quel, Lequel)

CHAPTER QUIZ 10

 TRACK 15

First, fill in the blanks, using the cues in parentheses. You will find the answers in the Answer Key. Then turn on your CD, and interact with the salesman while you play the role of the customer.

1. Le/La client(e): Monsieur, je cherche des baskets _____ (*brown*).

2. Le vendeur: Quelle est votre _____ ? (*shoe size*)

3. Le/La client(e): _____ quarante. (*It is*)

4. Le vendeur: Voici des baskets marron. Ils vous _____ ? (*fit*)

5. Le/La client(e): Oui, et ils me _____ . (*use* **plaire** *for liking*)

6. Le vendeur: Ils sont _____ . (*on sale*)

7. Le/La client(e): _____ bon prix! (*What*)

8. Le vendeur: Je _____ emballe les baskets? (*for you*)

9. Le/La client(e): Oui, merci. Voici ma _____ . (*credit card*)

10. Le vendeur: Et voici vos baskets et votre _____ . (*receipt*)

A. Préparatifs de voyage (*Trip preparations*). Circle the letter corresponding to the most logical reply for each of the following questions or instructions.

1. Depuis quand est-ce que tu désires faire ce voyage?

    a. Ça fait trois ans.   b. Bientôt!

2. Il coûte combien, ce voyage?

    a. Dix euros.   b. Deux mille euros.

3. Comment tu aimes voyager?

    a. En France.   b. En avion.

4. Tu as besoin d'argent?

    a. Non, je n'ai pas d'argent.   b. Non, j'ai des économies.

5. Qu'est-ce que tu veux visiter?

    a. J'aime les galeries d'art moderne.   b. Oui, j'aime le tourisme.

6. Tu as envie de prendre les petits déjeuners à l'hôtel?

    a. Non, je préfère aller au café.   b. Non, je ne veux pas dîner à l'hôtel.

7. Qu'est-ce que tu manges le matin?

    a. De la soupe et de la salade   b. Je ne prends que le café.

8. Tu n'as pas envie de faire du camping?

    a. Non, j'ai peur des insectes.   b. Si, j'aime dormir à l'hôtel.

9. Fais donc ta réservation de train immédiatement!

    a. Oui, depuis deux ans.   b. Oui, tu as raison.

10. Prends une place en première classe!

    a. Oh! C'est trop cher!   b. Oh! Ce n'est pas confortable!

B. C'est vrai ou faux? (*True or false?*) Decide if the following statements make sense by writing **V** for **vrai** (*true*) or **F** for **faux** (*false*) on the line provided.

_____ 11. On va à la salle de bains pour dormir.

_____ 12. On regarde la télé au grenier.

_____ 13. Les films au cinéma sont plus récents qu'à la télé.

_____ 14. On se dépêche quand on est en retard.

_____ 15. C'est bien d'avoir un meilleur ami ou une meilleure amie.

_____ 16. Il faut choisir des vêtements qui vous vont bien et qui vous plaisent.

_____ 17. On dîne généralement le matin.

_____ 18. On sert des spaghettis dans les restaurants chinois.

_____ 19. Un kilo est plus qu'une livre.

_____ 20. Beaucoup de gens prennent un litre de lait dans leur café.

_____ 21. D'abord, on enregistre les bagages. Ensuite, on monte dans l'avion.

_____ 22. On porte généralement une cravate au match de rugby.

_____ 23. On ne peut jamais commander de repas dans un hôtel.

_____ 24. On ne vend ni sandales ni bottes dans une pâtisserie.

_____ 25. On peut acheter du pain dans une boulangerie.

PART THREE

THE PAST AND FUTURE

CHAPTER 11

Talking About Memories and Celebrations

In this chapter you will learn:

Memories

*Using the **imparfait** (Imperfect Tense) to Reminisce*

Celebrations

*Using the **passé composé** to Describe Specific Moments in the Past*

Memories

Today Émilie and her father are looking at an old photo album together, and Émilie has a lot of questions for him.

 TRACK 16

ÉMILIE: Dis, papa, c'est toi le petit garçon dans la photo?

Hey, Dad, is that you, the little boy in the picture?

PAPA: Oui, c'est moi. J'étais mignon, tu ne penses pas?

Yes, that's me. I was cute, don't you think?

ÉMILIE: Oui, mais tu portais un drôle de maillot de bain.

Yes, but you were wearing a funny bathing suit.

PAPA: C'était à la mode à l'époque, ces maillots très courts!

It was fashionable at the time, those very short suits!

ÉMILIE: Et cette vieille dame, elle portait une robe à la plage!

And this old lady, she was wearing a dress at the beach!

PAPA: C'est ton arrière-grand-mère. Je passais toujours le mois d'août chez elle.

That's your great-grandmother. I always spent the month of August at her house.

ÉMILIE: Elle avait une maison sur la plage?

Did she have a house on the beach?

PAPA: Sa maison était à quelques minutes de la plage.

Her house was a few minutes away from the beach.

ÉMILIE: Tu aimais aller chez elle?

Did you like going to her house?

PAPA: Bien sûr! Je m'amusais toute la journée avec mes cousins.

Of course! I had fun all day with my cousins.

ÉMILIE: Qu'est-ce que vous faisiez?

What did you do?

PAPA: Oh! On nageait, on jouait au ballon et on faisait des châteaux de sable!

Oh! We swam, we played ball, and we made sand castles!

ÉMILIE: Vous passiez vraiment toute la journée à la plage?

Did you really spend the whole day at the beach?

PAPA: Généralement oui. Quelquefois mon oncle Joseph nous emmenait pêcher, mes cousins et moi.

Generally yes. Sometimes my Uncle Joseph would take us fishing, my cousins and me.

ÉMILIE: Qu'est-ce que vous pêchiez? Du thon?

What did you fish for? Tuna?

PAPA: Non, Émilie, on pêchait des sardines. L'oncle Joseph nous faisait une friture le soir chez lui.

No, Émilie, we fished for sardines. Uncle Joseph would make us fried sardines at night at his house.

ÉMILIE: C'était bon?

Was it good?

PAPA: Et comment! C'était délicieux!

And how! It was delicious!

Using the imparfait (Imperfect Tense) to Reminisce

Using the **imparfait** tense is absolutely necessary in French when reminiscing and sharing memories of what used to be. There are often several ways to translate into English a verb conjugated in this tense. Look at the following examples:

Quand j'étais petit, **je passais** toute la journée à la plage.

*When I was little, **I used to spend / I would spend** all day at the beach.*

Quand j'étais petit, **j'allais** souvent à la pêche avec mon oncle.

*When I was little, I often **went / would go** fishing with my uncle.*

As you learned in Chapter 5, there are two steps needed to conjugate a verb in the **imparfait**:

First, identify the **imparfait** stem by taking the present tense **nous** form of the verb and dropping its **-ons** ending. Look at the following examples of **imparfait** derived from the **nous** form of the present tense. They are in bold face.

Regular -er Verbs	Regular -ir Verbs	Regular -re verbs
nous jouons→**jou-**	nous choisissons→**choisiss-**	nous perdons→**perd-**
nous portons→**port-**	nous rôtissons→**rôtiss-**	nous répondons→**répond-**

This rule also applies to irregular verbs. Look at the following examples:

nous avons→**av-**	nous faisons→**fais-**	nous prenons→**pren-**
		nous voulons →**voul-**

Then add the appropriate **imparfait** ending to the stem: **je -ais, tu -ais, il/elle/on -ait, nous -ions, vous -iez, ils/elles -aient**. Here is the **imparfait** conjugation of the verb **avoir**:

j'av**ais**	*I had*	nous av**ions**	*we had*
tu av**ais**	*you had*	vous av**iez**	*you had*
il/elle av**ait**	*he/she had*	ils/elles av**aient**	*they had*
on av**ait**	*one/we had*		

Remember that the only verb with an irregular stem in the **imparfait** is **être** (*to be*). Start with the stem **ét-**, and add endings as follows:

j'**étais**	*I was*	nous ét**ions**	*we were*
tu ét**ais**	*you were*	vous ét**iez**	*you were*

| il/elle ét**ait** | *he/she was* | ils/elles ét**aient** | *they were* |
| on ét**ait** | *one was / we were* | | |

VOCABULARY: ADVERBS OF TIME AND FREQUENCY

When sharing memories using the **imparfait**, use words such as the following adverbs or adverbial expressions to indicate that events took place on a regular basis in the past.

toujours	*always*	tous les jours	*every day*
souvent	*often*	tout le temps	*all the time*
généralement	*generally*	toute la journée	*all day long*
fréquemment	*frequently*	jour et nuit	*day and night*
régulièrement	*regularly*	chaque jour/nuit	*every day/night*
quelquefois	*sometimes*	à l'époque	*at the time*

Oral Practice 11-1

Read aloud each of the following statements about Émilie's dad. Each statement will start with **Quand il était petit...** (*When he was little . . .*). You may listen to your CD to check pronunciation while you look at the translations on the right.

TRACK 17

1. ..., il allait chez sa grand-mère en août.   *..., he used to go to his grandmother's in August.*

2. ..., il jouait tout le temps avec ses cousins.   *..., he used to play all the time with his cousins.*

3. ..., il dînait quelquefois chez son oncle.   *..., he would sometimes eat dinner at his uncle's.*

4. ..., il pêchait souvent.   *..., he often went fishing.*

5. ..., il s'amusait beaucoup.   *..., he had a lot of fun.*

6. ..., il aimait les sardines.   *..., he liked sardines.*

7. ..., il faisait des châteaux de sable.   *..., he built sand castles.*

8. ..., il voulait jouer toute la journée.   *..., he wanted to play all day.*

In the following dialogue, Émilie and her dad continue to talk about his childhood.

 TRACK 18

ÉMILIE: Tu avais quel âge dans cette photo?

How old were you in this picture?

PAPA: Onze ans. Regarde, il y avait onze bougies sur le gâteau.

Eleven years old. Look, there were eleven candles on the cake.

ÉMILIE: Ah oui, c'était ton anniversaire?

Ah yes, was it your birthday?

PAPA: Comme je suis né le 14 juillet, on fêtait mon anniversaire le jour de la Bastille, c'est-à-dire, la Fête Nationale.

Since I was born on the fourteenth of July, we celebrated my birthday on Bastille Day, that is, our national holiday.

ÉMILIE: Avec des feux d'artifice!

With fireworks!

PAPA: Oui, enfin, les feux d'artifice étaient plutôt pour fêter la Fête Nationale.

Yes, well, the fireworks were more to celebrate the national holiday.

ÉMILIE: Quelle chance tu avais, papa!

You were lucky, Dad!

PAPA: La maison était toujours pleine d'amis et de membres de la famille et mon papa faisait des shish kebab.

The house was always full of friends and family members and my dad made shish kebab.

ÉMILIE: Il y avait une piñata?

Was there a piñata?

PAPA: Non, on n'avait pas ça à l'époque. Mais je jouais avec mes nouveaux cadeaux toute la journée.

No, we didn't have that then. But I played with my new presents all day long.

ÉMILIE: Quel était ton meilleur cadeau?

What was your best present?

PAPA: Ah! C'était un beau vélo à dix vitesses. Laisse-moi retrouver la photo.

Ah! It was a beautiful ten-speed bike. Let me find the photo.

WHEN TO USE THE IMPARFAIT

There are several past tenses in French. The most frequently used past tenses are the **imparfait** and the **passé composé**. The previous two dialogues in this chapter feature verbs almost exclusively in the **imparfait**. They are narratives about what used

Bastille Day

Bastille Day is the French national holiday, celebrated on July 14. In France, it is called **la Fête Nationale** or more commonly **le quatorze juillet**. It commemorates the 1790 **Fête de la Fédération** held on the first anniversary of the storming of the Bastille prison, a symbol of the abuses of the French monarchy under Louis XVI. Festivities are held on the morning of July 14, on the Avenue des Champs-Élysées in Paris. On the **Fête Nationale**, fireworks and street dances take place all over France.

to be and about things that took place regularly over a period of time in the past. The following descriptors help identify when the **imparfait** should be used:

1. An action that sets the background for a story by describing a state, that is, how things were. Verbs describing an unchanging condition or state of being such as **être** (*to be*) and verbs of state of mind such as **penser** (*to think*) are usually used in the **imparfait**. In the previous dialogue, note the frequency of verbs such as **être** and **avoir**, both of which describe a state.

2. A continuous action (often expressed in English by *was/were* plus the *-ing* form of the verb).

3. A customary or regularly repeated action (often expressed in English by *would* / *used to* plus the verb).

Note that in the second dialogue above, there is one verb (**je suis né** *I was born*) not in the **imparfait**. The action of being born cannot be perceived as an action occurring regularly, nor is it an unchanged state of being. It took place at a specific, unique point in time and must therefore be expressed in the **passé composé** (*compound past tense* or *present perfect*). You will see additional verbs in this tense in the next dialogue.

Written Practice 11-1

Write the verbs in parentheses in the **imparfait** to complete each French sentence.

1. Papa _____ onze ans. (avoir)

2. Il _____ en France. (être)

3. Son anniversaire _____ en été. (être)

4. Grand-père _____ des grillades de shish kebab. (faire)

5. Grand-mère _____ le gâteau. (préparer)

6. Ses amis lui _____ des cadeaux. (donner)

7. Papa et ses amis _____ beaucoup. (s'amuser)

8. Papa _____ toujours jouer. (vouloir)

Celebrations

In the following dialogue, Émilie and her friend Jacqueline talk on the phone about how each of them celebrated the winter holidays.

 TRACK 19

ÉMILIE: Allô Jacqueline, c'est Émilie. Comment ça va?

Hello Jacqueline, it's Émilie. How are you?

JACQUELINE: Bien, merci. Et toi? Tu as passé une bonne fête de Noël?

Fine, thank you. And you? Did you spend a good Christmas holiday?

ÉMILIE: Magnifique. Il a neigé le jour de Noël. C'était un vrai paysage de Noël.

Magnificent. It snowed on Christmas day. It was real Christmas scenery.

JACQUELINE: Tu as reçu de beaux cadeaux?

Did you get nice presents?

ÉMILIE: Oui, maman et papa m'ont offert une caméra numérique. Et toi, tu as reçu de beaux cadeaux de Hanoukka?

Yes, Mom and Dad gave me a digital camera. How about you, did you get nice Hanukkah presents?

JACQUELINE: Ah oui! Entre autres, j'ai reçu un joli collier et un bracelet en or.

Oh yes! Among other things, I received a pretty necklace and a gold bracelet.

ÉMILIE: Formidable!

Fantastic!

JACQUELINE: Évidemment, on a mangé toutes sortes de choses très délicieuses chaque soir.

Of course, we ate all kinds of delicious things each night.

ÉMILIE: Je n'en doute pas. Chez nous, la veille de Noël, on a mangé la dinde traditionnelle et la bûche de Noël de maman.

I don't doubt it. At our house on Christmas Eve we ate the traditional turkey and Mom's yule log.

JACQUELINE: Oh! Je me rappelle encore le jour où j'ai goûté de cette bûche chez toi. Quel régal!

Oh! I still remember the day I tasted that log at your house. What a treat!

ÉMILIE: Il faut que je te quitte. Mais je te rappelle très bientôt.

I have to go. But I'll call you back very soon.

JACQUELINE: D'accord. Je t'embrasse ainsi que tes parents.

OK. My love to you and your parents.

Using the passé composé **to Describe Specific Moments in the Past**

Using the **passé composé** is necessary in French when talking about what happened at a certain point in time. In the dialogue above, verbs were conjugated in the **passé composé** because they all related to what happened specifically on Christmas or Hanukkah. Whenever you refer to precise moments in time and what happened, you will likely use adverbs and adverbial expressions such as **ce jour-là** (*that day*) or **dimanche dernier** (*last Sunday*). Look at the following examples and see how they use such expressions of time:

Dimanche dernier, on **a mangé** de la dinde.

Last Sunday, we ate turkey.

Hier soir, nous **avons regardé** un film à la télé.

Last night, we watched a movie on TV.

Il y a deux ans, ma famille **a fait** un voyage en France.

Two years ago, my family went on a trip to France.

Vocabulary: Adverbs Used with the passé composé

aujourd'hui	*today*	soudain	*suddenly*
ce matin / ce soir	*this morning / this evening*	tout à coup	*all of a sudden*
		tout de suite	*right away*
hier	*yesterday*	d'abord	*first (of all)*
samedi dernier	*last Saturday*	alors/ensuite/après	*then/next*
la semaine dernière	*last week*	un jour / une fois	*one day / once*
il y a un mois	*a month ago*		

THE PASSÉ COMPOSÉ **OF VERBS CONJUGATED WITH** AVOIR

To conjugate a verb in the **passé composé**, you need an auxiliary verb and a past participle. The great majority of French verbs use **avoir** as an auxiliary verb. There are usually two English equivalents for the **passé composé**. Look at the following example:

Celebrations and Holidays in the Francophone World

There are many celebrations and holidays throughout the Francophone world. Some are faith-based, such as Christmas (**Noël**) and Hanukkah (**Hanoukka**). There are also numerous annual festivals such as **la Fête de la Musique** (*music*), **la Fête des Fleurs** (*flowers*), **la Fête du Vin** (*wine*), **la Fête Médiévale**, **la Fête Nationale** (*Bastille Day / July 14*) and, of course, **les mariages** (*weddings*), **les anniversaires** (*birthdays*), and **les anniversaires de mariage** (*wedding anniversaries*). Some other notable holidays are **Carnaval** (also called **Mardi Gras** *Fat Tuesday*) and la **Saint Valentin** (*Valentine's Day*).

Tu **as fait** les courses au marché ce matin!	*You shopped / You have shopped* at *the market this morning!*

Note: If you follow the English word order *you have shopped* (rather than *you shopped*), you will come up with the **passé composé** structure in French. (This equivalent does not always sound natural in English.)

The first step in forming the **passé composé** is to use the appropriate form of the auxiliary verb **avoir** (*to have*). You already know these forms: **j'ai, tu as, il/elle/on a, nous avons, vous avez, ils/elles ont**.

Second, create the *past participle* of the verb you are conjugating. Regular **-er**, **-ir**, and **-re** verbs have a set pattern of past participle formation: Replace the infinitive ending (**-er, -ir, -re**) with **-é, -i,** or **-u,** respectively. Look at the following examples:

Infinitive→Past Participle	Infinitive→Past Participle	Infinitive→Past Participle
to buy →bought	*to choose →chosen*	*to forbid →forbidden*
ache**ter** →ache**té**	chois**ir** →chois**i**	défen**dre** →défen**du**

The form of the auxiliary verb plus the past participle gives you the **passé composé**. Look at the **passé composé** conjugation of the verb **acheter**:

j'ai acheté	*I (have) bought*	nous avons acheté	*we (have) bought*
tu as acheté	*you (have) bought*	vous avez acheté	*you (have) bought*
il/elle a acheté	*he/she (has) bought*	ils/elles ont acheté	*they (have) bought*
on a acheté	*we (have) bought*		

Oral Practice 11-2

Listen to each statement about Émilie and Jacqueline. If the statement is *true*, say **oui**, and repeat the statement aloud. If it is *false*, say **non** followed by a correct statement. Look at number 1 which has been done for you as an example.

 TRACK 20

Example: 1. Émilie a fêté Hanoukka.   *Non, Émilie a fêté Noël.*

2. Jacqueline a fêté Noël.

3. La maman d'Émilie a fait une bûche de Noël.

4. Il a neigé le jour de Noël.

5. Émilie a reçu un collier et un bracelet en or.

6. Jacqueline a reçu une caméra pour Hanoukka.

7. Jacqueline a déjà goûté la bûche de Noël.

8. Émilie a mangé de la dinde le jour de Noël.

WEDDINGS

In the following dialogue, Joëlle is calling her friend Suzanne to tell her about a wedding she attended. Note that in this dialogue, there are verbs in the **imparfait** and others in the **passé composé**. This is very common in past narration: some elements describe a setting or a state of being and require the **imparfait** (how the weather and the dress *were*, for example), while others describe specific actions or moments that require the **passé composé** (where and how the wedding took place, as well as what was said or done).

TRACK 21

JOËLLE: Allô Suzanne, c'est Joëlle. Ça va? Tu as le temps de bavarder?

Hello Suzanne, it's Joëlle. How are you? Do you have time to chat?

SUZANNE: Ça va, merci. Tu vas me raconter comment s'est passé le mariage?

Fine, thank you. Are you going to tell me how the wedding went?

JOËLLE: Il s'est passé en plein air. Il faisait un temps magnifique!

It took place outdoors. The weather was fantastic!

SUZANNE: Et il y avait combien de personnes?

And how many people were there?

JOËLLE: Environ cinquante. Ils sont tous arrivés les bras chargés de cadeaux.

About fifty. They all arrived with their arms full of presents.

SUZANNE: Et la cérémonie? Elle était traditionnelle ou moderne?

And the ceremony? Was it traditional or modern?

JOËLLE: Très moderne! Ils ont écrit leurs propres vœux et c'était très émouvant.

Very modern! They wrote their own vows, and it was very moving.

SUZANNE: Et la robe de la mariée, elle était comment?

And the bride's gown, what was it like?

JOËLLE: Simple mais élégante! C'était une longue robe blanche avec un joli décolleté.

Simple but elegant! It was a long white dress with a pretty décolleté.

SUZANNE: Oh! La mariée devait être belle!

Oh! The bride must have been beautiful!

JOËLLE: Magnifique! Quand ils se sont embrassés, tout le monde a applaudi.

Magnificent! When they kissed, everyone applauded.

SUZANNE: Et la réception, elle a duré combien de temps?

What about the reception, how long did it last?

JOËLLE: Je ne suis pas sûre! Quand je suis partie, il y avait encore pas mal de monde.

I'm not sure! When I left, there were still a good many people there.

SUZANNE: Tu t'es bien amusée, j'espère!

You had fun, I hope!

JOËLLE: Je me suis amusée comme une folle. Attends les photos!

I enjoyed myself like crazy! Wait for the pictures!

THE PASSÉ COMPOSÉ **WITH THE AUXILIARY VERB** ÊTRE

In the previous dialogue, some of the verbs differ from the **passé composé** structure you just learned. Instead of using **avoir** as the auxiliary verb, these verbs use the verb **être**. There are two types of verbs that use the auxiliary verb **être**: verbs of *coming/going* and *reflexive* verbs.

Look at the following list of frequently used *coming* and *going* verbs conjugated with the auxiliary verb **être**. They are grouped to help you remember them better. Note that **naître** (*to be born*) and **mourir** (*to die*) are part of the list; you may remember them metaphorically as *coming into* and *leaving* the world.

aller/arriver	*to go / to arrive*	partir/sortir	*to leave / to go out*
descendre/ tomber	*to go down / to fall*	monter/ remonter	*to go up / to go back up*
entrer/rentrer/ retourner	*to enter / to come back*	venir/revenir	*to come / to come back*
naître/mourir	*to be born / to die*	passer/rester	*to pass by /drop in / to stay*

To form the past participle of these verbs, follow the rule you know: change the infinitive ending of the verb to -**é** for -**er** verbs, -**i** for -**ir** verbs, and -**u** for -**re** verbs, except for verbs with *irregular* past participles, such as:

(re)venir →(**re**)**venu**   naître →**né**   mourir →**mort**

Look at the conjugation of the verb **partir** (*to leave*) in the **passé composé**, below, and note that the past participle *agrees* in gender and number with the *subject* of the verb. The feminine ending -**e** and the masculine ending -**s** are silent, and therefore do not change the pronunciation of the past participle: **parti**.

je suis parti(**e**)	*I (have) left*	nous sommes partis/parti**es**	*we (have) left*
tu es parti(**e**)	*you (have) left*	vous êtes parti(**e**)(**s**)	*you (have) left*
il/elle est parti/parti**e**	*he/she (has) left*	ils/elles sont partis/parti**es**	*they (have) left*
on est parti	*we/people (have) left*		

To make these verbs negative, just insert **ne** (**n'** before a vowel sound) before the auxiliary and **pas** after the auxiliary. Look at the following example:

Il est parti.   *He left.*   Il **n'**est **pas** parti.   *He did not leave.*

The second group of verbs conjugated with the auxiliary **être** includes all *reflexive* (also called *pronominal*) verbs. You learned some reflexives in Chapter 7.

Reflexives are verbs like **se fâcher** (*to get mad/angry*) or **se promener** (*to go for a walk*) which include a reflexive pronoun. They indicate that the subject is doing the action of the verb *to itself*. See below the **passé composé** of the verb **s'amuser** (*to have fun*). Past participles agree with the subject of the verb, but note that they are always pronounced the same way, regardless of their feminine and/or plural written markers.

je me suis amusé(**e**)	*I (have) had fun*
tu t'es amusé(**e**)	*you (have) had fun*
il/elle s'est amusé(**e**)	*he/she (has) had fun*
on s'est amusé	*we/people (have) had fun*
nous nous sommes amusés/amusé**es**	*we (have) had fun*

vous vous êtes amusé(**e**)(**s**)   *you (have) had fun*
ils/elles se sont amusés/amus**ées**   *they (have) had fun*

To make these verbs negative, insert **ne** (**n'**) before the reflexive pronoun and **pas** after the auxiliary verb. Look at the following example:

Il s'est amusé.   *He had fun.*   Il **ne** s'est **pas** amusé.   *He did not have fun.*

Oral Practice 11-3

TRACK 22

Read each short sentence aloud, covering the English translations at the right. Then listen to your CD to check your pronunciation, uncovering the translations.

1. Il s'est amusé.   *He had fun.*
2. Nous sommes arrivés.   *We arrived.*
3. Elle est venue.   *She came.*
4. Ils sont morts.   *They died.*
5. Je suis descendu(e).   *I went down.*
6. Vous êtes monté(e).   *You went up.*
7. Tu es sorti(e).   *You went out.*
8. Elles sont entrées.   *They entered.*
9. Nous nous sommes embrassés.   *We kissed.*
10. Ils se sont fâchés.   *They got mad.*

Chapter Practice 11

A. L'enfance. Imagine that the following actions took place regularly when you were young. Write them in French using the **imparfait** of the verbs in parentheses.

1. I used to go to the beach. (**aller**) _____
2. We used to swim every day. (**nager**) _____
3. My cousins played ball all day long. (**jouer**) _____
4. My uncle went fishing all the time. (**pêcher**) _____

5. I loved sardines. (**aimer**) _____

6. I spent every summer at my grandparents'. (**passer**) _____

B. Le jour du mariage. Using the verbs provided, complete the following paragraph to reconstruct what Joëlle recounted about the wedding. Use the **imparfait** for the verbs **être** and **avoir** and the **passé composé** for all other verbs. Remember that verbs of *coming/going* and *reflexive* verbs use the auxiliary **être**.

1. aller 2. être 3. arriver 4. avoir 5. commencer 6. prononcer 7. s'embrasser 8. se passer 9. faire 10. s'amuser 11. partir 12. naître

Joëlle (1) _____ à un mariage. C' (2) _____ un mariage en plein air dans un parc. Quand Joëlle (3) _____ , il y (4) _____ une cinquantaine d'invités. La cérémonie (5) _____ à quatre heures. Les mariés (6) _____ leurs vœux. Après les vœux, ils (7) _____. La cérémonie et la réception (8) _____ dans le parc. Il (9) _____ un temps magnifique toute la journée. Joëlle et les autres invités (10) _____ ! Tous les invités (11) _____ à trois heures du matin. Un bébé (*baby*) (12) _____ dix mois plus tard.

CHAPTER QUIZ 11

L'anniversaire de Jacques. Yesterday was Jacques's birthday. Write the verbs in parentheses in the correct form of the **imparfait** or **passé composé** as appropriate.

1. Son anniversaire, c' _____ hier. (être)

2. Il _____ le 30 janvier 2000. (naître)

3. Avant-hier, maman _____ un beau gâteau d'anniversaire. (préparer)

4. Hier, nous _____ de jolies cartes à Jacques. (donner)

5. Les invités _____ chez nous à dix-huit heures. (arriver)

6. Il y _____ dix personnes. (avoir)

7. Après le gâteau, nous _____ de la musique rock. (jouer)

8. Ensuite, nous _____ à regarder les cadeaux. (s'amuser)

9. C' _____ une très bonne journée. (être)

10. Jacques _____ très heureux. (être)

CHAPTER 12

Talking on the Phone

In this chapter you will learn:

Talking on the Phone
Talking About Restaurants
*Using the Object Pronoun **y** When Referring to a Location*
Asking for Precise Information
*Using the Verbs **prendre**, **surprendre**, and **comprendre***

Talking on the Phone

Geneviève is in Switzerland getting training in a chef's school. She calls her brother Marc to tell him how her stay has been so far.

TRACK 23

GENEVIÈVE: Salut, Marc. Je viens de rentrer à l'hôtel et je suis fatiguée.

Hi, Marc. I just got back to the hotel and I'm tired.

MARC: Je comprends. Mais dis-moi comment se passe ton séjour.

I understand. But tell me how your stay is going.

GENEVIÈVE: L'hôtel où j'étais d'abord, c'était un désastre!

The hotel where I was at first, it was a disaster!

MARC: Oh non, je ne savais pas, mais pourquoi?

Oh no, I didn't know, but why?

GENEVIÈVE: Il était très loin de l'école, et si je rentrais après onze heures du soir, il n'y avait personne à la réception.

It was far from school, and if I came back after eleven o'clock at night, there was nobody at the reception desk.

MARC: Mais tu pouvais quand même rentrer dans ta chambre, non?

But you could still get into your room, no?

GENEVIÈVE: Justement pas! Figure-toi qu'une fois, ma clé n'a pas marché, et j'ai dû attendre jusqu'à deux heures du matin que quelqu'un arrive.

Well no! Just imagine, one time my key didn't work, and I had to wait until two o'clock in the morning for someone to arrive.

MARC: Quelle horreur! Qu'est-ce que tu as fait? Tu as changé d'hôtel?

How awful! What did you do? Did you change hotels?

GENEVIÈVE: Bien sûr. Maintenant je suis dans un hôtel en ville. Il est un peu plus cher, mais je n'ai plus de problèmes.

Of course. I'm now in a hotel in town. It's a little more expensive, but I don't have any more problems.

MARC: Heureusement que tu as pu trouver un autre hôtel. Comment est ta chambre?

It's lucky you were able to find another hotel. What's your room like?

GENEVIÈVE: J'ai eu de la chance! J'ai une chambre avec belle vue sur un parc, un grand lit et une jolie salle de bains.

I was lucky! I have a room with a beautiful view onto a park, a big bed, and a pretty bathroom.

MARC: Pas mal! Est-ce que le petit déjeuner est compris dans le prix de la chambre?

Not bad! Is breakfast included in the room rate?

GENEVIÈVE: Non, je paie un supplément pour ça. On sert du café, du chocolat, du jus d'orange, du pain frais et des croissants chaque matin dans la salle à manger.

No, I pay extra for that. They serve coffee, hot chocolate, orange juice, fresh bread, and croissants every morning in the dining room.

MARC: Formidable! Mais tu es en ville; ce n'est pas un peu bruyant?

Great! But you're in town; isn't it a bit noisy?

GENEVIÈVE: Généralement non; ma chambre donne sur un parc. Mais hier soir, il y eu un concert gratuit dans le parc et il a duré jusqu'à minuit.

Usually not; my room looks out onto a park. But last night, there was a free concert in the park, and it lasted 'til midnight.

MARC: La musique était bonne au moins?

Was the music good at least?

GENEVIÈVE: Peu importe. Je voulais me coucher et dormir!

It doesn't matter [That isn't the point]. I wanted to go to bed and sleep!

MARC: Bon, écoute, repose-toi bien ce soir. Je t'embrasse, et je te rappelle demain.

OK, listen, have a nice rest tonight. I love you, and I'll call back tomorrow.

NARRATING PAST EVENTS USING IRREGULAR VERBS IN THE PASSÉ COMPOSÉ

In the previous chapter, you learned the past participle of regular **-er**, **-ir**, and **-re** verbs and how to form the **passé composé** with the auxiliary verb **avoir** followed by the past participle. Review these examples:

CULTURE DEMYSTIFIED

Saying Good-Bye on the Phone

When ending a phone conversation with a close friend or a relative, the French will often refer to *kisses* rather than *love*. This is based on the Francophone custom of greeting and saying good-bye with kisses on the cheek. The number of kisses varies from one region to another and usually includes between two and four. Therefore, a phone conversation or a friendly letter will often end with the phrase **Je t'embrasse**, which literally means *I kiss you*, but should be interpreted as *I love you*.

acheter	choisir	répondre
(to buy)	*(to choose)*	*(to answer)*
j'ai ache**té** *I bought*	tu as choi**si** *you chose*	elle a répon**du** *she answered*

You also saw that, in addition to verbs conjugated with the auxiliary **avoir**, some are conjugated with **être**. Some of the **être** verbs have irregular past participles. Review them below:

(re)venir *(to come / to come back)*   **naître** *(to be born)*   **mourir** *(to die)*

il est **(re)venu** *he came (back)*   il est **né** *he was born*   il est **mort** *he died*

Many irregular verbs conjugated with **avoir** also have irregular past participles. These must be memorized. Study the following commonly used verbs with their irregular past participles:

avoir *(to have)*	**eu**	*had*	faire *(to do)*	**fait**	*done*
être *(to be)*	**été**	*been*	lire *(to read)*	**lu**	*read*
croire *(to believe)*	**cru**	*believed*	pouvoir *(to be able to)*	**pu**	*been able to*
devoir *(to have to)*	**dû**	*had to*	recevoir *(to receive)*	**reçu**	*received*
dire *(to say/tell)*	**dit**	*said/told*	savoir *(to know)*	**su**	*known*
écrire *(to write)*	**écrit**	*written*	vouloir *(to want)*	**voulu**	*wanted*

Once you know the past participle of a verb, you can conjugate that verb in the **passé composé** by changing the form of the auxiliary **avoir**. Look at the conjugation of the irregular verb **faire** *(to do)*:

j'**ai** fait	*I have done / I did*	nous **avons** fait	*we have done / we did*
tu **as** fait	*you have done / you did*	vous **avez** fait	*you have done / you did*
il/elle **a** fait	*he/she has done / he/she did*	ils/elles **ont** fait	*they have done / they did*
on **a** fait	*one has done / one did / we have done / we did*		

Written Practice 12-1

Match the English and French sentences below, writing the letter of the corresponding English sentence on the line provided.

_____	1.	Nous avons fait notre exercice.	a. *You wrote a letter.*
_____	2.	Elle a dit merci.	b. *You got lucky.*
_____	3.	Tu as écrit une lettre.	c. *They died in an accident.*
_____	4.	Ils ont voulu revenir.	d. *You read a lot.*
_____	5.	Il a été surpris.	e. *We did our exercise.*
_____	6.	Tu as eu de la chance.	f. *They received presents.*
_____	7.	Ils sont morts dans un accident.	g. *I believed this story.*
_____	8.	Vous avez beaucoup lu.	h. *She said thank you.*
_____	9.	Elles ont reçu des cadeaux.	i. *He was surprised.*
_____	10.	J'ai cru cette histoire.	j. *They wanted to come back.*

NARRATING PAST EVENTS USING VERBS OF STATE OF MIND IN THE IMPARFAIT AND PASSÉ COMPOSÉ

In the previous chapter, you saw that verbs establishing a *state of being*, like the verbs **être** (*to be*) and **avoir** (*to have*), as well as verbs of *state of mind*, like **penser** (*to think*), are usually expressed in the past in the **imparfait**. (Why? Because they rarely refer to an action completed at a specific point of time.) Here is a list of some verbs in this category:

aimer	*to like / to love*	espérer	*to hope*
avoir	*to have*	penser	*to think*
être	*to be*	pouvoir	*to be able to (can)*
croire	*to believe*	savoir	*to know*
devoir	*to have to (must)*	vouloir	*to want*

However, verbs of state of being and state of mind can sometimes be used in the **passé composé**. In this case, they show that the event occurred and was over at a precise point in time. Choosing between the **imparfait** and the **passé composé** allows the speaker or writer to express a nuanced perspective. Compare the following examples. Note that the **imparfait** describes an unchanging state, while the **passé composé** emphasizes something unusual, unexpected, or sudden.

J'**aimais** toujours la cuisine française.	*I always liked French cuisine.*
Mais j'**ai aimé** ce plat chinois hier soir.	*But I liked that Chinese dish last night.*
Je ne **pouvais** jamais prononcer ce mot.	*I could never pronounce this word.*
Mais hier j'**ai** finalement **pu** prononcer ce mot.	*But yesterday I was finally able to pronounce this word.*

Je ne **savais** pas où tu étais.	*I didn't know where you were.*
Mais quand j'ai entendu ta voiture, j'**ai su** que tu rentrais.	*But when I heard your car, I knew that you were coming home.*
Il y **avait** beaucoup de bruit.	*There was a lot of noise.*
Il y **a eu** un soudain coup de tonnerre.	*There was a sudden thunderbolt.*

SPECIAL MEANINGS OF THE VERB DEVOIR

Devoir (*to be obliged to*), a high-frequency verb, is irregular in the present tense. It is most often used in front of an infinitive. Look at its conjugation, and note its various meanings:

je **dois**	*I must / have to / owe*	nous **devons**	*we must / have to / owe*
tu **dois**	*you must / have to / owe*	vous **devez**	*you must / have to / owe*
il/elle/on **doit**	*he/she/one must / has to / owes*	ils/elles **doivent**	*they must / have to / owe*

Look at the following examples in the present and past, and note the various meanings of **devoir**:

Je **dois** finir cet exercice.	*I **must / have to** finish this exercise.*
Je **dois** dix euros à ma sœur.	*I **owe** my sister ten euros.*
J'**ai dû** changer d'hôtel hier soir.	*I **had to** change hotels last night.*
Je **devais** être au cours à huit heures, mais j'étais en retard.	*I **was supposed to** be in class at eight o'clock, but I was late.*

The verb **devoir** (plus infinitive) is often used in the **imparfait** with the meaning of *was/were supposed to*.

Sa mère **devait** envoyer les invitations.	*Her mother **was supposed to** send the invitations.*
Nous **devions** les imprimer.	*We **were supposed to** print them.*

The verb **devoir** (plus infinitive) used in the **passé composé** often means *must have* as in a supposition or assumption of *probability*.

Il **a dû** oublier la date.	*He **must have** forgotten the date.*
Ils **ont dû** manquer le train.	*They **must have** missed the train.*

Oral Practice 12-1

Pretend you just spent a week in a hotel. Read each sentence aloud, selecting the correct verb tense from the choices given. Then turn on your CD, and check your answers.

TRACK 24

1. (Je suis arrivé(e) / J'arrivais) à l'hôtel le 9 avril vers dix-sept heures.
2. (J'ai donné / Je donnais) mon numéro de réservation à la réceptionniste.
3. Elle (m'a donné / me donnait) la clé de la chambre 208.
4. La chambre (a été / était) petite.
5. Il y (a eu / avait) une jolie salle de bains.
6. (Je suis resté[e] / Je restais) une semaine.
7. Le prix du petit déjeuner (n'a pas été / n'était pas) compris.
8. L'agent de voyage (a dû / devait) oublier de me le dire.
9. Alors (j'ai dû / je devais) payer un supplément.
10. Heureusement tous les petits déjeuners (ont été / étaient) inclus.

Talking About Restaurants

In the following dialogue, Marc calls his sister to see how she is doing. This time, Geneviève tells him about a restaurant where she dined.

TRACK 25

MARC: Salut, Geneviève. Ça va aujourd'hui?

Hi, Geneviève. Are you OK today?

GENEVIÈVE: Je suis sortie au restaurant avec des amis hier soir, et nous sommes rentrés tard.

I went out to a restaurant last night, and we came back late.

MARC: Vous vous êtes bien amusés?

Did you have fun?

GENEVIÈVE: Je croyais que les Suisses étaient plutôt sérieux, mais je t'assure qu'ils aiment s'amuser!

I thought that the Swiss were rather serious, but I assure you they like to have fun!

MARC: Tant mieux pour toi et pour eux!

Good for you and for them!

GENEVIÈVE: Le restaurant où nous étions est un restaurant à trois étoiles. Très très cher!

The restaurant where we were is a three-star restaurant. Very, very expensive!

MARC: Combien tu as dépensé?

How much did you spend?

GENEVIÈVE: Pas trop! Notre école de cuisine nous a donné des bons.

Not too much! Our cooking school gave us vouchers.

MARC: Alors, qu'est-ce que tu as commandé?

So what did you order?

GENEVIÈVE: Un soufflé aux pommes de terre comme plat principal et une tarte aux myrtilles comme dessert.

A potato soufflé for the main dish and a blueberry tart for dessert.

MARC: Et le vin, comment était-il?

And how was the wine?

GENEVIÈVE: Alors là, j'ai été vraiment surprise. Je ne l'ai pas aimé.

As for that, I was really surprised. I didn't like it.

MARC: Qu'est-ce que c'était? Du vinaigre?

What was it? Vinegar?

GENEVIÈVE: Non, pas tout à fait! Mais il n'était pas à mon goût.

No, not quite! But it was not to my taste.

MARC: Et le service? Il devait être bon.

What about the service? It had to be good.

GENEVIÈVE: Super! Nous avions un serveur très professionnel.

It was great! We had a very professional waiter.

MARC: Il a dû recevoir un bon pourboire alors.

He must have received a good tip then.

GENEVIÈVE: Eh oui! En plus du service qui était compris, nous lui avons laissé cinquante francs suisses.

Yes! In addition to the service charge, which was included, we left him fifty Swiss francs.

MARC: Quand est-ce que tu y retournes?

When will you go back there?

GENEVIÈVE: Je voudrais bien y retourner. J'espère que l'école a encore des bons à nous donner!

I'd like to go back there. I hope the school has more vouchers to give us!

VOCABULARY: RESTAURANTS

Look at the following essential words and phrases to use in restaurants:

le maître d'hôtel	*maître d'*	l'entrée (f.)	*first course*
le serveur	*waiter*	le plat principal	*main dish / entrée*
la serveuse	*waitress*	le dessert	*dessert*

l'addition (*f.*) / la note   *bill/check*   le pourboire   *tip*
le service est compris   *service is included*

Using the Object Pronoun y When Referring to a Location

The pronoun **y** is generally used to replace a prepositional phrase representing a *location*. Look at the following examples of prepositional phrases which might be replaced by the pronoun **y** in a sentence:

à la plage	*at/on/to the beach*	devant l'hôtel	*in front of the hotel*
à l'hôtel	*at/in/to the hotel*	derrière le parc	*behind the park*
au restaurant	*at/in/to the restaurant*	en face du café	*across from the café*
sur la table	*on the table*	loin de l'école	*far from the school*
sous le lit	*under the bed*	près de la maison	*near the school*
dans la chambre	*in the bedroom*	à côté du jardin	*next to the garden*

When **y** replaces the name of a location, it is translated as *there*. Although the adverb *there* is often omitted in English, it should not be omitted in French. Like other object pronouns, the pronoun **y** is placed before the verb. Look at the following examples:

Tu es **à l'école**? —Oui, j'**y** suis.	*Are you at school? —Yes, I am (there).*
Quand est-ce qu'elle va **au restaurant**? —Elle **y** va ce soir.	*When is she going to the restaurant? —She is going (there) tonight.*
Il reste **dans sa chambre**? —Oui, il **y** reste.	*Is he staying in his room? —Yes, he is (staying there)!*

When the verb is in the **passé composé**, the pronoun **y**, like other object pronouns, is placed *before* the auxiliary verb. Look at the following examples:

Quand est-ce qu'elle est partie **à la plage**? —Elle **y** est partie ce matin.	*When did she leave for the beach? —She left (for there) this morning.*
Tu étais **à l'aéroport**? —Oui, j'**y** ai accompagné ma sœur.	*Were you at the airport? —Yes, I accompanied my sister (there).*

The Michelin Guides

Michelin Guides (**les guides Michelin**) have been used for over a century in Europe, and are now available for some cities in the United States. They use a system of symbols to identify the best hotels and restaurants within categories that vary according to amenities and price. The very best restaurants are awarded from one to three stars, based on five criteria: quality of products, mastery of flavor and cooking, "personality" of the cuisine, value for the money, and consistency between visits. A three-star restaurant is truly exceptional.

Ton téléphone cellulaire est **sur la table**? —Non, il n'**y** est pas.	*Is your cell phone on the table?—No, it isn't (there).*
Paul est **à la maison**? —Non, il n'**y** est pas.	*Is Paul at home? —No, he is not (there).*

The only structure where object pronouns are placed *after* the verb is the affirmative command. (You learned this form with reflexive pronouns in Chapter 7.) Compare the following negative and affirmative commands using the pronoun **y**:

N'**y** va pas!	*Don't go!* (familiar, singular)	N'**y** allez pas!	*Don't go!* (plural and formal singular)	N'**y** allons pas!	*Let's not go!*
Vas-**y**!	*Go!* (familiar)	Allez-**y**!	*Go!* (plural and formal singular)	Allons-**y**!	*Let's go!*

Written Practice 12-2

Answer each question in writing, affirmatively or negatively according to the cue. Use a command form for item numbers 7 and 8. Be sure to use the pronoun **y** in each answer.

1. Le concert est dans le parc? —Oui, il _____ .

2. Tu vas au parc? —Non, je _____ .

3. Jacques est en face de l'hôtel? —Oui, il _____ .

4. Tu restes dans ta chambre? —Oui, j'_____ .

5. Tu dînes dans ta chambre? —Non, je _____ .

6. Tu vas au restaurant ce soir? —Oui, j'_____ .

7. Je dois aller au concert, moi? —Oui, _____ !

8. On va au café ensemble? —Oui, _____ !

Asking for Precise Information

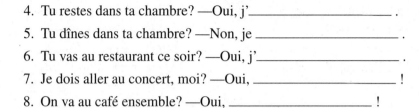 TRACK 26

In the following dialogue, Geneviève calls Marc to share her good news with him. She is very excited about having been selected to evaluate the cuisine in several restaurants.

GENEVIÈVE: Marc, j'ai des nouvelles sensationnelles.

Marc, I have sensational news.

MARC: Tu as gagné un prix?

Did you win a prize?

GENEVIÈVE: Quelque chose comme ça. J'ai été choisie pour goûter la cuisine de plusieurs restaurants. Je dois en visiter trois cette semaine.

Something like that. I've been chosen to taste the food in several restaurants. I have to visit three of them this week.

MARC: Ça veut dire que tu vas manger dans tous ces restaurants? Gratuitement?

Does it mean you're going to eat in all those restaurants? For free?

GENEVIÈVE: Je dois payer, mais l'école me rembourse!

I have to pay, but the school reimburses me!

MARC: Formidable! Ce sont des restaurants à trois étoiles?

Great! Are they three-star restaurants?

GENEVIÈVE: Ah non! Ce sont des restos à une étoile, mais je suis bien contente.

Oh no! They are one-star restaurants, but I'm quite happy.

MARC: Bien sûr! Tu vas te régaler.

Of course! You're really going to enjoy yourself.

GENEVIÈVE: Pour mon premier, j'ai choisi un petit resto suisse près de mon hôtel.

For my first one, I chose a little Swiss restaurant near my hotel.

MARC: Tu as bien fait de t'inscrire à cette école de cuisine.

It was a good idea (You did well) to enroll at that cooking school.

GENEVIÈVE: Pour sûr! Elle est un peu loin de la maison, mais j'y apprends beaucoup.

For sure! It is a little far from home, but I am learning a lot there.

MARC: Et à part ce petit resto suisse?

And aside from that little Swiss restaurant?

GENEVIÈVE: Mon deuxième c'est un café marocain à côté de la gare, où on trouve des spécialités comme le poulet tagine.

My second one is a Moroccan restaurant next to the train station, where they serve specialties like chicken tagine.

MARC: Et ton troisième?

And your third?

GENEVIÈVE: Dans l'hôtel Mercure, il y a un restaurant provençal.

In the Mercure Hotel, there is a Provençal restaurant.

MARC: Sans blague! La cuisine provençale, on la connaît quand on habite en Provence, comme nous!

No kidding! Provençal cuisine, that's something you know when you live in Provence, like we do!

GENEVIÈVE: Oui, mais tu sais, depuis que je suis ici, je mange beaucoup de pommes de terre.

Yes, but you know, since I've been here, I've been eating a lot of potatoes.

USING THE QUESTION WORDS OÙ, QUI, QUAND, POURQUOI, AND COMMENT

To ask for precise information, you must learn *interrogative adverbs* (question words) and their structures. Look at the following questions starting with **où** (*where*) and **qui** (*who*). Note that **où** and **qui** are immediately followed by the verb when they are used to say **Où est/sont... ?** (*Where is/are . . .?*) or **Qui est/sont... ?** (*Who is/are . . . ?*)

Où est le café du Maroc?   *Where is the Café du Maroc?*

Qui était votre serveuse?   *Who was your waitress?*

Look at the questions below starting with **quand** (*when*), **pourquoi** (*why*), and **comment** (*how*). There are three possible interrogative structures. First, these adverbs can be followed immediately by the subject of the sentence (*extremely informal*). Second, they can be followed by **est-ce que** (or **est-ce qu'** before a vowel sound) plus the subject. Third, the adverb is followed by an inverted verb-subject structure. (Review Asking Questions in Chapter 7.)

CULTURE DEMYSTIFIED

Cuisine

French cuisine is quite diversified and features many regional cooking styles that influence and are also influenced by neighboring countries. For example, Provençal cuisine, from Provence in the south, has a uniquely Mediterranean flavor and almost always features ingredients such as olive oil, garlic, and tomatoes. Alsatian cuisine, from the Alsace-Lorraine region in the east, features specialties influenced by nearby Germany, such as **choucroute garnie** (*sauerkraut with meats*). The French Burgundy region (**la Bourgogne**) features dishes such as **bœuf bourguignon** (*beef cooked in Burgundy wine*).

Swiss cuisine also enjoys regional influences from its neighbors (mainly Italy, France, and Germany). However, the Swiss also have their own dishes such as **fondue au fromage** (*melted cheese into which bread is dipped*), **raclette** (*melted cheese dribbled over potatoes, served with gherkins and pickled onions*), and **fondue bourguignonne** (*meat cooked in oil at the table*).

Europeans also enjoy the foods of other ethnicities. Paris, for example, has numerous North African restaurants featuring the cuisine of Morocco, Tunisia, and Algeria, where French is spoken. At the heart of this cuisine is **couscous** (*semolina wheat granules*). Many markets, stores, and restaurants in Europe feature **tajines** (also spelled **tagines**). These casserole-type dishes consist of lamb, beef, or chicken, often served with couscous. The name **tajine** comes from the circular clay pot covered with a dome in which it is cooked.

Quand on mange? Quand est-ce qu'on mange? Quand mange-t-on?	*When do we eat?*
Pourquoi tu ne sors pas? Pourquoi est-ce que tu ne sors pas? Pourquoi ne sors-tu pas?	*Why don't you go out?*
Comment il paie? Comment est-ce qu'il paie? Comment paie-t-il?	*How does he pay / is he paying?*

Of course many other verbs may follow **où** or **qui** in a question:

Où tu vas? Où est-ce que tu vas? Où vas-tu?	*Where are you going?*
Qui tu cherches? Qui est-ce que tu cherches? Qui cherches-tu?	*Who(m) are you looking for?*

Oral Practice 12-2

Say aloud the question that would elicit the answer shown. Important elements are in boldface. Then turn on your CD to verify your question.

 TRACK 27

1. **Paul** est arrivé.

2. **Le serveur** apporte la note.

3. Le café est **à côté du parc**.

4. La note était **sur la table**.

5. **Moi, je** vais payer.

Next, use the phrase **est-ce que/est-ce qu'** with **quand**, **pourquoi**, and **comment** to ask your question. Verify your question by listening to the CD.

6. Sarah est rentrée **ce matin**.

7. Elle est arrivée **en taxi**.

8. **Elle est fatiguée;** elle ne va pas au cours.

Now, use the inverted verb-subject structure with **quand**, **pourquoi**, or **comment** to ask your question. Then verify your question by listening to the CD.

9. Ils vont au café **ce soir**.

10. Ils ont mangé au café; **ils n'ont rien à la maison**.

11. Ils ont **bien** mangé.

GRAMMAR DEMYSTIFIED

The Inverted Interrogative Structure in the passé composé

Pay particular attention to the inverted verb-subject structure for interrogatives when the verb is in the **passé composé**. In this case, invert the auxiliary verb and the subject following the adverb. Look at the following examples:

Quand **avez-vous** mangé?	*When did you eat? / When have you eaten?*
Pourquoi **es-tu** parti?	*Why did you leave? / Why have you left?*

Also, when you use inversion, remember to insert a **-t-** in the third-person singular with the subjects **il**, **elle**, and **on** between the auxiliary verb and the subject. (This avoids the proximity of two vowel sounds.)

Comment a-**t**-il payé?	*How did he pay? / How has he paid?*

Using the Verbs prendre, surprendre, and comprendre

You learned the irregular present tense conjugation of the verb **prendre** (*to take*) in Chapter 6. You may review that section at this time. The verbs **surprendre** (*to surprise*) and **comprendre** (*to understand / to include*) follow the same pattern as the verb **prendre**. Study the conjugation of the verb **comprendre** in the present tense:

je compren**ds**	*I understand*	nous compren**ons**	*we understand*
tu compren**ds**	*you understand*	vous compren**ez**	*you understand*
il/elle compren**d**	*he/she/it understands/ includes*	ils/elles compren**nent**	*they understand/ include*
on compren**d**	*one understands / we understand*		

Note that the verb **comprendre** in the third person can have two equivalents in English. Look at the examples:

Marie comprend le français.   *Marie **understands** French.*

Le prix comprend le petit déjeuner.   *The price **includes** breakfast.*

The verbs **prendre**, **apprendre**, **comprendre**, and **surprendre** have irregular past participles as follows:

prendre →**pris**   apprendre →**appris**   comprendre →**compris**   surprendre→**surpris**

Remember to conjugate the auxiliary verb **avoir** in the **passé composé**. Look at some examples:

J'ai pris le poulet.   *I took/had the chicken.*   **Elle a** pris la quiche.   *She took/had the quiche.*

On a compris.   *We understood.*   **Nous avons** compris.   *We understood.*

SPECIAL USES OF COMPRIS **AND** SURPRIS

The past participle **compris** (*included*) is often used as an adjective. The expression **y compris** is a fixed form meaning *including*. Look at these examples:

Le déjeuner est **compris** dans le prix.   *Lunch is included in the price.*

Le service est **compris** dans la note.	*Service is included in the bill.*
J'ai tout payé, **y compris** la taxe.	*I paid everything, including the tax.*

Similarly, the past participle of the verb **surprendre** (*to surprise*) can be used as an adjective after the verb **être** (*to be*).

J'ai été très **surpris(e)** par le vin.	*I was very surprised by the wine.*
Il va être **surpris** par ma visite.	*He is going to be surprised by my visit.*

Written Practice 12-3

Surprise! Complete each sentence with the appropriate form of the verb **prendre**, **surprendre**, or **comprendre**. Follow the instructions in parentheses.

1. Aujourd'hui, Jasmine _____ le taxi. (prendre / passé composé)

2. Elle _____ son ami Alain au restaurant. (surprendre / passé composé)

3. Alain _____ le déjeuner. (prendre / passé composé)

4. Maintenant ils _____ un apéritif ensemble. (prendre / présent)

5. Alain ne _____ pas pourquoi le serveur donne la note à Jasmine. (comprendre / présent)

6. Tout à coup cinq autres amis arrivent; Alain est _____! (surprendre / participe passé / adjectif)

7. C'est l'anniversaire d'Alain et ses amis paient la note du déjeuner, _____ l'apéritif avec Jasmine. (*including*, expression using a form of **comprendre**)

8. Le service est _____ mais Jasmine et ses amis laissent un pourboire. (comprendre / participe passé / adjectif)

Chapter Practice 12

A. L'apprentissage de Geneviève. Recount Genevieve's apprenticeship by writing the verbs indicated in the present and past tenses as suggested below.

*1. être / présent 2. vouloir / présent 3. s'inscrire / passé compose
4. apprendre / passé composé 5. comprendre / présent 6. être / imparfait
7. faire / imparfait 8. être / présent*

Geneviève (1) _____ provençale. Elle adore faire la cuisine et elle
(2) _____ être chef un jour. Alors, le mois dernier elle
(3) _____ à une école culinaire suisse. Elle (4) _____ à
faire toutes sortes de plats. Maintenant elle (5) _____ la gastronomie.
Avant elle (6) _____ toujours un peu hésitante quand elle
(7) _____ la cuisine mais maintenant elle (8) _____ plus sûre
d'elle-même.

B. Réponses. Answer questions 1-3 affirmatively and 4-5 negatively using the
pronoun **y**. Turn on your CD, and verify your answers. You may also uncover the
printed answers on the right.

 TRACK 28

1. Tu es allé(e) au café ce matin?   *[Oui, j'y suis allé(e).]*

2. Tu étais au cinéma?   *[Oui, j'y étais.]*

3. Ton copain est arrivé au concert à l'heure?   *[Oui, il y est arrivé à l'heure.]*

4. Vous étudiez à l'hôtel?   *[Non, nous n'y étudions pas.]*

5. Tes amis sont dans ta chambre?   *[Non, ils n'y sont pas.]*

C. Questions. You are in a restaurant, and you ask the following questions. Use
est-ce que, except for numbers 1 and 4. Check your answers by uncovering the
answers on the right.

1. Where is the waiter?   *[Où est le serveur?]*

2. When is he going to bring the   *[Quand est-ce qu'il va apporter la
   bill?   note?]*

3. Why isn't he here?   *[Pourquoi est-ce qu'il n'est pas là?]*

4. Who is the maître d'?   *[Qui est le maître d'hôtel?]*

5. How and whom do I pay?   *[Comment et à qui est-ce que je paie?]*

CHAPTER QUIZ 12

Complete this dialogue between two friends using the words provided.

*allons-y / ce soir / comprends / étoiles / j'espère / la réceptionniste / où /
pourquoi / surprise / y*

JEAN: Tu veux retourner au restaurant de l'hôtel (1) _____?

ARLÈNE: Non, on (2) _____ était hier soir. Allons dans un restaurant italien aujourd'hui!

JEAN: D'accord. Il y a un restaurant italien à deux (3) _____ en face de l'hôtel.

ARLÈNE: Super! (4) _____!

JEAN: (5) _____ que ce n'est pas trop cher.

ARLÈNE: Demande à (6) _____ de l'hôtel. Elle doit avoir leurs prix.

JEAN: (7) _____ est-elle?

ARLÈNE: Je ne sais pas. Mais (8) _____ on ne regarde pas sur Internet?

JEAN: Bonne idée, mais voilà le taxi! Tu es (9) _____?

ARLÈNE: Oui, je ne (10) _____ pas comment il est arrivé si vite.

CHAPTER 13

Dreams and Aspirations

In this chapter you will learn:

Comparing Old and New Dreams
Sharing Hopes for the Future
Making Predictions Using the Simple Future Tense
Expressing Possibilities Using the Present Conditional

Comparing Old and New Dreams

Jean-Claude and Kelly are two adolescents sitting on the terrace of a café. It's a beautiful afternoon.

 TRACK 29

JEAN-CLAUDE: Tu sais, Kelly, quand j'étais petit, je voulais devenir chauffeur d'autobus.

You know, Kelly, when I was little, I wanted to become a bus driver.

KELLY: C'est drôle. Je ne te vois pas comme chauffeur d'autobus du tout.

That's funny. I don't see you at all as a bus driver.

JEAN-CLAUDE: Plus tard, quand j'étais au collège, je voulais devenir chanteur de rock.

Later, when I was in middle school, I wanted to become a rock singer.

KELLY: Oh non, qu'est-ce qu'ils ont dit, tes parents?

Oh no, what did they say, your parents?

JEAN-CLAUDE: Mon père m'a acheté une guitare et m'a payé des leçons, mais j'ai vite réalisé que je n'avais pas trop de talent pour la musique.

My dad bought me a guitar and paid for lessons, but I quickly realized that I had no talent for music.

KELLY: Pauvre Jean-Claude! Tu sais ce que je voulais devenir, moi?

Poor Jean-Claude! Do you know what I wanted to be?

JEAN-CLAUDE: Dis-le-moi!

Tell me!

KELLY: Depuis toujours j'ai voulu devenir actrice.

I have always wanted to become an actress.

JEAN-CLAUDE: Tu as de la chance d'être si sûre. Moi j'hésite.

You are lucky to be so sure. I am undecided.

KELLY: Tu es bon en maths, n'est-ce pas?

You are good at math, right?

JEAN-CLAUDE: Oui, je pourrais faire des études d'informatique.

Yes, I could study computer science.

KELLY: Tu souhaites être le prochain Bill Gates?

Do you aspire to be the next Bill Gates?

JEAN-CLAUDE: Être connu dans le monde entier, être incroyablement riche! Pas mal comme rêve!

To be known throughout the world, to be incredibly rich! Not a bad dream!

KELLY: Et moi, être une Audrey Tautou ou une Angelina Jolie!

And me, to be an Audrey Tautou or an Angelina Jolie!

JEAN-CLAUDE: C'est beau de rêver!

It is nice to dream!

VOCABULARY DEMYSTIFIED

Le collège

French children, like American children, go through three educational cycles: the primary cycle (**le cycle primaire**), the middle school cycle (**le collège**) and the high school cycle (**le lycée**). However, it is only upon passing a rigorous examination called **le baccalauréat** in their senior year of the **lycée**, that students may enroll at the university (**l'université**). All universities are state-sponsored and fees for attendance are minimal. (There is no French equivalent word for the American *college*. The words *college* and **collège** are false cognates.)

VOCABULARY: EXPRESSING WISHES, DREAMS, AND ASPIRATIONS

Look at the following verbs that express wishes, dreams, and aspirations:

désirer	*to desire*	rêver	*to dream*
espérer	*to hope*	souhaiter	*to wish*
penser	*to think*	vouloir	*to want*

Now look at the following examples, noting that these verbs are followed by an infinitive (the equivalents of *to become, to be, to study*, etc.)

Avant, je **désirais devenir** chanteuse. Maintenant je **veux être** professeur.

Before, I wanted to become a singer. Now I want to be a teacher.

Avant, il **souhaitait devenir** chanteur de rock. Maintenant, il **espère étudier** l'informatique.

Before, he wished to become a rock singer. Now he hopes to study computer science.

Note that the verb **rêver** is followed by the preposition **de/d'** and an infinitive.

Avant, elle **rêvait d'être** riche. Maintenant elle **veut** simplement **être** heureuse.

Before, she dreamed of being rich. Now she simply wants to be happy.

The verbs **aimer** (*to like*) and **vouloir** (*to want*) are frequently used in the *conditional mood* to express wishes. Here are the conditional endings; note that they are identical to **imparfait** endings: **-ais, -ais, -ait, -ions, -iez, -aient**. The conditional

stems of **aimer** (a regular verb) and **vouloir** (an irregular verb) are shown in bold-face below:

j'**aimer**ais / je **voudr**ais	*I would like*	nous **aimer**ions / nous **voudr**ions	*we would like*
tu **aimer**ais / tu **voudr**ais	*you would like*		
il/elle **aimer**ait / il/elle **voudr**ait	*he/she would like*	vous **aimer**iez / vous **voudr**iez	*you would like*
on **aimer**ait / on **voudr**ait	*one/we would like*	ils/elles **aime**raient / ils/elles **voudr**aient	*they would like*

Aimer and **vouloir** in the conditional are very often followed directly by an infinitive.

> Ils **aimeraient être** célèbres.   *They would like to be famous.*
>
> Nous **voudrions réaliser** nos rêves.   *We would like to realize our dreams.*

Here is a list of occupations that could be part of a dream:

l'acteur / l'actrice	*actor/actress*	l'infirmier / l'infirmière	*nurse*
l'archéologue (*m., f.*)	*archeologist*	l'inventeur / l'inventrice	*inventor*
l'artiste (*m., f.*)	*artist*	le/la journaliste	*journalist*
l'avocat(e)	*lawyer*	le médecin	*physician*
le chanteur / la chanteuse	*singer*	le peintre	*painter*
le/la cycliste	*bicyclist*	le/la photographe	*photographer*
le danseur / la danseuse	*dancer*	le professeur	*teacher/professor*
l'écrivain (*m.*)	*writer*	le reporter	*reporter*

Now look at these adjectives which could convey a dream or aspiration. Both masculine and feminine forms are provided except where the form is the same in both genders.

célèbre	*famous*	heureux/heureuse	*happy*
créatif/créative	*creative*	bien nanti / bien nantie	*well-off*
marié/mariée	*married*	riche	*rich*

Oral Practice 13-1

Restore each person's dreams by saying what he/she wanted to be and what he/she would now like to be. Number 1 has been done for you as an example. Use **voulait devenir** followed by **aimerait être** in each sentence. After saying the sentence aloud, listen to it on your CD.

 TRACK 30

1. Josette: actrice/femme d'affaires   *Elle voulait devenir actrice. Maintenant, elle aimerait être femme d'affaires.*

2. Paul: inventeur/écrivain

3. Ginette: exploratrice/archéologue

4. Luc: peintre / professeur d'art

5. Cécile: infirmière/médecin

6. Marc: coureur cycliste / reporter de sports

7. Jeanine: mannequin / hôtesse de l'air

8. Kevin: chanteur/journaliste

Sharing Hopes for the Future

In the following dialogue, Jean-Claude and Kelly continue their conversation about the future in a playful manner.

 TRACK 31

KELLY: Il y a une chose qui m'intéresserait aussi à l'avenir.

There is one thing that would also interest me in the future.

JEAN-CLAUDE: Ah oui, à part le cinéma et le théâtre?

Oh yes, aside from movies and theater?

KELLY: Oui, j'aimerais faire du travail bénévole ou être ambassadrice pour une bonne cause.

I would like to do volunteer work or be an ambassador for a good cause.

JEAN-CLAUDE: Pourquoi pas? Il y a beaucoup de vedettes de cinéma qui mettent leur célébrité au service de l'humanité.

Why not? There are many movie stars who put their celebrity at the service of humanity.

KELLY: Ce qui me tenterait le plus, c'est de partager mes talents artistiques avec des enfants de pays en voie de développement.

What would tempt me most is to share my artistic talents with children in developing countries.

JEAN-CLAUDE: C'est une aspiration très noble, mais tu ne crois pas qu'ils ont besoin de manger et d'apprendre à lire?

That's a noble aspiration, but don't you think that they need to eat and learn to read?

KELLY: Jean-Claude! Tu ne sais donc pas qu'on peut apprendre par les arts dramatiques?

Jean-Claude! Don't you know that we can learn through dramatic art?

JEAN-CLAUDE: Peut-être! Mais qu'est-ce que tu apprendras à des enfants qui ont le ventre vide?

Perhaps! But what can you teach children who have empty bellies?

KELLY: Justement! Ce qu'il me faut, c'est une organisation qui veut nourrir le ventre et la tête.

That's just it! What I need is an organization whose goal is to feed the belly and the brain.

JEAN-CLAUDE: Moi, ce qui me fascine, c'est le travail de l'organisation Médecins Sans Frontières.

What fascinates me is the work of Doctors Without Borders.

KELLY: Oui, ce sont des gens qui procurent des soins médicaux dans des zones dangereuses.

Yes, they are people who provide medical care in dangerous areas.

JEAN-CLAUDE: Un spécialiste en informatique pourrait leur être utile.

A computer scientist could be useful to them.

KELLY: Eh bien, un jour, je te rencontrerai peut-être en Afrique ou en Asie.

Well, some day maybe I'll meet you in Africa or in Asia.

JEAN-CLAUDE: On ne sait jamais, Kelly! Tu seras peut-être célèbre et bénévole!

One never knows, Kelly! You may be famous and involved in charity work!

KELLY: Toi aussi, tu mettras peut-être ton talent au service d'une bonne cause.

You too might put your talent in the service of a good cause.

JEAN-CLAUDE: Voilà! Le rêve continue. Nous serons connus, riches et généreux.

There! The dream continues. We'll be well-known, rich, and generous.

Making Predictions Using the Simple Future Tense

To predict how things will be in the future, the *simple future* tense is generally used in French. As with the conditional, the stem of the simple future is normally the entire infinitive of the verb. Endings are as follows: **-ai**, **-as**, **-a**, **-ons**, **-ez**, **-ont**. The future endings are easy to remember because they resemble the forms of the verb

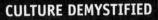
Médecins Sans Frontières

The organization **Médecins Sans Frontières** is known as **MSF** in most of the world, but is more commonly referred to as *Doctors Without Borders* in the United States and Canada. It was created in 1971 by a small group of French doctors. It has no political affiliation, and its unique goal is to provide humanitarian aid in war-torn regions and disaster areas, usually in developing countries.

avoir in the present. See below the regular **-er** verb **étudier** (*to study*) conjugated in the simple future. The future stem (here, the infinitive) is highlighted in boldface.

j'**étudier**ai	*I will study*	nous **étudier**ons	*we will study*
tu **étudier**as	*you will study*	vous **étudier**ez	*you will study*
il/elle **étudier**a	*he/she will study*	ils/elles **étudier**ont	*they will study*
on **étudier**a	*one/we will study*		

See below the examples of the regular **-re** verb **attendre** (*to wait*), and the regular **-ir** verb **finir** (*to finish*), conjugated in the simple future. The future stem is highlighted in boldface. Note that the final **-e** of **-re** verbs is dropped before the ending is added.

-re **Verb**		-ir **Verb**	
j'**attendr**ai	*I will wait*	je **finir**ai	*I will finish*
tu **attendr**as	*you will wait*	tu **finir**as	*you will finish*
il/elle **attendr**a	*he/she will wait*	il/elle **finir**a	*he/she will finish*
on **attendr**a	*one/we will wait*	on **finir**a	*one/we will finish*
nous **attendr**ons	*we will wait*	nous **finir**ons	*we will finish*
vous **attendr**ez	*you will wait*	vous **finir**ez	*you will finish*
ils/elles **attendr**ont	*they will wait*	ils/elles **finir**ont	*they will finish*

Here are examples of regular verbs in the future tense:

L'année prochaine, j'**étudier**ai pour le baccalauréat.	*Next year, I will study for the baccalauréat.*
Nous **finir**ons nos études secondaires.	*We will finish our secondary studies.*
On **attendr**a les résultats.	*We will wait for the results.*
Dans dix ans, nous nous **marier**ons.	*In ten years, we will get married.*

Some verbs that are irregular in the present tense also follow this model in the future. Although **apprendre** (*to learn*) is irregular in the present, it uses the infinitive form **apprendr-** (dropping the final **-e**) as the future stem. Thus, in the future, **prendre**, **comprendre**, and **surprendre** are conjugated like other **-re** verbs. Compare the present and future tense conjugations of **apprendre**:

Présent	**Futur simple**
j'apprends	j'**apprendr**ai
tu apprends	tu **apprendr**as
il/elle/on apprend	il/elle/on **apprendr**a
nous apprenons	nous **apprendr**ons
vous apprenez	vous **apprendr**ez
ils/elles apprennent	ils/elles **apprendr**ont

There are a few high-frequency verbs that have irregular stems in the simple future. Once you have memorized them, you may conjugate them in the future simply by changing the endings. Look at the following irregular stems:

aller (*to go*) → **ir-**	pouvoir (*to be able to*) → **pourr-**
avoir (*to have*) → **aur-**	recevoir (*to receive*) → **recevr-**
devenir (*to become*) → **deviendr-**	savoir (*to know*) → **saur-**
être (*to be*) → **ser-**	voir (*to see*) → **verr-**
faire (*to do/make*) → **fer-**	vouloir (*to want*) → **voudr-**

Look at the following examples of irregular verbs in the future. Note also the English equivalents of sentences containing the adverb **peut-être** (*maybe/perhaps*).

Un jour je **serai** peut-être bien nanti(e).	*One day I will perhaps be well-off. / I may one day be well-off.*
Elle **deviendra** peut-être célèbre et riche.	*She will perhaps become famous and rich. / She may become famous and rich.*
Ils **feront** peut-être du bénévolat.	*They will perhaps do volunteer work. / They may do volunteer work.*

Written Practice 13-1

Complete each sentence with the future tense of the verb in parentheses.

1. Laurent et moi, nous _____ à l'université. (aller)
2. Laurent _____ des études d'informatique. (faire)

3. Un jour, il _____ programmeur. (être)

4. Il _____ peut-être dans un bureau. (travailler)

5. Moi, je _____ infirmière. (devenir)

6. Je _____ travailler dans un hôpital. (pouvoir)

7. J'espère que nous _____ d'être amis. (continuer)

8. Nous nous _____ peut-être. (marier)

Jean-Claude and Kelly's discussion of the future takes on a more serious tone.

 TRACK 32

KELLY: Quand je serai à l'université, je chercherai un programme de bénévolat qui me permettra d'enseigner.

When I am at the university, I will look for a volunteer program which will allow me to teach.

JEAN-CLAUDE: Moi, dès que j'aurai mes résultats du bac, je me renseignerai sur les programmes d'échange avec l'Afrique.

As for me, as soon as I have my results from the baccalauréat, I will get information on exchange programs in Africa.

KELLY: Pourquoi l'Afrique? Pourquoi pas l'Asie?

Why Africa? Why not Asia?

JEAN-CLAUDE: Parce qu'en Afrique, il y a une grande communauté francophone.

Because in Africa, there is a large French-speaking community.

KELLY: Tu ne voudrais pas apprendre une nouvelle langue, c'est ça?

You wouldn't want to learn another language, is that it?

JEAN-CLAUDE: Je ne suis pas fort en langues, tu sais.

I am not good at languages, you know.

KELLY: Mais Jean-Claude! Tu étudies l'anglais depuis trois ans. Lorsque tu voyageras, ce sera une langue très utile.

But Jean-Claude! You've been studying English for three years. When you travel, it will be a useful language.

JEAN-CLAUDE: J'espère bien!

I hope so!

DISCUSSING FUTURE EVENTS USING QUAND, LORSQUE, DÈS QUE, **AND** AUSSITÔT QUE

Unlike in English, the conjunctions **quand/lorsque** (*when*) as well as **dès que** / **aussitôt que** (*as soon as*) are followed by the *future tense* whenever the action of

the verb refers to the future. Look at the following sentences, and compare the tenses in French and English. You will notice that in French the future is used in both clauses, while the English present tense is always used after *when*.

Lorsqu'ils voyageront, ils **apprendront** beaucoup.	*When they **travel**, they **will** learn a lot.*
Dès qu'on saura l'heure de départ, nous **partirons**.	*As soon as we **know** the departure time, we **will** leave.*

Oral Practice 13-2

Respond to each of the questions below with the answer provided. You may listen to the answers on your CD.

 TRACK 33

1. Quand est-ce que tu me téléphoneras? —Dès que j'arriverai.
2. Quand est-ce que vous voyagerez? —Aussitôt que nous aurons des vacances.
3. Quand partiront-ils en Afrique? —Lorsqu'ils auront leurs passeports.
4. Quand écrira-t-elle? —Quand elle sera installée à l'hôtel.
5. Quand est-ce que je pourrai venir? —Quand tu voudras.

VOCABULARY DEMYSTIFIED

Enseigner **and** apprendre

The verb **enseigner** means to teach and is used in educational settings. The verb **apprendre** can mean *to learn* or *to teach*.

Le professeur Dupuis **enseigne les maths**.	*Professor Dupuis teaches math.*
Les étudiants **apprennent les maths**.	*The students are learning math.*

However, when it means *to teach*, **apprendre** is always followed by the preposition **à** plus infinitive. The person being taught is an *indirect object* noun following **à** or an indirect object pronoun (**me, te, lui, nous, vous, leur**). Here are some examples:

J'**apprends** *à* ma sœur *à* **faire** du ski.	*I'm teaching my sister to ski.*
Il va **leur apprendre** *à* **résoudre** des problèmes difficiles.	*He is going to teach them to solve difficult problems.*

Expressing Possibilities Using the Present Conditional

There are two tenses in the *conditional mood*: present and past. The present conditional (*would*) expresses both present and future possibilities. The formation of the present conditional is similar to that of the simple future.

Compare below the future and conditional conjugations of the regular **-ir** verb **nourrir** (*to nourish / to feed*). Note that the stem **nourrir-** is the same in both the future and the conditional; only the endings differ. The present conditional endings are the same as those of the **imparfait**: **-ais, -ais, -ait, -ions, -iez, -aient**, while the future tense endings parallel the forms of **avoir**: **-ai, -as, -a, -ons, -ez, -ont**.

Future		**Conditional**	
je nourrir**ai**	*I will feed*	je nourrir**ais**	*I would feed*
tu nourrir**as**	*you will feed*	tu nourrir**ais**	*you would feed*
il/elle/on nourrir**a**	*he/she/one will feed*	il/elle/on nourrir**ait**	*he/she/one would feed*
nous nourrir**ons**	*we will feed*	nous nourrir**ions**	*we would feed*
vous nourrir**ez**	*you will feed*	vous nourrir**iez**	*you would feed*
ils/elles nourrir**ont**	*they will feed*	ils/elles nourrir**aient**	*they would feed*

Verbs with irregular stems in the future use the same stem in the present conditional, followed by the appropriate conditional endings. Look at these examples:

Vous **aimeriez** travailler pour nous?	*Would you like to work for us?*
Un membre de MSF **pourrait** faire beaucoup de bien.	*A member of MSF could (would be able to) do a lot of good.*
Est-ce qu'elle **apprendrait** une autre langue?	*Would she learn another language?*

THE VERB DEVOIR

The verb **devoir** in the present and future tenses is translated as *must have* or *has/have to*. However, in the present conditional, it is generally translated as *should* (suggestion or obligation). Look at the following examples:

Ils **doivent** rester.	*They must / have to stay.*	(present)
Ils **devront** rester.	*They will have to stay.*	(future)
Ils **devraient** rester.	*They should stay.*	(conditional)

The verb **devoir** is irregular in the present tense. It also has an irregular future and conditional stem. Look at those conjugations:

Present	Future	Conditional
je **dois**	je **devr**ai	je **devr**ais
tu **dois**	tu **devr**as	tu **devr**ais
il/elle/on **doit**	il/elle/on **devr**a	il/elle/on **devr**ait
nous **devons**	nous **devr**ons	nous **devr**ions
vous **devez**	vous **devr**ez	vous **devr**iez
ils/elles **doivent**	ils/elles **devr**ont	ils/elles **devr**aient

Oral Practice 13-3

Complete each sentence in writing with the present conditional of the verb in parentheses. Then say the sentences aloud, and check the pronunciation by listening to each answer on your CD. You may also uncover the answers on the right.

 TRACK 34

1. En France, on _____ vite le français.
   (apprendre)   *apprendrait*

2. Nous _____ parler français. (aimer)   *aimerions*

3. Nos amis québécois _____ contents. (être) *seraient*

4. On _____ mieux se comprendre. (pouvoir) *pourrait*

5. On _____ beaucoup plus de fun! (avoir)   *aurait*

6. Moi, je _____ tout de suite! (partir)   *partirais*

7. Et toi, tu _____ avec moi? (venir)   *viendrais*

8. Tu _____ venir avec moi. (devoir)   *devrais*

EXPRESSING ASPIRATIONS AND HOPES USING CE QUI AND CE QUE

Ce qui and **ce que** are both translated as *what*. **Qui** is a relative pronoun functioning as the *subject* (immediately preceding a verb), and **que** is a relative pronoun functioning as the *direct object* of the verb. Look at the following sentences to see how **ce qui** is used *before a verb* and **ce que/qu'** is used *before a subject* (a pronoun such as **je, te, il, elle, on, nous, vous, ils, elles** or a noun subject such as **Paul**).

Ce qui sera super, c'est de jouer dans des films.

What will be great is to play in movies.

Ce qui intéresserait ma sœur le plus, c'est de faire du droit.

What would interest my sister the most is to study law.

Ce qu'on voudrait, c'est de travailler avec des enfants.

What we would like is to work with children.

Ce que Paul fera le mieux, c'est de leur apprendre à lire.

What Paul will do best is teach them to read.

Written Practice 13-2

Complete the following with **Ce qui** or **Ce que**.

1. _____ sera super, c'est d'aller en Afrique.
2. _____ tu pourrais faire, c'est de t'inscrire à MSF.
3. _____ j'aimerais faire, c'est de voyager.
4. _____ lui plairait, c'est de devenir acteur.
5. _____ Claire souhaiterait, c'est d'être mannequin.
6. _____ fascinera Jean, c'est le travail d'informatique.

Chapter Practice 13

A. Le futur. Write the verbs in parentheses in the future.

1. Quand nous _____ en France, tu viendras. (aller)
2. Lorsqu'on sera en France, on _____ la Tour Eiffel. (voir)
3. Nous _____ monter sur la Tour. (pouvoir)
4. La vue _____ magnifique. (être)
5. Nous _____ dans des restaurants connus. (manger)

B. Les rêves. Write the verbs in parentheses in the conditional.

1. Moi, je _____ devenir journaliste. (vouloir)
2. André _____ être footballeur. (aimer)
3. Élise _____ être danseuse professionnelle. (préférer)
4. Nous _____ célèbres et riches. (être)
5. Nous _____ des fans. (avoir)

C. L'avenir de Jean. Answer each question as indicated in parentheses to complete the following dialogue. Write your answer on the line provided.

1. Alors, Jean, quand est-ce que tu partiras? (*As soon as I have my passport.*)

   _____.

2. Où voudrais-tu voyager? (*I would like to travel in Africa.*)

   _____.

3. Qu'est-ce que tu espères faire en Afrique? (*I hope to be a volunteer.*)

   _____.

4. Qu'est-ce que tu veux faire? (*What I would like to do is teach children how to read.*)

   _____.

5. Tu souhaites être professeur? (*I want to be a programmer, but I could teach too.*)

   _____.

6. Tu ne veux pas être riche? (*No, happy.*)

   _____.

CHAPTER QUIZ 13

Complete each line of dialogue with a word from the list provided, and reconstruct the discussion between two young people.

aimerions / ce que / ce qui / devenir / devrais / étudierai / peut-être / serai / seras / voudrais

MÉLANIE: Moi, je pense (1) _____ astronaute.

STÉPHANE: Moi, je (2) _____ être chanteur.

MÉLANIE: Eh bien, tu (3) _____ riche et célèbre.

STÉPHANE: (4) _____ ! On ne sait jamais.

MÉLANIE: (5) _____ est sûr, c'est que nous avons de beaux rêves.

STÉPHANE: Pourquoi pas? Quand je (6) _____ au conservatoire de musique, on verra.

MÉLANIE: Et quand j' (7) _____ les maths, on verra.

STÉPHANE: Voilà, mes parents pensent que je (8) _____ être avocat. C'est plus sûr.

MÉLANIE: (9) _____ tu penses est plus important.

STÉPHANE: Oui, nous (10) _____ réaliser nos rêves.

CHAPTER 14

Opportunities and Goals

In this chapter you will learn:

Talking About Opportunities
Talking About Goals
Stating Conditions

Talking About Opportunities

Monique, an American university student, has been offered the opportunity to apply for a scholarship to study in Belgium. She shares her news with a friend.

 TRACK 35

MONIQUE: Marie-Claude, ma prof de français a suggéré que je pose ma candidature à une bourse d'études.

Marie-Claude, my French professor suggested that I apply for a scholarship.

MARIE-CLAUDE: Chouette. Mais ça paierait quoi exactement?

Great. But exactly what would it pay for?

MONIQUE: Des cours d'été dans une université en Belgique.

Summer classes at a university in Belgium.

MARIE-CLAUDE: Si j'étais à ta place, je le ferais tout de suite!

If I were in your place, I'd do it right away!

MONIQUE: J'aimerais bien aller en Belgique, mais j'allais travailler cet été.

I'd really like to go to Belgium, but I was going to work this summer.

MARIE-CLAUDE: Si tu ne peux pas y aller cet été, est-ce que tu pourras poser ta candidature l'an prochain?

If you can't go there this summer, will you be able to apply next year?

MONIQUE: Il paraît que c'est une bourse qu'on offre chaque année.

It appears to be a scholarship that's offered each year.

MARIE-CLAUDE: Alors, qu'est-ce qui t'empêcherait de saisir cette occasion plus tard?

So what would prevent you from taking this opportunity later?

MONIQUE: Des cours de français en été me prépareraient mieux pour mes cours d'automne.

French classes during the summer would prepare me better for my fall classes.

MARIE-CLAUDE: Bon, alors, si tu ne travailles pas cet été, quelles seront les conséquences?

OK, so if you don't work this summer, what will be the consequences?

MONIQUE: Si je ne travaille pas, je serai fauchée cet automne.

If I don't work, I'll be broke this fall.

MARIE-CLAUDE: Quel dilemme! Qu'est-ce que tu vas faire? Enfin, c'est à toi de décider.

What a dilemma! What are you going to do? In the end, it's up to you to decide.

DISCUSSING OPPORTUNITIES USING CONDITIONAL SENTENCES

A conditional sentence conveys that something (a condition) must first be realized in order for something else (an outcome) to take place. It consists of a si-*clause* where a condition is stated and a *main clause* that expresses the result or consequence. French has two types of conditional sentences.

In the first type of conditional sentence, the verb following **si** is in the *present tense* and the verb in the main clause is in the *present* or *future tense*. The main clause can also be in the *imperative*. (See Chapter 6 to review the imperative.)

GRAMMAR DEMYSTIFIED

Qu'est-ce qui **and** qu'est-ce que

These two phrases are used to ask *What?* questions. **Qu'est-ce qui** is the *subject* of the verb and thus always precedes the verb, while **Qu'est-ce que/qu'** is the *direct object* of the verb and precedes a subject pronoun such as **je, tu, il, elle, on, nous, vous, ils, elles,** or a subject noun. Look at the following examples:

Qu'est-ce qui change?	*What is changing?*
Qu'est-ce qui est arrivé?	*What happened?*
Qu'est-ce que vous désirez?	*What would you like?*
Qu'est-ce que Jean-Claude voulait?	*What did Jean-Claude want?*
Qu'est-ce qu'on ferait?	*What would we do?*

Si tu **travailles**, tu **gagnes** de l'argent.	*If you work, you earn money. (present)*
Si tu ne **travailles** pas, tu n'**auras** pas d'argent.	*If you don't work, you will not have any money. (future)*
Si tu ne **travailles** pas, **va** en Belgique!	*If you don't work, go to Belgium! (imperative)*

In the second type of conditional sentence, the verb in the **si**-clause is in the **imparfait**, and the verb in the main clause is in the *present conditional*. Look at the following examples, noting that the conjunction **si** becomes **s'** before the vowel **i-**.

Si elle **allait** en Belgique, elle **perfectionnerait** son français.	*If she went to Belgium, she would perfect her French. (present conditional)*
S'il posait sa candidature à la bourse, il **aurait** une chance d'étudier à l'étranger.	*If he applied for the scholarship, he would have a chance to study abroad. (present conditional)*

Written Practice 14-1

Match the most logical consequence listed in the right column to the corresponding condition in the left column. Write the letter on the line provided.

_____ 1. S'il partait à l'étranger...
_____ 2. S'il m'écrivait...
_____ 3. Si je pouvais payer mon voyage...
_____ 4. Si tu veux...
_____ 5. Si la prof ne le suggère pas...
_____ 6. Si on travaille...

    a. je répondrais.
    b. on n'est pas fauché.
    c. ne le fais pas.
    d. je poserai ma candidature.
    e. il irait en Europe.
    f. je l'accompagnerais.

EVALUATING A DECISION

Monique has now made a decision about the scholarship to study in Belgium. She tells her friend Marie-Claude.

TRACK 36

MONIQUE: Marie-Claude, j'ai pris une décision.

Marie-Claude, I made a decision.

MARIE-CLAUDE: Qu'est-ce que tu as décidé?

What did you decide?

MONIQUE: Mon problème, c'était que si je ne travaillais pas cet été, je serais fauchée cet automne.

My problem was that if I didn't work this summer, I'd be broke this fall.

MARIE-CLAUDE: Oui, je sais. Alors, qu'est-ce qui a changé?

Yes, I know. So what changed?

MONIQUE: Si je suis sélectionnée, la bourse comprendra non seulement les frais de voyage mais aussi une somme de trois mille euros en espèces.

If I am selected, the scholarship will include not only travel costs but also three thousand euros cash.

MARIE-CLAUDE: C'est vraiment magnifique, ça! Et où est-ce que tu vas vivre?

That's really fantastic! And where will you live?

MONIQUE: Je pourrai vivre chez la sœur de ma prof à Bruxelles.

I'll be able to live at the home of my teacher's sister in Brussels.

MARIE-CLAUDE: Dis donc, elle est sympa, ta prof!

Say, she is nice, your teacher!

MONIQUE: Oui, c'est vrai. Si j'obtiens la bourse, je lui devrai beaucoup!

Yes, that's true. If I get the scholarship, I'll owe her a lot!

Prepositions in Geographical Expressions

In French, continents, countries, and regions, like other nouns, are accompanied by articles.

la France *France* **le** Canada *Canada* **les** États-Unis *the United States*

The preposition used to say *in* or *to* a geographical area varies according to the gender and number of the noun representing the area. The preposition **en** is used before feminine nouns (without the article); the preposition **au** is used before masculine nouns, and **aux** is used before masculine plural nouns. Look at the following examples:

en Afrique, **en** Amérique, **en** Asie, **en** Australie, **en** Europe	*in/to Africa, in/to America, in/to Asia, in/to Australia, in/to Europe*
en Algérie, **en** Belgique, **en** France, **en** Suisse,	*in/to Algeria, in/to Belgium, in/to France, in/to Switzerland*
en Alsace, **en** Bourgogne, **en** Bretagne, **en** Provence	*in/to Alsace, in/to Burgundy, in/to Brittany, in/to Provence*
au Canada, **au** Luxembourg, **au** Maroc, **au** Québec	*in/to Canada, in/to Luxembourg, in/to Morocco, in/to Québec*
aux États-Unis, **aux** Pays-Bas	*in/to the United States, in/to the Netherlands*

However, the names of cities, with a few exceptions, do not have articles. The preposition **à** is used to express *in* or *to* the city: **à** Bruxelles, **à** Genève, **à** Paris, etc.

Some exceptions are: **Le Caire (au Caire)** (*Cairo*), **La Havane (à La Havane)** (*Havana*), **La Nouvelle-Orléans (à La Nouvelle-Orléans)** (*New Orleans*).

Oral Practice 14-1

Complete each sentence as indicated. The answers are in your Answer Key. Then say each sentence aloud, and verify by listening to it on your CD.

 TRACK 37

What will people do in the following circumstances? Use the future tense.

1. S'il fait mauvais temps, nous _____ à la maison. (rester)

2. Si un ami téléphone, vous _____ une discussion. (avoir)

3. S'ils ont des exercices, ils les _____ . (faire)

Now, give people instructions to follow in the following circumstances (use the imperative).

4. Si tu es fatigué, _____ dormir! (aller)

5. Si vous avez besoin d'argent, _____ ! (travailler)

What would people do in the following circumstances (use the present conditional)?

6. Simone _____ en Suisse si elle avait une bourse. (aller)

7. Elle _____ chez une amie si elle y était. (habiter)

8. Ses amis lui _____ souvent si elle voyageait. (écrire)

Talking About Goals

In the following dialogue, Monique talks to her French professor. She has decided to apply for the scholarship to study in Belgium. Now she has to prove that she can meet the requirements and is the perfect candidate for the scholarship.

 TRACK 38

MME SOUSY: Monique, si vous voulez aller en Belgique, remplissez les formulaires, et obtenez les lettres de recommandation aussitôt que possible.

Monique, if you want to go to Belgium, fill out the forms, and get the letters of recommendation as soon as possible.

MONIQUE: Si j'obtiens les lettres la semaine prochaine, est-ce que ça ira?

If I get the letters next week, will that be OK?

MME SOUSY: Il me faut votre dossier complet avant le 30 mars.

I need your complete dossier before March 30th.

MONIQUE: Il me faut aussi une transcription de mes cours et de mes notes.

I also need a transcript of my courses and my grades.

MME SOUSY: Si vous faites votre demande en ligne, vous la recevrez beaucoup plus vite.	*If you make your request online, you will get it much faster.*
MONIQUE: Oui, c'est vrai. Je vais signaler que c'est urgent.	*Yes, that's true. I'm going to point out that it's urgent.*
MME SOUSY: Si vous signalez que la date limite est le 30 mars, le service des transcriptions vous le procurera à temps.	*If you point out that the deadline is March 30th, the transcript service will provide it to you on time.*
MONIQUE: Et si, par hasard, je ne reçois pas le document avant le 30 mars?	*And what if, by chance, I do not receive the document by March 30th?*
MME SOUSY: Il faudra aller le chercher personnellement, même si vous devez attendre toute la journée!	*You'll have to go get it in person, even if you have to wait all day!*

THE VERBS OBTENIR AND TENIR

The verb **obtenir** (*to obtain*) is derived from the verb **tenir** (*to hold*). Verbs in this group (the group **venir** *to come*) have an irregular present tense conjugation, as well as an irregular future/conditional stem (**viendr-**, **tiendr-**) and an irregular past participle (**venu**, **tenu**).

Present Tense

j'**obtiens**	*I obtain*	je **tiens**	*I hold*
tu **obtiens**	*you obtain*	tu **tiens**	*you hold*
il/elle/on **obtient**	*he/she/one obtains*	il/elle/on **tient**	*he/she/one holds*
nous **obtenons**	*we obtain*	nous **tenons**	*we hold*
vous **obtenez**	*you obtain*	vous **tenez**	*you hold*
ils/elles **obtiennent**	*they obtain*	ils/elles **tiennent**	*they hold*

Future/Conditional Stem: **obtiendr-/tiendr-**

Past Participle: **obtenu**, **tenu**

Look at these verbs used in various tenses:

Ils **ont obtenu** leurs passeports hier.	*They obtained their passports yesterday.*

Ils les **tiennent** en main.	*They're holding them in their hands.*
Nous **obtiendrons** les nôtres demain.	*We'll obtain ours tomorrow.*

Vocabulary: Scholarship Application

la bourse	*scholarship*	faire une demande	*to make a request / an application*
le bureau	*office*		
le bureau	*office*	obtenir une	*to obtain a*
le document	*document*	recommandation	*recommendation*
le dossier	*dossier/portfolio*	poser sa candidature	*to apply*
le service	*service/section*	rédiger un essai	*to write an essay*
la transcription	*transcript*	remplir des formulaires	*to fill out forms*
		respecter la date limite	*to respect the deadline*

Written Practice 14-2

Complete each sentence with the appropriate noun or verb to reconstruct all the conditions necessary to apply for a scholarship. Use the vocabulary presented above.

1. L'étudiant doit poser sa _____ .

2. Il doit _____ des formulaires.

3. Il doit _____ des recommandations de ses professeurs.

4. Il doit faire une _____ de transcription à l'université.

5. Il doit _____ un essai.

6. Il doit _____ la date limite.

7. Il doit vérifier tous les _____ .

8. Il doit déposer son _____ au Bureau des Langues.

Stating Conditions

There are several ways to state conditions that must be met before a goal can be achieved.

STATING CONDITIONS WITH A SI-CLAUSE

One of the main ways to express a condition is with a **si**-clause.

For Future Realization If an expected result or outcome is to take place in the *future*, the verb in the outcome or result clause is in the *present* or *future* tense, as follows:

Tu **as/auras** une bonne chance de recevoir une bourse...	*You have / will have a good chance of receiving a scholarship . . .*

In this case, the verb immediately following **si** (*if*) must be expressed in the *present tense*, as shown here:

si tu **travailles** dur.	*if you work hard.*
si tu **as** de bonnes notes.	*if you have good grades.*
si tu **participes** à beaucoup d'activités.	*if you participate in a lot of activities.*
si tu **es** vraiment motivé(e).	*if you are truly motivated.*
si tu **montres** beaucoup d'enthousiasme.	*if you show a lot of enthusiasm.*

For Immediate Realization If an expected result or outcome is to take place in the immediate present, the verb in the outcome or result clause is in the *present conditional*, as follows:

Tu **aurais** une bonne chance de recevoir une bourse...	*You would have a good shot at getting a scholarship . . .*

In this case, the verb immediately following **si** (in the conditional clause) must be expressed in the **imparfait**, as shown here:

si tu **travaillais** bien.	*if you worked hard.*
si tu **avais** de bonnes notes.	*if you had good grades.*
si tu **participais** à beaucoup d'activités.	*if you participated in a lot of activities.*
si tu **étais** vraiment motivé(e).	*if you were truly motivated.*
si tu **montrais** beaucoup d'enthousiasme.	*if you showed a lot of enthusiasm.*

The **si-** (conditional) clause and the outcome (result) clause can be expressed in either order within a sentence.

Oral Practice 14-2

Plus tard (*Later*). Say each French sentence aloud starting with the conditional clause. Then listen to each sentence on your CD.

TRACK 39

1. Si les étudiants aiment le français, ils s'inscriront au cours. — *If students like French, they will enroll in the course.*

2. Si le professeur est bon, ils apprendront beaucoup. — *If the teacher is good, they will learn a lot.*

3. S'il y a un club de français, ils y participeront. — *If there is a French club, they will participate in it.*

4. S'il y a une bourse d'études, ils poseront leur candidature. — *If there is a scholarship, they will apply.*

5. S'il y a une date limite, ils la respecteront. — *If there is a deadline, they will respect it.*

Written Practice 14-3

Maintenant (*Now*). Change each sentence in the previous exercise so that the possibility of realization is in the present instead of the future. Remember to use the **imparfait** in the **si**-clause and the *present conditional* in the outcome/result clause.

1. Si les étudiants _____ le français, ils _____ au cours.

2. Si le professeur _____ bon, ils _____ beaucoup.

3. S'il y _____ un club de français, ils y _____ .

4. S'il y _____ une bourse d'études, ils _____ leur candidature.

5. S'il y _____ une date limite, ils la _____ .

STATING CONDITIONS WITH THE VERB FALLOIR

The verb **falloir** (*to have to / must*), followed by an infinitive, can also be used to express a condition to be met if the realization is in the present or future. It is used in various tenses but is only conjugated in the third-person singular, with **il** (*it*) as the subject. **Falloir (il faut)** is an impersonal verb of obligation that has several meanings. Look at the following examples:

Il faut étudier pour obtenir un diplôme.	*One must study in order to obtain a diploma.*
Il faudra partir en voyage en Belgique, Mademoiselle.	*You will have to travel to Belgium, Miss.*
Il faudrait obtenir nos passeports.	*We should obtain our passports.*

Because **falloir** is impersonal, context clues help determine who must fulfill the obligation. In the previous two examples, the clues were words such as **Mademoiselle** (*Miss*) and **nos** (*our*).

When the verb **falloir** is used to state conditions, the prepositions **pour** (*in order to*) and an infinitive often introduce the outcome/result. Look at the following examples:

Il faut acheter votre billet d'avion très tôt **pour avoir un bon prix**.	*You have to buy your plane ticket very early to get a good price.*
Il faudrait contacter une agence de voyage **pour obtenir des brochures**.	*One/You/We should contact a travel agency in order to obtain brochures.*

Written Practice 14-4

State the conditions using the forms **Il faut**, **Il faudra**, or **Il faudrait** as suggested in English.

1. _____ faire des études pour bien parler français. (*One must*)

2. _____ apprendre le français pour vivre en France. (*One should*)

3. _____ trouver notre hôtel. (*We will have to*)

4. _____ apporter vos passeports. (*You will have to*)

5. _____ prendre le taxi. (*You should*)

6. _____ voir la Tour Eiffel. (*One/They must*)

Chapter Practice 14

A. Possibilities in the future. Match the possible realization with each condition. Write the letter of the possible realization on the line provided.

_____ 1. Si tu aimes le français...   a. il restera au bureau.

_____ 2. Si tes amis te téléphonent...   b. remplis le formulaire aujourd'hui!

_____ 3. S'il a beaucoup de travail...   c. il ne fera pas la demande de bourse d'études.

_____ 4. S'il obtient un bon job...   d. réponds!

_____ 5. Si tu veux respecter la date limite...   e. tu iras à ton cours!

_____ 6. S'il préfère rester aux États-Unis...   f. il aura de la chance.

B. Possibilities in the immediate present. Match the possible realization with each condition.

_____ 1. Elle serait riche...   a. si nous ne travaillions pas.

_____ 2. Elle deviendrait célèbre...   b. si elle était amoureuse.

_____ 3. Nous aurions le temps de nous reposer   c. si elle avait un million de dollars.

_____ 4. Nous irions en Belgique...   d. si on nous attendait à Montréal.

_____ 5. Nous partirions au Canada...   e. si nous avions de la famille à Bruxelles.

_____ 6. Elle se marierait...   f. si elle avait le rôle principal dans un film.

C. State the condition indicated in parentheses using **il faut**, **il faudra**, or **il faudrait**, plus an infinitive.

1. _____ le travail à temps pour respecter les dates limites. (*One must do*)

2. _____ en France pour voir la Tour Eiffel. (*We must go*)

3. _____ le taxi pour aller à l'aéroport. (*We should call*)

4. _____ aux États-Unis pour apprécier les États-Unis. (*You will have to live*)

5. _____ sa candidature pour une bourse pour étudier au Canada. (*One must apply for*)

6. _____ apporter vos passeports. (*You will have to bring*)

CHAPTER QUIZ 14

Complete each sentence in the following dialogue with the appropriate word from the list provided.

date limite / devrais / dossier / faut / ferais / finissez / pour / recommandation / remplir / voulez

MONIQUE: Qu'est-ce qu'il (1) _____ faire pour obtenir une bourse d'études?

LE PROFESSEUR: D'abord, (2) _____ vos cours de français, Monique!

MONIQUE: Oui, bien sûr, mais je voudrais commencer à (3) _____ les formulaires.

LE PROFESSEUR: Oui, il vous faudra tout un (4) _____ .

MONIQUE: Est-ce que vous pourriez m'écrire une lettre de (5) _____ ?

LE PROFESSEUR: Certainement, Monique. Mais la (6) _____ est dans six mois.

MONIQUE: Je préfère faire les choses à l'avance (7) _____ ne pas être stressée.

LE PROFESSEUR: Si j'étais à votre place, je (8) _____ de mon mieux afin d'obtenir de bonnes notes.

MONIQUE: Et je (9) _____ participer aux activités du Club de français.

LE PROFESSEUR: C'est vrai. Si vous (10) _____ avoir une bonne chance de gagner, faites tout ce que vous pouvez!

CHAPTER 15

Regrets and Missed Opportunities

In this chapter you will learn:

Expressing Regret

Talking About Missed Opportunities

Enriching Communication with Adverbs

Expressing Regret

Michel is very sorry that he disappointed his friend Anne. He was supposed to buy concert tickets, but waited till the last minute when they were already sold out.

TRACK 40

MICHEL: Anne, j'ai de mauvaises nouvelles. Je n'ai pas réussi à obtenir les billets de concert que je t'avais promis.

Anne, I have bad news. I've not been able to get the concert tickets I had promised you.

ANNE: Oh zut! Mais pourquoi pas?

Oh darn! But why not?

MICHEL: J'ai attendu trop longtemps. J'aurais dû le faire le mois dernier.

I waited too long. I should have done it last month.

ANNE: Il n'y a plus du tout de tickets?

There are no more tickets at all?

MICHEL: Malheureusement non, je suis vraiment désolé.

Unfortunately not, I'm really sorry.

ANNE: Oh! Je n'aurais jamais dû te laisser cette responsabilité.

Oh! I never should have left you with this responsibility.

MICHEL: Je sais. C'est vraiment ma faute!

I know. It's really my fault!

ANNE: Si tu m'avais demandé de les acheter, je l'aurais fait tout de suite.

If you had asked me to do it, I would have done it right away.

MICHEL: La prochaine fois, je t'assure que je saisirai l'occasion dès le premier jour.

Next time, I assure you that I will seize the opportunity on the very first day.

ANNE: Que je suis malheureuse! Si seulement j'avais acheté les billets moi-même!

I'm so unhappy! If only I'd bought the tickets myself!

THE USES OF QUE

The word **que** is used many ways in French. Note that **que** becomes **qu'** before a vowel sound.

First, **que** following verbs such as **penser** and **croire** (*to think*), **assurer** (*to assure*), and **imaginer** (*to imagine*) is translated as *that. That* is often omitted in English, but not in French.

Je pense **que** c'est triste.

I think (that) it's sad.

Je t'assure **que** je serai fiable.

I assure you (that) I will be trustworthy.

Second, **que** used at the beginning of an exclamatory sentence is translated as *how*.

Qu'il est gentil!	*How nice he is!*
Qu'elle est malheureuse!	*How unhappy she is!*

Third, **que** is used as a relative pronoun that functions as a *direct object* in a subordinate clause. It replaces a noun already mentioned in the main clause. Look at the following sentences, and note that the English equivalent of **que** (*that/which/whom*) may be omitted in English but not in French.

Le **billet qu'**elle veut est cher.	*The ticket (that/which) she wants is expensive.*
La **personne que** tu cherches n'est plus là.	*The person (whom) you are looking for is no longer here.*

EXPRESSING REGRETS USING EXCLAMATORY STRUCTURES

Two types of exclamatory sentences express regret. The first consists of the adjective **quel** followed by a noun, as in the following examples:

Quel dommage!	*What a shame!*	**Quel** malheur!	*What misfortune!*

The second consists of **que/qu'** followed by a subject + verb, as in the following:

Que c'est dommage!	*What a shame!*	**Qu'**elle est triste!	*How sad she is!*
Que c'est regrettable!	*How regrettable!*	**Que** tu es déçu!	*How disappointed you are!*

EXPRESSING REGRET USING INFINITIVES AND PAST INFINITIVES

To express regret, you may use the following verbs followed by the preposition **de/d'** and an infinitive.

être désolé(e) de	*to be sorry*	regretter de	*to regret*

The regret may pertain to a current situation. Look at the examples below, noting that the preposition **de/d'** is followed by an infinitive:

Nous sommes désolés **d'arriver** en retard.	*We are sorry to be late.*
Il regrette **de décevoir** sa copine.	*He regrets disappointing his girlfriend.*

The regret may pertain to a past situation. Look at the following examples, noting that the preposition **de/d'** is followed by the auxiliary **avoir** or **être** and a *past participle*. This structure is called the *past infinitive*.

Il regrette **d'avoir déçu** sa copine.	*He regrets having disappointed his girlfriend.*
Elle est désolée **d'avoir raté** la date limite.	*She is sorry to have missed the deadline.*
Nous sommes désolés **d'être arrivés** en retard.	*We are sorry to have arrived late.*

GRAMMAR DEMYSTIFIED

Agreement of Past Participles

In the *past infinitive*, just as in the **passé composé**, past participles agree in gender and number with the *subject* of the verb when they are conjugated with the auxiliary **être**. Look at the following examples, noting how the past participle adds -s when the subject is plural, -e when the subject is feminine, and -es when the subject is feminine plural.

Ils regrettent d'être sorti**s** sans moi.	*They are sorry to have gone out without me.*
Elles regrettent d'être all**ées** si loin.	*They regret having gone so far.*

In addition, as in the **passé composé**, in past infinitive structures, past participles agree in gender and number with the *direct object pronoun that precedes* verbs conjugated with the auxiliary **avoir**. Look at the following examples, and note how the past participle adds -s when the direct object is plural, -e when the direct object is feminine, and -es when the direct object is feminine plural.

Les billets? Il est désolé de **les** avoir perdu**s**.	*The tickets? He is sorry to have lost them.*
La bourse? Il regrette de ne pas **l'**avoir gagn**ée**.	*The scholarship? He regrets not having won it.*
Les clés? Il regrette de **les** avoir oubli**ées**.	*The keys? He regrets having forgotten them.*

EXPRESSING REGRETS USING SI-CLAUSES AND THE PLUPERFECT

Regret can be expressed in **si**-clauses that include the adverb **seulement** (*only*) and a verb in the pluperfect tense. The pluperfect is a compound tense like the **passé composé**, but the auxiliary verb **avoir** or **être** is conjugated in the **imparfait**. Review the **imparfait** stems of **avoir** and **être**: **av-** and **ét-**. The **imparfait** endings are **-ais, -ais, -ait, -ions, -iez, -aient**.

Avoir **Verbs**		Être **Verbs**	
j'**avais** terminé	*I had finished*	il **était** sorti	*he had gone out*
elles **avaient** compris	*they had understood*	elle **était** née	*she was / had been born*

Look at the following examples of **si seulement** + pluperfect to express regret:

Si seulement j'**étais parti**(e)!	*If only I had left!*
Si seulement ils **n'étaient pas tombés**!	*If only they hadn't fallen!*
Si seulement vous **aviez été prudents**!	*If only you had been cautious!*
Si seulement elle **avait eu** le courage!	*If only she had had the courage!*
Si seulement nous **avions compris**!	*If only we had understood!*

Oral Practice 15-1

Say each sentence aloud. You may verify your pronunciation on the CD and refer to the translation on the right if necessary.

 TRACK 41

1.	Elle a fait un faux pas. Quel dommage!	*She made a blunder. What a shame!*
2.	Ils n'ont pas gagné le prix. Qu'ils sont déçus!	*They did not win the prize. How disappointed they are!*
3.	Elle est désolée d'être arrivée en retard.	*She is sorry to have arrived late.*
4.	Ils regrettent de ne pas avoir répondu.	*They regret not having answered.*

5. Tu regrettes d'être parti si tôt?   *Do you regret having left so early?*

6. Je suis désolé de vous avoir déçu.   *I am sorry to have disappointed you.*

7. Désolé! Je ne sais pas.   *Sorry! I don't know.*

8. Si seulement ils avaient été ici.   *If only they had been here!*

9. Ah. Si seulement nous avions eu de l'argent.   *Ah! If only we had had money!*

10. Si seulement vous étiez restés!   *If only you had stayed!*

Talking About Missed Opportunities

In the following dialogue, Michel confides in his friend Anouk, telling her how he missed out on a good opportunity. He was supposed to buy concert tickets, but waited till the last minute when they were sold out.

TRACK 42

MICHEL: Zut alors, Anouk! Je suis terriblement gêné. Anne est si fâchée avec moi.   *Darn, Anouk, I am terribly embarrassed. Anne is so angry with me.*

ANOUK: Pourquoi? Qu'est-ce que tu as fait?   *Why? What did you do?*

MICHEL: J'avais promis d'acheter des billets de concert, mais maintenant il n'y en a plus.   *I had promised to buy concert tickets, but now there are none left.*

ANOUK: Oh Michel! Je comprends Anne. À sa place, je me serais fâchée aussi.   *Oh Michel! I understand Anne. In her place, I would have gotten angry too.*

MICHEL: Si seulement j'avais acheté les billets tout de suite!   *If only I had bought the tickets right away!*

ANOUK: Oui, évidemment, tu aurais dû faire cela.   *Yes, of course, you should have done that.*

MICHEL: Si nous avions eu les billets, nous aurions pu célébrer son anniversaire en allant au concert.   *If we had gotten the tickets, we would have been able to celebrate her birthday by going to the concert.*

ANOUK: Quel dommage! On dirait que tu avais imaginé une belle soirée!

What a shame! Looks like you had imagined a beautiful evening!

MICHEL: Eh oui, on aurait pu avoir un dîner romantique après le concert, et on serait devenus meilleurs amis.

Well yes, we could have had a romantic dinner after the concert, and we would have become best friends.

ANOUK: Mon pauvre Michel! J'ai l'impression que tu as raté une belle occasion!

My poor Michel! I get the impression that you missed a beautiful opportunity!

MAKING REPROACHES USING THE PAST CONDITIONAL

The *past conditional* is used in sentences that imply an *unmet condition* in the past. Like the **passé composé**, the past conditional is a compound tense. In this case, the auxiliary verb **avoir** or **être** is in the present conditional. Review the conditional stems of **avoir** and **être**: **aur-** and **ser-**. The conditional endings are the endings used for the **imparfait**: **-ais, -ais, -ait, -ions, -iez, -aient**.

Avoir **Verbs**		Être **Verbs**	
j'**aurais** mangé	*I would have eaten*	nous **serions** revenu(e)s	*we would have come back*
tu **aurais** saisi	*you would have seized*	ils se **seraient** mariés	*they would have gotten married*
ils **auraient** compris	*they would have understood*	je **serais** né(e)	*I would have been born*

Here are examples of sentences that include verbs in the past conditional:

VOCABULARY DEMYSTIFIED

On dirait

The expression **on dirait** includes the verb **dire** (*to say/tell*) in the present conditional. Its English equivalent is *It looks like* or *It would seem*.

On dirait qu'il est gêné.	*It looks like / It seems (that) he is embarrassed.*
On dirait qu'ils sont contents.	*It looks like they're happy. / They seem happy.*

Je n'**aurais pas dit** cela.	*I would not have said that.*
Moi, je **serais rentrée** chez moi.	*I would have gone back home.*
À leur place, j'**aurais remercié** la prof.	*In their place, I would have thanked the teacher.*

The past conditional of the verbs **devoir** and **falloir** (*to have to / must*) are frequently used to express reproach or regret regarding unmet conditions in the past. Look at the following sentences:

Tu **aurais dû** le faire!	*You should have done it!*
J'**aurais dû** acheter les billets.	*I should have bought the tickets.*
Il **n'aurait pas dû** attendre.	*He shouldn't have waited.*
Nous **aurions dû** saisir l'occasion.	*We should have seized the opportunity.*

Remember that **falloir** is an impersonal verb only conjugated in the third person singular with **il**. It expresses obligation; in the past conditional it conveys disappointment about what did *not* occur. Look at these examples:

| Il **aurait fallu** le faire tout de suite. | *We/They/One should have done it right away.* |
| Il **aurait fallu** écouter. | *We/They/One should have listened.* |

Written Practice 15-1

Write the following sentences in French. Use the cues in parentheses.

1. I would have gone on this trip. (**faire ce voyage**)

   _____

2. My friend would have come with me. (**ami / venir avec moi**)

   _____

3. We would have bought the plane tickets right away. (**acheter les billets d'avion**)

   _____

4. I would not have waited. (**ne pas attendre**)

   _____

5. My friend should have applied. (**poser sa candidature**)

_____

6. We should have done it. (**le faire** / _use_ **falloir**)

_____

EXPRESSING UNREALIZED DESIRES USING THE PAST CONDITIONAL

Use conditional sentences when making assumptions about _what would or could have happened in the past_, if circumstances had been different. The unmet outcome is stated in the _past conditional_, and the circumstance that stood in the way is stated with **si** + the _pluperfect_. Look at the examples below. Note that the sentence may start with either clause (the **si**-clause or the unmet realization).

Si elle **avait su** quelle heure il était, elle **serait partie**.	_If she had known what time it was, she would have left._
Il **serait venu** si nous l'**avions invité**.	_He would have come if we had invited him._
Je t'**aurais écrit** ou **téléphoné** si j'**avais eu** mon mobile.	_I would have written or called you if I had had my cell phone._
Si Michel **avait acheté** les billets, Anne **aurait été** contente.	_If Michel had bought the tickets, Anne would have been happy._

Written Practice 15-2

Match the unrealized outcome with the corresponding condition. Write the letter of the most logical unrealized outcome on the line provided.

_____ 1. S'ils avaient eu leurs billets...   a. il les auraient achetés.

_____ 2. S'il avait demandé à sa copine...   b. je les aurais invités.

_____ 3. Si les billets n'avaient pas été si chers...   c. je serais rentrée chez moi.

_____ 4. Si mes copains avaient voulu venir...   d. ils seraient allés au concert.

_____ 5. S'il y avait eu trop de spectateurs...   e. il n'aurait pas pu venir.

_____ 6. S'il avait dû travailler...   f. elle aurait dit oui.

In the following dialogue, Mario finds out that his girlfriend Sonia just missed her train and will meet him much later than expected that day.

TRACK 43

MARIO: Tu as raté ton train, Sonia? Zut! Je t'attendais impatiemment, tu sais.

You missed your train, Sonia? Darn! I was waiting impatiently for you, you know.

SONIA: Je suis vraiment désolée.

I am really sorry, Mario.

MARIO: J'étais tellement heureux de te voir bientôt. À quelle heure est le prochain train?

I was so happy to be seeing you soon. What time is the next train?

SONIA: Tu sais, j'ai conduit aussi vite que possible mais il y avait des bouchons partout.

You know, I drove as quickly as possible but there were traffic jams everywhere.

MARIO: Je comprends parfaitement, Sonia. Mais quand est-ce que tu arrives alors?

I understand perfectly, Sonia. But when are you arriving then?

SONIA: Si j'étais partie une demi-heure plus tôt, je serais arrivée à temps! C'est trop bête!

If I had left a half hour earlier, I would have arrived on time! It's too stupid!

MARIO: Je suis sincèrement désolé! Mais est-ce que tu pourrais répondre à ma question?

I am sincerely sorry. But could you answer my question?

SONIA: C'est si long jusqu'à dix-sept heures. Tu dois être drôlement fâché.

It is so long till five P.M. You must be really mad.

MARIO: Mais non, Sonia. Je ne suis pas du tout fâché. Je suis très impatient, c'est tout.

No, Sonia. I am not mad at all. I'm impatient, that's all.

SONIA: Oh Mario. Franchement, qu'est-ce que je ferais sans toi?

Oh Mario! Frankly, what would I do without you?

Enriching Communication with Adverbs

Sometimes adjectives and adverbs are preceded by adverbs that modify their meaning. Look at the following adverbs placed before adjectives or other adverbs:

très tôt	*very early*	plus patient	*more patient*
si tard	*so late*	presque heureux	*almost happy*
aussi gentil	*as nice*	sincèrement désolé	*sincerely sorry*
drôlement triste	*really sad*	tellement beau	*so beautiful*
franchement surpris	*frankly surprised*	trop franc	*too frank*
moins attentif	*less attentive*	vraiment déçu	*really disappointed*

In addition to the adverbs that enrich the meaning of adjectives or other adverbs, many adverbs are used to modify or clarify the meaning of verbs. Often adverbs are derived from adjectives. If you recognize the feminine form of an adjective, you will easily recognize the corresponding adverb. Look at the following feminine adjectives and their corresponding adverbs, noting the **-ment** ending of the adverbs:

facile	*funny*	facilement	*easily*	heureuse	*happy*	heureusement	*fortunately*
franche	*frank*	franchement	*frankly*	rapide	*quick*	rapidement	*fast*
furieuse	*furious*	furieusement	*furiously*	sérieuse	*serious*	sérieusement	*seriously*

Other adverbs are related to adjectives using a different pattern. Look at these adjectives ending in **-ent/-ant**, noting the **-mment** ending of the resulting adverbs:

élégant	*elegant*	élégamment	*elegantly*
fréquent	*frequent*	fréquemment	*frequently*
récent	*recent*	récemment	*recently*

Some adverbs are not related to adjectives at all. Look at these examples:

bien	*well*	parfois	*sometimes*	aussi	*as/too*
déjà	*already*	quelquefois	*sometimes*	mieux	*better*
mal	*badly*	souvent	*often*	moins	*less*
vite	*quickly*	toujours	*always*	plus	*more*

Unlike adverbs of time, such as **aujourd'hui** (*today*) and **demain** (*tomorrow*), which generally appear at the beginning or end of a sentence, most adverbs are placed directly after the verb.

Je **vois mal** sans lunettes.	*I see badly without glasses.*
On **parle bien** le français.	*We speak French well.*
Tu **vas fréquemment** au restaurant.	*You frequently go to restaurants.*
Elle **s'habille élégamment**.	*She dresses elegantly.*

When verbs are in a compound form, such as the **passé composé**, pluperfect, and past conditional, the adverb usually follows the auxiliary verb.

Nous sommes **souvent** allés en France. *We often went to France.*

Ils avaient **beaucoup** mangé. *They had eaten a lot.*

Elle aurait **facilement** pleuré. *She would have easily cried.*

Oral Practice 15-2

Say each of the following sentences aloud. Then listen to it on your CD. You may check the English translation on the right for comprehension.

 TRACK 44

1. Elle est franche. Elle parle franchement. *She is frank. She speaks frankly.*

2. Elle est sérieuse. Elle travaille sérieusement. *She is serious. She works seriously.*

3. Elle est furieuse. Elle répond furieusement. *She is furious. She answers furiously.*

4. On parle facilement français. *One speaks French easily.*

5. Il faut toujours être honnête. *One must always be honest.*

6. On mange très fréquemment des fruits. *We eat fruit very often.*

7. Les exercices sont faciles! On les fait facilement. *The exercises are easy. We do them easily.*

8. Nous avons bien appris la leçon. *We learned the lesson well.*

9. Si nous avions pu, nous serions déjà allés en Europe. *If we had been able to, we would have already gone to Europe.*

10. S'il avait parlé moins vite, nous aurions compris. *If he had spoken more slowly, we would have understood.*

Chapter Practice 15

A. Translate the following sentences into English. They include various meanings of **que**.

1. Que c'est dommage! _____

2. Je croyais que tu arriverais bientôt. _____

3. La vendeuse qu'il cherche fait la pause. _____

4. Nous pensons qu'il est l'heure de partir. _____

5. Ils ont raté le train. Zut! Que c'est irritant! _____

B. Regrets! In the following exercise, Paul regrets *doing* something in sentences 1, 2, and 3 (use **de/d'** + infinitive). He regrets *having done* something in sentences 4, 5, and 6 (use **de/d'** + past infinitive). Write the answer on the line provided.

1. Il regrette _____ (*to leave*).

2. Il regrette _____ une copine. (*to disappoint*)

3. Il regrette _____ absent. (*to be*)

4. Il est désolé _____ une faute. (*to have done*)

5. Il est désolé _____ fâché. (*to have been*)

6. Il est désolé _____ en retard. (*to have arrived*)

C. Si seulement! Use **si seulement** + pluperfect to complete the following sentences in which you express regret.

1. Si seulement tu _____ venir! (*had been able to*)

2. Si seulement on _____ ! (*had finished*)

3. Si seulement il _____ ! (*had left*)

4. Si seulement nous _____ ! (*had listened*)

5. Si seulement elles _____ ! (*had telephoned*)

D. Peut-être, peut-être pas! Complete the following sentences with the past conditional of the verb in parentheses to express what *would have* or *would not have* happened.

1. S'ils m'avaient demandé, j' _____ . (répondre)

2. Si elle avait fait une liste, elle n'_____ pas _____ . (oublier)

3. Si nous étions descendus, nous t'_____ . (voir)

4. Si tu n'avais pas travaillé, tu _____ en France. (aller)

5. S'il avait été minuit, il _____ rentrer. (falloir)

E. Comment? Complete each sentence with an appropriate adverb from the list to tell how something was done.

déjà / facilement / furieusement / mal / sincèrement

1. Hier soir, j'ai _____ dormi. J'étais malade.

2. Il était _____ parti quand elle est arrivée.

3. Nous étions _____ désolés.

4. Elles ont _____ appris le français. Elles le parlent très bien.

5. Il était fâché et il est parti _____ sans dire un mot.

CHAPTER QUIZ 15

Match each phrase with the logical completion. Write the corresponding letter in the space provided.

_____ 1. Tu aurais dû me demander...
_____ 2. À ma place...
_____ 3. Il est mort!
_____ 4. Zut! On dirait...
_____ 5. Voilà la boutique...
_____ 6. Elles sont désolées...
_____ 7. Vous pensez...
_____ 8. Si seulement...
_____ 9. Quand il était petit, il y allait...
_____ 10. S'il faisait beaucoup de fautes...

a. que le train est déjà parti.
b. de ne pas avoir répondu.
c. qu'ils ont mal compris?
d. nous pouvions voyager!
e. fréquemment.
f. elle serait rentrée plus tôt.
g. on ne l'écouterait pas.
h. si tu ne savais pas.
i. que je cherchais.
j. Quel malheur!

CHAPTER 16

Needs and Desires

In this chapter you will learn:

Talking About Needs

Anne's French university has a study abroad program, and Anne can earn credits toward her master's degree by studying at an American university for a year. She is going over the information she received and discussing it with her mother.

TRACK 45

ANNE: Bon, avant de prendre certaines décisions, il va falloir que je comprenne tous les renseignements qu'on m'a envoyés.

Well, before making certain decisions, I will have to understand all the information they sent me.

MAMAN: Ils sont en français ou en anglais?

Is it in French or in English?

ANNE: Pour la plupart, c'est en français, mais, tu sais, notre système d'éducation est totalement différent du système américain.

For the most part, it's in French, but, you know, our educational system is totally different from the American system.

MAMAN: Tu n'as pas discuté avec tes profs d'anglais ce que tu vas étudier?

Haven't you discussed what you are going to study with your English professors?

ANNE: Si, si. Mais il y a par exemple des fiches à remplir en anglais et je ne suis pas toujours sûre de savoir la signification de certains mots.

Yes, I have. But, for example, there are forms to fill out in English, and I'm not always sure I know the meaning of certain words.

MAMAN: Eh bien, cherche dans le dictionnaire!

Well, look in the dictionary!

ANNE: Les explications du dictionnaire ne sont pas toujours suffisantes, maman. Il faut connaître le contexte culturel.

The explanations in the dictionary aren't always sufficient, Mom. You have to know the cultural context.

MAMAN: Il faudrait que tu fasses une liste de questions et que tu ailles voir tes profs.

You should make a list of questions and go see your professors.

ANNE: Oui, mais il faut que je sache d'abord ce que je dois éclaircir et quelles questions je dois poser!

Yes, but first I must know what I have to clarify and what questions I need to ask!

MAMAN: Eh bien, je pense que tu dois d'abord savoir où tu vas loger, sur le campus ou en dehors, et ensuite quels cours tu vas suivre. Finalement tu dois savoir où et comment tu vas aller aux cours.

Well, I think that you must first know where you are going to live, on campus or off, and then what classes you're going to take. Finally, you need to know where and how you'll get to class.

ANNE: Je dois remplir ce formulaire pour obtenir un studio sur le campus dans une résidence pour étudiants étrangers.

I have to fill out this form to get a studio apartment on campus in a residence for foreign students.

MAMAN: Eh bien, voilà, remplis-la! — *Well then, fill it out!*

ANNE: Oui, mais on dit qu'un logement n'est pas garanti, et que je n'aurai la réponse qu'en mai. — *Yes, but it says that lodging is not guaranteed, and that I will not get an answer 'til May.*

MAMAN: Ah. Ça, c'est un problème. — *Oh, that is a problem.*

ANNE: Oui, il y a aussi une liste d'immeubles avec des studios à louer juste en dehors du campus. — *Yes, there is also a list of buildings with studios to rent just off campus.*

MAMAN: Pourrais-tu obtenir une liste d'étudiants français qui cherchent un logement pour l'année comme toi? — *Could you get a list of French students who are looking for lodging for the year like you?*

ANNE: Oui, mais si je loge avec des Français, je serai tentée de parler français au lieu de parler anglais. — *Yes, but if I room with French people, I will be tempted to speak French instead of speaking English.*

Expressing Necessity, Possibility, and Uncertainty

We can express necessity, possibility, and uncertainty in different ways.

USING DEVOIR, FALLOIR, OR POUVOIR WITH AN INFINITIVE

For example, we can use verbs such as **devoir**, **falloir**, or **pouvoir** followed by an infinitive.

You have already seen how to use the verb **devoir** (*to have to / must*) and an infinitive to express obligation.

Je **dois partir**.	*I have to / must leave.*
Anne **doit étudier**.	*Anne must study.*

You have also learned how to use **il faut** + *infinitive* to express *it is necessary* (*for someone to do something*). However, this structure forces interpretation on the part of the listener as to *who* is obliged to accomplish the action. Context clues can help.

Suzanne, **il faut** partir!	*Suzanne, **you/we** have to leave.*
Anne, **il faudrait** remplir le formulaire!	*Anne, **you** should fill out the form!*

French Higher Education

The only way to access higher education in France is to pass the **baccalauréat** exam at the end of high school (**le lycée**). There are a number of tracks, such as Science, Math and Physics, Literature, and Technology, which prepare students for the **baccalauréat** exams (also called **le bac**) corresponding to the respective tracks.

There are many public universities in France, generally named after the big cities where they are located. Although the French higher education system is currently undergoing reform, it is still relatively rigid. Students usually have few course options once they enroll in a particular degree program, and it is extremely difficult to change majors during one's undergraduate studies.

French higher education is funded by the state, and health insurance is free up to the age of twenty-five. Therefore, with school fees generally under 1000 euros a year, students are responsible only for their books and living costs. It is not rare for students to continue living with their parents until they complete their studies at the nearest university; this allows them to graduate debt-free from the university system.

Some prestigious French universities require a **concours d'entrée** (*entrance exam*) in addition to the **baccalauréat** diploma. These specialized programs are called **Grandes Écoles** and are very competitive. **L'École Polytechnique**, for instance, is one of the most prominent engineering schools in the world.

Similarly, to express a *possibility* or an *uncertainty*, you may use a conjugated form followed by an infinitive, as in the following examples. (This is done when the subject of the conjugated verb is also the subject of the infinitive.)

Anne **peut demander** des conseils à ses profs.	*Anne can ask advice from her professors.*
Elle **n'est pas sûre de trouver** un studio sur le campus.	*She is not sure she'll find a studio apartment on campus.*
Sa maman **pourra** peut-être **l'aider à prendre** des décisions.	*Her mom may be able to help her make some decisions.*

USING IMPERSONAL EXPRESSIONS

Now see how we express necessity, possibility, or uncertainty using impersonal expressions, such as **il faut que/qu'** (*it is necessary that*). In the examples below,

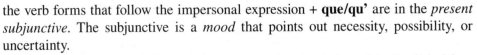

the verb forms that follow the impersonal expression + **que/qu'** are in the *present subjunctive*. The subjunctive is a *mood* that points out necessity, possibility, or uncertainty.

Note that literal translations of this structure can be awkward in English. More natural equivalents are shown in parentheses.

Il faut qu'Anne **étudie** beaucoup de renseignements.	*It is necessary that Anne (Anne must) study many pieces of information.*
Il se peut qu'elle **demande** des conseils à ses profs.	*It is possible that she will ask advice (She may ask advice) from her professors.*
Il n'est pas certain qu'elle **trouve** un studio sur le campus.	*It is not certain that she will find (She may not find) a studio apartment on campus.*
Il faut que sa mère l'**aide**.	*It is necessary that her mom (Her mom must) help her.*

Here are several other impersonal expressions of necessity, possibility, and uncertainty followed by the subjunctive:

Il est impératif que/qu'	*It is imperative that*	Il n'est pas probable que/qu'	*It is not probable that*
Il est nécessaire que/qu'	*It is necessary that*	Il n'est pas sûr que/qu'	*It is not sure that*
Il est possible que/qu'	*It is possible that*	Il semble que/qu'	*It seems that*

USING THE SUBJUNCTIVE MOOD

The subjunctive mood must be used in the clause following impersonal expressions + **que/qu'** that convey necessity, possibility, and uncertainty. There are two tenses in the subjunctive mood: present and past. The *present subjunctive* is used whenever the action of the verb is in the present or future.

The conjugation of regular **-er** verbs in the present subjunctive is simple. Don't forget that **-er** verbs are the most common French verbs. Present tense indicative and present tense subjunctive forms of regular **-er** verbs are the *same*, except in the **nous** and **vous** forms. Compare the present indicative and present subjunctive conjugations of the verb **parler** (*to speak*).

Present Indicative	Present Subjunctive
je parle	je parle
tu parles	tu parles
il/elle/on parle	il/elle/on parle
nous parl**ons**	nous parl**ions**
vous parl**ez**	vous parl**iez**
ils/elles parlent	ils/elles parlent

For other groups of verbs, the present subjunctive stem is derived from the **ils/elles** (*they*) form of the present indicative (minus the **-ent** ending). Look at these examples:

Infinitive	ils/elles **Form /** Present Indicative	Present Subjunctive Stem
finir (*to finish*)	finissent	**finiss-**
vendre (*to sell*)	vendent	**vend-**
mettre (*to put / to put on*)	mettent	**mett-**

The present subjunctive endings are **-e**, **-es**, **-e**, **-ions**, **-iez**, **-ent**. Note that these are the same as the present indicative endings, except for **-ions** and **-iez** (**nous** and **vous** forms).

Look at the present subjunctive conjugations of **finir** (*to finish*), a regular **-ir** verb, **vendre** (*to sell*), a regular **-re** verb, and **mettre** (*to put / to put on*), an irregular verb in the indicative. Note the verb stems in boldface.

que je **finiss**e	que je **vend**e	que je **mett**e
que tu **finiss**es	que tu **vend**es	que tu **mett**es
qu'il/elle/on **finiss**e	qu'il/elle/on **vend**e	qu'il/elle/on **mett**e
que nous **finiss**ions	que nous **vend**ions	que nous **mett**ions
que vous **finiss**iez	que vous **vend**iez	que vous **mett**iez
qu'ils/elles **finiss**ent	qu'ils/elles **vend**ent	qu'ils/elles **mett**ent

Oral Practice 16-1

 TRACK 46

A. Je dois. Starting with **Je dois...** , state that you must do the following activities. Say each one aloud, and then verify your answer by listening to your CD.

1. sleep (**dormir**)

2. eat (**manger**)

3. go to work (**aller au travail**)

4. go home (**rentrer**)

5. rest (**me reposer**)

B. Chéri(e), il faut! Pretend you are telling your sweetheart (**chéri[e]**) that he/she must do the following things. Starting with **Chéri(e), il faut...** say each one aloud, then verify your answer by listening to your CD.

1. prepare dinner (**préparer le dîner**)

2. set the table (**mettre la table**)

3. take out the napkins (**sortir les serviettes**)

4. turn the TV off (**fermer la télé**)

5. serve dinner (**servir le dîner**)

C. Il se peut! State a list of possibilities for your future, starting each sentence with **Il se peut que je/j'**. Say each one aloud, then verify your answer by listening to your CD.

1. studying in France (**étudier en France**)

2. staying on a campus (**rester sur un campus**)

3. sharing a room (**partager une chambre**)

4. improving my French (**perfectionner mon français**)

5. lose my American accent (**perdre mon accent américain**)

6. finishing my studies over there (**terminer mes études là-bas**)

Talking About Desires

Anne and her mom continue discussing Anne's needs when she starts her coursework in the United States. Mom worries about how Anne will get to class every day.

 TRACK 47

MAMAN: Dis, Anne! Si tu louais un studio en dehors du campus, est-ce que tu pourrais aller aux cours en bus?

Say, Ann! If you rented a studio off campus, would you be able to go to class by bus?

ANNE: Aux États-Unis, on n'utilise pas les transports en commun autant que chez nous.

In the United States, they don't use public transportation as much as we do.

MAMAN: Ah oui. Tout le monde conduit là-bas. Est-ce qu'il vaudrait mieux que tu achètes une bicyclette?

Oh yes. Everybody drives over there. Would it be better if you bought a bike?

ANNE: En plus, à Miami, il fait toujours chaud, maman. Alors, attendre le bus dans la chaleur humide, ce ne serait pas drôle.

Plus, in Miami, it's always hot. So, waiting for a bus in the humid heat, that wouldn't be fun.

MAMAN: Eh bien, tu vas te trouver dans un pays dont tu ne connais pas grand-chose et aussi dans un climat tropical.

Well, you're going to find yourself in a country you don't know much about and also in a tropical climate.

ANNE: Il faudrait peut-être que je fasse mon permis de conduire avant de partir.

Maybe I should get my driver's license before leaving.

MAMAN: Est-ce qu'il n'est pas plus facile d'obtenir un permis de conduire là-bas?

Isn't it easier to get a driver's license over there?

ANNE: Je ne suis pas sûre que ce soit plus facile. Mais c'est un autre système, plus flexible, c'est vrai. En tout cas, je voudrais bien pouvoir conduire.

I am not sure it's easier. But it's a different system, more flexible, that's true. At any rate, I'd like to be able to drive.

MAMAN: Je préfère que tu ailles au cours à pied ou en vélo.

I prefer that you go to class on foot or by bike.

ANNE: Oui, évidemment. Je rêvais!

Yes, of course. I was dreaming!

MAMAN: Écoute, Anne, j'ai vu un documentaire dans lequel les étudiants américains se déplaçaient en roller et en skate.

Listen, Ann, I saw a documentary where American students got around on rollerblades and skates.

ANNE: Ça, c'est super, maman, pourvu qu'il n'y ait ni carrefours ni grandes routes à traverser!

That's great, mom, provided there aren't any intersections or big roads to cross!

MAMAN: Je voudrais vraiment que tu sois mieux renseignée, Anne!

I would really like you to be better informed, Anne!

Obtaining a Driver's License in France

The countries of the European Union will soon institute a common driver's license for all their citizens. This should take effect toward the end of 2012. In France, the current driver's license examination consists of two parts: the written exam (**le code de la route**) and a road test (**l'épreuve pratique**). To prepare for the exam, people take classes in an accredited driving school. This is relatively expensive because the average person requires twenty to thirty hours of class. After successfully passing the exam, new drivers enter a probationary period during which they must take extra classes if they lose any "points." Unlike the American system, the driver's license for an adult driver in France is initially issued with twelve points. Losing all one's points means losing one's license. Adolescents may start driving at the age of sixteen under the supervision of an adult, as long as they attend a driving school and meet certain requirements. Their probationary permit is issued with only six points.

Expressing Desires Using the Present Subjunctive

You have already seen how people express personal wishes and desires by using a conjugated verb followed by an infinitive. Review with these examples:

Il **aimerait devenir** ingénieur.	*He would like to become an engineer.*
Nous **désirons partir** en vacances.	*We would like to leave on vacation.*
Je **voudrais voyager**.	*I would like to travel.*

However, whenever a person expresses a desire that relates to the present or future of *another person*, the present subjunctive is likely to be used. Look at the following examples, noting the more natural English translation of the French clause containing the subjunctive.

Il aimerait **que je sois** avec lui.	*He would like me to be with him.*
Je voudrais **que tu aies** plus de patience.	*I would like you to have more patience.*
Nous désirons **que vous veniez**.	*We would like you to come.*
Ils veulent **qu'on fasse** attention.	*They want us to pay attention.*
J'ai envie **qu'on prenne** le train.	*I would like us to take the train.*

Ils souhaitent **qu'elle aille** au Québec. *They would like her to go to Québec.*

Elle préfère **que nous sachions** le *She prefers that we know*
français. *French.*

Some verbs in the present subjunctive have *irregular* stems (that is, the stems are not derived from the **ils/elles** form of the present indicative); other verbs have unpredictably irregular conjugations. These must be memorized. Here are some frequently used verbs with irregular stems in the subjunctive:

faire (*to do*)	**savoir** (*to know*)
que je **fasse**	que je **sach**e
que tu **fasses**	que tu **sach**es
qu'il/elle/on **fasse**	qu'il/elle/on **sach**e
que nous **fass**ions	que nous **sach**ions
que vous **fass**iez	que vous **sach**iez
qu'ils/elles **fass**ent	qu'ils/elles **sach**ent

The following frequently used verbs also have irregular stems in the present subjunctive. In addition, the stems of this group change in the **nous** and **vous** forms.

aller (*to go*)	**prendre** (*to take*)	**venir** (*to come*)
que j'**aille**	que je **prenne**	que je **vienn**e
que tu **ailles**	que tu **prenn**es	que tu **vienn**es
qu'il/elle/on **aille**	qu'il/elle/on **prenne**	qu'il/elle/on **vienn**e
que nous **all**ions	que nous **pren**ions	que nous **ven**ions
que vous **all**iez	que vous **pren**iez	que vous **ven**iez
qu'ils/elles **aill**ent	qu'ils/elles **prenn**ent	qu'ils/elles **vienn**ent

The following common verbs have very irregular conjugations in the subjunctive. It is best to memorize them.

avoir (*to have*)	**être** (*to be*)
que j'**aie**	que je **sois**
que tu **aies**	que tu **sois**
qu'il/elle/on **ait**	qu'il/elle **soit**
que nous **ayons**	que nous **soyons**
que vous **ayez**	que vous **soyez**
qu'ils/elles **aient**	qu'ils/elles **soient**

Written Practice 16-1

Complete each sentence with the appropriate form from the choices given.

1. Elle désire que nous _____ nos devoirs. (fassions, soyons)

2. Vous voulez qu'ils _____ leurs études. (aillent, finissent)

3. Moi, j'aimerais qu'il _____ son examen. (réussisse, vende)

4. Ils souhaitent que les enfants _____ gentils. (aient, soient)

5. Tu as envie qu'on _____ la vérité. (soit, sache)

6. Elle voudrait que je/j' _____ le bus. (aie, prenne)

7. Il vaudrait mieux que tu _____ en Suisse. (aies, ailles)

8. Je veux que vous _____ le français. (appreniez, veniez)

Enriching, Clarifying, and Refining Communication

The message conveyed by a speaker is made clearer when organized thoughts are communicated with precise language. Clarity can be achieved by the use of accurate vocabulary and structures. It can also be enhanced by the right choice of transitional words.

TRANSITIONAL AND LINKING WORDS

One way to enrich and refine communication is to organize and link sentences using transitional or linking words. Here are some commonly used coordinating conjunctions along with sentences that use them:

et	*and*	mais	*but*
ou	*or*	donc	*so/then*
ni... ni	*neither . . . nor*		

Je voudrais voyager **et** visiter d'autres. pays.	*I would like to travel and visit other countries.*
Elle veut que j'étudie le français **ou** l'espagnol.	*She wants me to study French or Spanish.*
Tu ne parles **ni** anglais **ni** français?	*You speak neither English nor French?*
Je ne parle pas très bien, **mais** j'essaie.	*I do not speak very well, but I try.*
Je prends des leçons, **donc** je fais des progrès.	*I'm taking lessons, so I'm making progress.*

Ideas within a sentence can also be linked by subordinating conjunctions. Look at the following sentences, noting that the conjunctions listed here are followed by a verb in the *indicative*:

parce que	*because*	pendant que	*while*	tandis que/ alors que	*while (expressing contrast)*

Moi, je faisais la cuisine **alors qu'**elle, elle lisait.

*I was doing the cooking **while** she was reading.*

Nous avons remercié la serveuse **parce qu'**elle était si serviable.

*We thanked the waitress **because** she was so helpful.*

Now look at the following conjunctions and example sentences, noting that these conjunctions are always followed by a verb in the *subjunctive* mood.

avant que	*before*	pour que / afin que	*so that*
bien que / malgré que	*although*	pourvu que	*provided that*
jusqu'à ce que	*until*	sans que	*without*

Je resterai **pourvu que** tu fasses le dîner.

I will stay, provided you make dinner.

Elle lui envoie son numéro par mail **pour qu'**il l'ait dans son mobile.

She e-mails him her number so that he will have it in his cell phone.

Nous insisterons **jusqu'à ce qu'**il vienne.

We will insist until he comes.

Il réussit toujours **bien qu'**il n'étudie jamais.

He always passes although he never studies.

Written Practice 16-2

Match the two ideas that complete each other best, and write the letter of the completion on the line provided.

_____ 1.	Attends...	a.	pendant que vous regardiez la télé.
_____ 2.	Rentrons...	b.	donc vous n'allez pas au travail.
_____ 3.	Je parle toujours anglais...	c.	et visiter des pays étrangers.
_____ 4.	Nous faisions nos devoirs...	d.	jusqu' à ce que j'arrive.
_____ 5.	Elles voulaient voyager...	e.	parce que c'est ma langue préférée.
_____ 6.	Vous ne désirez...	f.	mais nous essayons de communiquer.

        7. Vous êtes en vacances...   g. avant qu'il ne pleuve.

        8. Nous ne parlons pas bien   h. ni café ni thé?
             le français...

TRANSITIONAL WORDS IN REPLIES

You may reply to a person's comments by pointing out a contrast or by objecting, disagreeing, agreeing, or expressing your own point of view. Look at the sentence examples below featuring the adverbs and adverbial phrases listed here:

bien sûr	*of course*	malgré tout	*in spite of it all*
cependant	*however*	naturellement	*naturally*
certainement	*certainly*	pourtant	*yet*
en effet	*indeed*	sinon	*otherwise*
en fait	*in fact*	sûrement	*surely*

> Tu dis qu'il est absent. **Pourtant** je l'ai vu.
>
> *You say he's absent. And yet I saw him.*

> Viens vite! **Sinon** tu vas rater le bus.
>
> *Come quickly! Otherwise you'll miss the bus.*

> **Certainement**, nous serons là!
>
> *Certainly, we will be there!*

The verbs **espérer** (*to hope*), **croire** (*to think/believe*), and **penser** (*to think*) can also be used to make transitional replies. Look at the following exchanges featuring these verbs:

> Tu vas loger sur le campus? —Je **crois que** oui.
>
> *Are you going to live on campus? —I think so.*

> Tu auras un camarade de chambre? —Je **pense que** non.
>
> *Will you have a roommate? —I don't think so.*

> La chambre sera petite? —J'**espère que** non.
>
> *Will the room be small? —I hope not.*

Espérer is never followed by the subjunctive.

> Nous **espérons qu'il trouvera** un emploi.   *We hope he'll find a job.*

Croire and **penser** are generally followed by a verb in the *indicative*. Look at these examples:

> Je crois **qu'il va** pleuvoir.   *I think (that) it is going to rain*

> Je pense **que nous sommes arrivés**.   *I think (that) we've arrived.*

However, when **croire** and **penser** are in the inverted interrogative form, they are often followed by a verb in the *subjunctive*. From the speaker's perspective, there is a higher degree of uncertainty about the outcome.

Crois-tu que je puisse le faire?	*Do you believe (that) I can do it?*
Pensez-vous qu'ils soient à l'heure?	*Do you think (that) they will be on time?*

Croire and **penser** may be followed by a verb in the subjunctive when they are negative. But negative **croire** and **penser** may also be followed by the indicative. The speaker's choice is dictated by his/her feeling of certainty (indicative) or uncertainty (subjunctive) about the outcome.

Je ne crois pas **que tu réussiras**.	*I don't believe (that) you will succeed.*
Je ne crois pas **que tu réussisses...**	*I don't think (that) you will succeed . . .*

Oral Practice 16-2

TRACK 48

Listen to the question on your CD, pause the CD, and answer according to the cue in parentheses. Listen to the answers on the CD.

1. Est-ce que vous allez venir au cinéma avec nous?
   —(*Certainly!*)   Certainement!

2. Venez immédiatement! —(*Yet*) nous avons le temps!   Pourtant

3. Vous êtes occupé(e)? —Oui, (*but*) j'ai envie de sortir.   mais

4. Votre cours est rigoureux? —(*Indeed!*)   En effet!

5. Ce n'est pas trop difficile? —Oh! (*I think that*) je   Je pense / Je
   réussirai.   crois que

6. Vous avez une chambre sur le campus? —(*I think so.*)   Je pense que /
                                                                 Je crois que oui.

Chapter Practice 16

A. Nécessité et possibilité. Use **devoir**, **falloir**, or **pouvoir** as indicated to complete each sentence.

1. Il _____ comprendre les renseignements. (falloir)

2. Nous _____ remplir ce formulaire. (devoir)

3. Tu _____ l'envoyer avant le 30 mars. (devoir)

4. Il _____ respecter la date limite. (falloir)

5. Tu _____ recevoir une réponse en mai. (pouvoir)

B. Les besoins et les doutes d'Anne. Complete each of the following sentences with the present subjunctive of the verb in parentheses.

1. Il faut qu'Anne _____ les renseignements. (comprendre)

2. Il faut aussi qu'elle _____ un formulaire. (remplir)

3. Il faudrait qu'elle _____ ce travail le 30 mars. (finir)

4. Il faudra qu'elle _____ la date limite. (respecter)

5. Il se peut qu'elle _____ la réponse en mai. (savoir)

6. Elle n'est pas sûre que la réponse _____ positive. (être)

C. Les désirs et les souhaits d'Anne. Select the appropriate word from the list provided to complete the following sentences.

avoir / étudier / passer / pense / permette / soit

1. Anne espère _____ aux États-Unis.

2. Elle veut _____ une année là-bas.

3. Elle voudrait que sa mère lui _____ de conduire.

4. Elle souhaite aussi que sa chambre _____ sur le campus.

5. Elle voudrait surtout _____ beaucoup d'amis américains.

6. Sa mère _____ qu'Anne doit être mieux informée.

D. Les transitions. In the following passage, fill in the blanks with transition words from the list below.

donc / et / je crois / mais / ni / en effet

Cette année, je voudrais finir mes études (1) _____ passer le baccalauréat. Je ne voudrais ni travailler (2) _____ continuer mes études. Je préfere aller en vacances pour quelques mois. (3) _____ il me faudra un peu d'argent pour payer mes dépenses. (4) _____, les vacances coûtent cher! (5) _____ il faudra que je

travaille pendant mes études et avant le baccalauréat! Est-ce possible?
(6) _____ que non. Zut!

CHAPTER QUIZ 16

TRACK 49

Play Anne's role in the following dialogue between her and her mother. For questions 1–5, find the appropriate answer among choices a–e. For questions 6–10, find the appropriate answer among choices f–j. Say the response aloud, and check it on your CD. You will also find the answers in the Answer Key.

1. Pourquoi es-tu si stressée, Anne?

2. Mais quelle est la date limite, Anne?

3. Ah oui, tu dois finir ça rapidement.

4. Oui, bien sûr, tu veux que je mette des renseignements généraux sur ce formulaire?

5. Je pense que oui. Ça ne devrait pas être trop difficile.

   a. En effet, maman. Tu peux m'aider?

   b. Merci maman. Tu crois qu'il est possible que je sois reçue?

   c. Maman, il faut que je finisse de remplir tous ces formulaires!

   d. Oui, vas-y, maman! Tu crois que tu peux aussi m'organiser ce dossier?

   e. L'université veut tous mes documents avant le premier avril.

6. Naturellement, Anne! Tu iras aux États-Unis, tu verras!

7. Il faudra que tu sois patiente et que tu attendes la réponse.

8. Je sais, Anne. Pourtant c'est une qualité nécessaire dans la vie.

9. Tu pourrais peut-être téléphoner à l'université pour obtenir une réponse plus rapide.

10. Espérons que oui. Ce serait super!

   f. Ce sera super pourvu que la réponse soit positive!

   g. Attendre jusqu'à ce que cette lettre arrive le 30 mai, oh là là!

   h. La patience n'est pas une de mes qualités.

   i. Tu crois qu'on me répondra au téléphone?

   j. Tu es si sûre, maman. Mais moi, je voudrais savoir tout de suite.

A. La famille Sarclos (*The Sarclos family*). Choose the most logical completion for each sentence, and write the corresponding letter in the space provided.

1. Il y a dix ans, la famille Sarclos passait toujours les _____ d'été à la mer.

   a. vacances   b. hôtels

2. Ils restaient dans un petit hôtel à _____ , sur la Côte d'Azur.

   a. France   b. Nice

3. Puis, il y a cinq ans, M. Sarclos _____ d'acheter une petite maison dans les Alpes en Provence (les Hautes-Alpes).

   a. décidait   b. a décidé

4. _____ il faut savoir, c'est que la Provence a des plages et des montagnes.

   a. Ce qui   b. Ce qu'

5. _____ Provence, on peut faire des sports d'hiver et des sports d'été.

   a. À   b. En

6. _____ ce temps, toute la famille Sarclos va passer des vacances de neige dans les Alpes.

   a. Depuis   b. Alors

7. Ils y _____ Noël l'an dernier.

   a. ont fêté   b. fêtaient

8. Si M. Sarclos avait pu, il _____ cette maison de vacances plus tôt.

   a. avait acheté   b. aurait acheté

9. Il regrette de ne pas avoir eu assez d'argent pour le faire. C'est _____ .

   a. dommage   b. tant mieux

10. _____ est bien, c'est que maintenant les Sarclos ont des vacances en famille deux fois par an.

   a. Ce qui   b. Ce que

B. Le rêve de Nicolas (*Nicolas's dream*). Choose the most logical completion for each sentence, and write the corresponding letter in the blank space. Then listen to the dialogue on your CD.

🔘 **TRACK 50**

MME SARCLOS: Alors, Nicolas, (11) _____ plus tard dans la vie?

a. qu'est-ce que tu veux faire   b. ce qui te plaît

NICOLAS: Je veux (12) _____ manager de restaurant.

a. apprendre   b. devenir

MME SARCLOS: Ah oui? Pourquoi? (13) _____ faire des études pour ça aussi, tu sais.

a. Il faut   b. Il obtient

NICOLAS: Je (14) _____ bien aller à l'école et apprendre des tas de choses.

a. veux   b. tiens

MME SARCLOS: Mais (15) _____ dans les carrières de restaurant?

a. qu'est-ce que   b. qu'est-ce qui te plaît

NICOLAS: Les managers ne travaillent pas beaucoup. (16) _____ travailler les employés.

a. Ils font   b. Ils ont

MME SARCLOS: Je crois que (17) _____ , Nicolas. Ils doivent travailler pendant les fêtes, tu sais.

a. tu te fâches   b. tu te trompes

NICOLAS: Oui, mais ils peuvent manger tout ce qu'ils (18) _____ tous les jours.

a. veut   b. veulent

MME SARCLOS: Oh! Que tu aimes (19) _____ les bons plats, toi!

a. mal   b. bien

NICOLAS: Oui. Si je ne deviens pas manager, je (20) _____ chef!

a. serai   b. pourrai

C. Comprenez-vous? (*Do you understand?*) Listen to the following dialogue, then translate it into English, and check your answers in the Answer Key. Finally, listen to the dialogue on your CD.

🔘 **TRACK 51**

21. Bonjour, Monsieur. Veuillez entrer.

22. Bonjour, Madame. Je vous remercie de m'avoir accordé cette interview.

23. Je vous assure que votre dossier était très impressionnant!

24. Je suis ravi que vous soyez intéressée, Madame.

25. Vous êtes très apprécié de vos collègues. Je suis sure que vous êtes un excellent candidat.

FINAL EXAM

Circle the letter of the word or phrase that best completes each sentence.

1. Dis, chéri, si on _____ à l'exposition?
   a. aller   b. allait   c. ira

2. C'est _____ , ce restaurant célèbre?
   a. quand   b. qui   c. où

3. Allez _____ ! C'est à dix minutes d'ici.
   a. tout droit   b. pardon   c. merci

4. Bonjour, Marie. Enchanté de faire ta _____ .
   a. sœur   b. famille   c. connaissance

5. Tu es la cousine _____ Cécile?
   a. chez   b. de   c. pour

6. Au revoir, Marie. Je _____ te revoir bientôt.
   a. cherche   b. voudrais   c. parle

7. Tu _____ canadienne ou française?
   a. es   b. êtes   c. est

8. Ces étudiantes sont _____ .
   a. américains   b. italiennes   c. française

9. Elles vont _____ France.
   a. à   b. en   c. au

10. Comment ça _____ ? —Très bien, merci.
    a. vont   b. allez   c. va

11. _____ est ton numéro de téléphone?
    a. Quels   b. Quel   c. Quelle

12. Invite Jean-Luc! Il est très _____ .
    a. arrogant   b. petit   c. sympa

13. Est-ce qu'il _____ , ton père?
    a. dort   b. va   c. fait

14. Ma mère est _____ .
    a. grand   b. joli   c. généreuse

15. Elle défend des clients. Elle est _____ .
    a. avocate   b. ingénieur   c. médecin

257

16. Ses films sont connus. C'est une _____ française.

    a. danseuse   b. chanteuse   c. actrice

17. Il _____ froid aujourd'hui et il neige.

    a. est   b. a   c. fait

18. Ce film est super! Il _____ plaît beaucoup.

    a. se   b. me   c. moi

19. Je veux aller au cinéma avec _____ .

    a. toi   b. te   c. tu

20. Mes copains _____ les sports.

    a. adores   b. adorons   c. adorent

21. Ils vont _____ au stade cet après-midi.

    a. partent   b. partir   c. partez

22. Marc fait des études de/d' _____ . Il veut être programmeur.

    a. informatique   b. journalisme   c. lettres

23. Il doit étudier ce soir parce qu'il a un examen _____ .

    a. ce matin   b. hier   c. demain

24. C'est urgent! Fais ce travail _____ !

    a. le mois prochain   b. après-demain   c. tout de suite

25. Quand il fait beau, ma famille fait _____ au parc.

    a. un pique-nique   b. des achats   c. du ski

26. C'est un emploi normal. Je travaille _____ heures par semaine.

    a. dix   b. soixante   c. quarante

27. Le vol direct de Floride en France dure environ _____ heures.

    a. neuf   b. quinze   c. quatre

28. Tu as _____ ? Voilà une limonade.

    a. faim   b. soif   c. peur

29. Je pense que tu as _____ . Ce concert n'est pas bon du tout. Partons!

    a. raison   b. envie   c. besoin

30. Je/J' _____ toujours sommeil vers vingt-deux heures.

    a. ai   b. suis   c. fais

31. _____ ! Il y a un Stop au coin de la rue.

    a. Pars   b. Arrête   c. Sache

32. _____ attention, Christophe! Nous avons presque eu un accident.

    a. Sois   b. Fais   c. Observe

33. _____ d'omelettes, s'il te plaît. Commandons une pizza!

    a. Plus   b. Ni   c. Personne

34. Je ne veux _____ . Je n'ai pas faim ce soir.

    a. pas   b. rien   c. que

35. Oh! Je _____ ai ni chèque ni carte de crédit.

    a. pas   b. n'   c. plus

36. Il n'y a jamais _____ ici à six heures du matin.

    a. personne   b. touristes   c. quelque chose

37. Oh là là! Nous n'avons plus rien en banque. Nous devons _____ de l'argent.

    a. sauver   b. économiser   c. payer

38. Tu as envie de _____ un tour en vélo. Allons-y!

    a. prendre   b. partir   c. faire

39. Je suis trop fatigué. Je travaille _____ ce matin.

    a. avant   b. après   c. depuis

40. Où est _____ d'embarquement pour le vol 215?

    a. le départ   b. la porte   c. l'enregistrement

41. Regarde! Le vol est _____ . Il faut encore attendre.

    a. en avance   b. remis   c. arrivé

42. Ne prends pas _____ dans l'avion! Elle est trop grande.

    a. la valise   b. l'escale   c. la carte d'embarquement

43. Nous sommes au deuxième étage. Il faut _____ l'escalier pour aller au premier.

    a. perdre   b. monter   c. descendre

44. Tu es trop nerveuse, Sophie. Calme-_____ !

    a. te   b. tu   c. toi

45. Bon, d'accord! Je vais _____ reposer.

    a. te   b. me   c. nous

46. Nous sommes en retard. Dépêchons-_____ !

    a. vous   b. nous   c. se

47. J'ai mon passeport. Mais où est _____ ?

    a. le tien   b. la sienne   c. les miennes

48. Où sont _____ bagages, Monsieur?

    a. vos   b. tes   c. son

49. Je n'ai rien à _____ , Monsieur le douanier.

    a. chercher   b. acheter   c. déclarer

50. Pouvez-vous me/m' _____ demain matin?

    a. monter   b. réveiller   c. apporter

51. Je voudrais des _____ sur les hôtels dans cette ville.

    a. horaires   b. réservations   c. renseignements

52. _____ c'est la bonne route?

    a. Est   b. Est-ce que   c. Est-ce

53. _____ -vous un plan de la ville, Monsieur?

    a. Avoir   b. Avez   c. As

54. Il te faut _____ dans la salle de bains?

    a. quand   b. combien de temps   c. comment

55. Voilà _____ savon et une serviette.

    a. de la   b. des   c. du

56. Quand je mange _____ , je grossis.

    a. un peu   b. assez   c. trop

57. Mon père a _____ au bureau.

    a. son ordinateur   b. sa voiture   c. son vin

58. _____ je rentre dîner avec ma famille.

    a. Le matin   b. L'hiver   c. Le soir

59. Je me brosse les dents _____ le dîner.

    a. pendant   b. avant   c. après

60. Quelquefois les films à la télévision sont _____ ennuyeux!

    a. si   b. pas   c. comme ci
                                                           comme ça

⊙ TRACK 52

Now listen to the questions on your CD. Press pause after each question, and say the answer you think is the best for the question. Listen to the recording, and repeat. Then go to the next question and repeat the process.

61. a. avril trente-trois   b. le neuf avril   c. avril deux

62. a. À une heure dix.   b. Il est deux heures trois.   c. C'est samedi.

63. a. Le soir   b. À Paris   c. Canada

64. a. deux et demie   b. un kilo   c. dix grammes

65. a. Oui, j'ai le reçu.   b. Oui, je suis dans le salon d'essayage.   c. Oui, demain.

66. a. Oui, c'est la bonne taille.   b. Oui, c'est ma pointure.   c. Oui, elles me font mal.

67. a. Non, à l'école, elle ne faisait pas les devoirs.   b. Non, elle ne voyageait jamais.   c. Oui, elle ne faisait ni le ménage ni les devoirs.

68. a. Je vais en Chine.   b. Je fais du sport.   c. Je travaille lundi.

69. a. Oui, c'était la semaine de Thanksgiving.   b. Oui, depuis l'année dernière.   c. Oui, j'ai continué à travailler.

70. a. Je ne sais pas ce que tu veux.   b. Je me suis bien amusé(e).   c. Mal, parce qu'il a fait beau temps.

71.
a. Oui, j'y resterai deux mois.
b. Oui, il y a quelques jours.
c. Oui, je pars dans deux heures.

72.
a. On pourrait sortir au restaurant.
b. Non, je ne veux pas.
c. Oui, d'accord.

73.
a. Je crois que c'est bientôt.
b. Ce n'est pas au parc de la Villette?
c. Je ne connais pas du tout le chanteur.

74.
a. Oui, je comprends.
b. Je ne sais pas comment y aller.
c. Je serai probablement professeur.

75.
a. Je me suis amusé aujourd'hui.
b. Je ferai des découvertes scientifiques.
c. Hier soir je n'ai pas fait de rêves.

76.
a. Je voulais être cuisinier.
b. J'étais toujours content.
c. J'avais peur de tout.

77.
a. Oui, je veux écouter la musique.
b. Non, je ne veux pas dormir.
c. Non, merci. Je n'ai pas faim.

78.
a. Très bien, il fait toujours chaud dans les hôtels.
b. Excellent. J'ai toujours froid dans les hôtels.
c. Très bien, j'ai toujours sommeil.

79.
a. Oui, mon lit.
b. Oui, mes clefs.
c. Oui, mon nom.

80.
a. Oui, d'une couverture pour mon lit.
b. Oui, d'un serveur pour porter mes bagages.
c. Oui, d'un concierge pour me servir le dîner.

81. a. Je préfère prendre le taxi.
    b. C'est très loin d'ici; on peut aller à pied.
    c. Je n'aime pas les films d'horreur.

82. a. Un sandwich au jambon.
    b. De la soupe au poulet.
    c. Du pain et de la confiture, s'il vous plaît.

83. a. Au grenier.
    b. Au garage.
    c. Au salon.

84. a. Épatant! J'ai dormi.
    b. Excellent! Je suis parti avant la fin.
    c. Super! Le meilleur que j'ai vu.

85. a. Il faut que j'écrive un essai en anglais.
    b. J'ai fait du jogging.
    c. Il vaut mieux dormir comme moi.

86. a. Oui, pas mal.
    b. Mais si, je l'aime beaucoup!
    c. Donc tu ne l'aimes pas!

87. a. Ils font du français.
    b. Ils font un tour.
    c. Ils font du cheval.

88. a. Quand la piscine sera fermée.
    b. Dès qu'il fera beau.
    c. Pas au magasin.

89. a. Oui, ils sont vraiment en avance.
    b. Oui, tu as raison, ils sont à l'heure.
    c. Oui, ils sont un peu en retard.

90. a. Je t'assure que oui.
    b. En bus, je pense.
    c. Comment veux-tu que je sache?

91.
a. Vers dix-neuf heures.
b. Jamais.
c. Pendant deux heures.

92.
a. Tiens! Elle doit se fâcher.
b. Tiens! Elle doit se dépêcher.
c. Tiens! Elle doit avoir mangé.

93.
a. C'est possible. Elle a trop de cours à suivre.
b. Elle l'obtiendra si elle réussit à ses examens.
c. Peut-être si elle a des profs absents.

94.
a. Il a reçu une bourse
b. Il a eu une note.
c. Il a envoyé un formulaire.

95.
a. Bien sûr!
b. Plus rien!
c. Mais si!

96.
a. Oui, il est respecté et indulgent.
b. Je ne l'aime pas; il me fait peur.
c. Tu as tort; il donne des D à tout le monde.

97.
a. d'avoir étudié peu de français.
b. d'avoir un emploi qui me plaît.
c. d'être en forme.

98.
a. Je ne pourrais jamais avoir de cancer.
b. Je pourrais inventer une galaxie.
c. Je pourrais faire le tour du monde.

99.
a. Une nouvelle voiture.
b. Un professeur patient.
c. Des amis avares.

100.
a. J'espère qu'il est arrivé.
b. Il faut que je finisse cet examen.
c. D'accord. Je vais le faire.

ANSWER KEY

CHAPTER 1

Written Practice 1-1
1. visite   2. rapports   3. suave   4. l'étiquette

Chapter Quiz 1
1. Sophie loves art nouveau and jazz.
2. Rémi loves going to the restaurant.
3. The restaurant is called "Chez Antoine."
4. The chef won the Cordon Bleu prize.
5. Sophie suggests an apéritif / a cocktail.
6. Rémi suggests champagne.
7. At the restaurant, Rémi wants the beef bourguignon.
8. Sophie wants the quiche and a salad.
9. The maître d' is excellent.
10. Sophie's parents respect social étiquette.

CHAPTER 2

Written Practice 2-1
1. Elle   2. Ils   3. eux   4. Ils   5. elle   6. elle

Chapter Practice 2

Dialogue 1
Salut; va; bien; toi; Pas; demain

Dialogue 2
Bonjour; comment; comme; moi; Il; Oui

Chapter Quiz 2

1. Salut.   2. Bonjour, Monsieur.   3. Bonjour, Madame.   4.Bonjour, maman!
5. Bonjour, tout le monde!   6. Salut; Ça va   7. Bien; toi   8. Pas mal; Au revoir;
9. À demain

CHAPTER 3

Written Practice 3-1

1. C'est Laura. C'est la correspondante de Josiane. Elle est américaine.

2. C'est Guy. C'est le copain de Josiane. Il est français.

3. C'est Kevin. C'est le copain de Guy. Il est américain.

4. C'est M. Dupuis. C'est le professeur d'anglais. Il est anglais.

Written Practice 3-2

1. Josiane est grande, blonde et curieuse.

2. La dame est belle, calme et gentille.

3. Nick est jeune, sportif et ambitieux.

4. Le frère de Bruno est grand, blond et gentil/sympathique.

5. La maman de Bruno est petite, intelligente et vive. Elle a les cheveux noirs.

6. Rémi, le mari de Sophie, est beau et chanceux.

Chapter Practice 3

4-3-5-6-2-8-7-1-9-10

Chapter Quiz 3

1. Bien, merci.   2. Pascal   3. Oui, de San Francisco.   4. Pas très bien.   5. brune
6. Elle s'appelle Lisette.   7. marocain   8. Oui, il est sérieux.   9. canadienne
10. C'est Dubois.

CHAPTER 4

Written Practice 4-1

1. Il est fonctionnaire.   2. Elle est viticultrice.   3. Il est cuisinier.   4. Elle est
actrice.   5. Il est chanteur.   6. Elle est avocate.

Written Practice 4-2

1. fait un tour   2. plaît   3. font une promenade   4. assure   5. pense/espère
6. pense/espère

Chapter Practice 4

Dialogue 1

1. F   2. V   3. V   4. F

Dialogue 2
1. F   2. V   3. V   4. V
Dialogue 3
1. F   2. F   3. V   4. V
Chapter Quiz 4
1. fait   2. un pique-nique   3. travailler   4. serveuse   5. serveur   6. Demain
7. faire un tour   8. vont   9. pense   10. voudrait

CHAPTER 5

Oral Practice 5-1

1. Q: Pardon, Mademoiselle. Où est la station Saint-Michel, s'il vous plaît? /
   Pardon me, Miss. Where is the Saint-Michel station, please?

   A: À cinq minutes d'ici. Tout droit devant vous. / *Five minutes from here,
   straight ahead.*

2. Q: Pardon, Monsieur. La rue de Rivoli c'est tout droit? / *Pardon me, Sir.
   The rue de Rivoli, is that straight ahead?*

   A: Ah non. Retournez en arrière et c'est à gauche. / *Oh no. Go back, and it
   is on the left.*

3. Q: Pardon, Madame. Le Jardin du Luxembourg, c'est près d'ici? / *Pardon
   me, Madam. The Luxembourg Garden, is that near here?*

   A: Oui, c'est à trois rues d'ici à droite. / *Yes, it is three blocks from here on
   the right.*

4. Q: Pardon, Madame. Où est le grand magasin Le Printemps, s'il vous plaît?
   / *Pardon me, Madam. Where is the Le Printemps department store,
   please?*

   A: Il faut tourner à droite au coin, aller tout droit, et c'est à gauche. / *You
   have to turn right at the corner, go straight, and it is on the left.*

5. Q: Pardon, Monsieur. Où sont les toilettes, s'il vous plaît? / *Pardon me, Sir.
   Where are the restrooms, please?*

   A: Les voici! / *Here they are!*

Written Practice 5-1

1. Si on allait au cinéma?

2. Si on dansait?

3. Si nous visitions un monument historique?

4. Si tu cherchais les copains?

5. Si nous faisions une promenade en ville?

6. Si nous déjeunions au café?

Oral Practice 5-2

1. Oui, avec plaisir. À lundi.   2. Désolé(e). Je ne peux pas.   3. D'accord.
À samedi.

Chapter Practice 5

A. 1. e   2. d   3. a   4. c   5. b

B. 1. déjeunait   2. faisait   3. allait   4. regardait   5. visitait

C. 1. vendredi, le 1 juin   2. jeudi, le 19 août   3. mardi à seize heures quinze
   4. samedi vers huit heures   5. lundi, le 5 mai

Chapter Quiz 5

1. Pardon   2. Où   3. tout   4. c'est   5. faut   6. Merci   7. veux   8. Si
9. heure   10. Vers

Part One Test

14. Hi Johnny. How are you?

15. The chef is excellent in this French restaurant.

16. He makes superb dishes.

17. The special of the day is delicious today.

18. Would you like snails as an appetizer?

19. I adore exotic salads.

20. You like chicken and beef.

21. Shall we go to the classical music concert?

22. You love jazz, I know.

23. Parking is a problem in Paris.

24. There are a lot tourists.

25. Good, we are going home.

26. There is the taxi!

CHAPTER 6

Written Practice 6-1

A. 1. Elle n'est pas sympathique.   2. Nous n'avons plus de compte d'épargne.
   3. Ils ne sont jamais ici.   4. Je préfère ne pas aller au cinéma.
   5. Il n'invite personne.

B. 1. a/f   2. b/c/e   3. b/e   4. a/f   5. b/c/e   6. a/d

Oral Practice 6-3

1. Je fais du yoga.

2. Tu prends le petit déjeuner.

3. Ils font du sport.

4. Vous prenez / Nous prenons des notes.

5. On fait appel à la police.

6. Je prends le bus.

7. Non, je ne prends jamais de pot le matin.

8. Non, elle ne prend pas le train.

9. Non, ils ne font plus de ski dans les Alpes.

10. Non, je ne fais ni chinois ni arabe.

Chapter Practice 6

A. 4-3-1-5-2

B. 1. F   2. V   3. V   4. F   5. F   6. V

C. 1. Il voudrait faire des promenades à pied.   2. Il voudrait faire une croisière.   3. Il voudrait faire du vélo.   4. Il voudrait sortir au restaurant. 5. Il voudrait prendre le bus.

Chapter Quiz 6

1. Je voudrais faire du vélo.

2. Tu ne fais jamais de croisières.

3. Nous ne prenons ni le train ni le bus.

4. Je ne prends pas le petit déjeuner.

5. Plus de soda!

6. Prenons un pot!

7. Va au cinéma, John!

8. Je préfère ne pas sortir.

9. Il faut économiser six cents euros.

10. Je travaille depuis deux heures.

CHAPTER 7

Written Practice 7-1

1. c   2. e   3. f   4. d   5. a   6. b

Written Practice 7-2

1. Nous attendons l'avion.

2. Les passagers descendent.

3. Elle entend le steward / l'hôtesse.

4. Vous perdez votre carte d'embarquement.

5. Tu réponds.

6. Ils défendent de fumer.

Oral Practice 7-1

1. nous   2. nous   3. toi   4. toi   5. me   6. se   7. te/m'   8. t'

Written Practice 7-3

1. ma   2. Ta   3. tienne   4. tienne   5. nos   6. notre   7. nôtre   8. tes

Oral Practice 7-2

1. Les voici!   2. Voici un soda.   3. Les voilà derrière vous.   4. Voilà une serviette en papier!   5. Voici vos écouteurs!   6. La voilà!

Chapter Practice 7

D. 1. se fâche   2. me dépêche   3. nous lavons   4. sien   5. nôtres/miens.
   6. sienne

Chapter Quiz 7

1. f   2. g   3. e   4. i   5. c   6. j   7. b   8. a   9. d   10. h

CHAPTER 8

Written Practice 8-1

1. des   2. des   3. de la   4. un peu de   5. assez de   6. trop de   7. du   8. du
9. beaucoup de

Oral Practice 8-2

1. e   2. g   3. a   4. f   5. c   6. h   7. b   8. d

Chapter Practice 8

B. 1. C/a   2. A/f   3. H/b   4. E/h   5. B, G/e   6. F/d   7. D/c   8. G/g

C. 1. plus   2. moins   3. meilleur   4. mieux   5. le mieux   6. meilleur

D. 1. Oui.   2. Si.   3. Oui.   4. Oui.   5. Oui.   6. Si.

CHAPTER 9

Written Practice 9-1

1. S/M   2. S   3. S   4. S/M   5. S/M   6. S   7. S/M   8. S

Oral Practice 9-2

1. des   2. Ces   3. quelques   4. un   5. Ce   6. ces   7. les   8. les

Written Practice 9-2

1. BP   2. BC   3. BC   4. BP   5. BP   6. BC   7. BP   8. BC

Written Practice 9-3

1. finissons   2. rôtissent   3. choisis   4. remplit   5. veulent   6. pouvez
7. veux   8. peut

Written Practice 9-4

1. servons   2. sortent   3. sort   4. sert   5. sortez   6. sers

Chapter Practice 9

   A. un / ce / ci / de / Ces / quelques / voulez / en / les / kilo

   B. 1. choisis   2. rôtissons   3. servir   4. veut   5. peux   6. remplis

Chapter Quiz 9

1. PL   2. L   3. PL   4. L   5. L   6. PL   7. L   8. PL   9. PL   10. L

CHAPTER 10

Written Practice 10-1

   A. 1. Quel   2. Quelle   3. Quels   4. Quelles   5. Quelle   6. Quelles

   B. 1. Laquelle   2. Lequel   3. Lesquelles   4. Lesquels

Written Practice 10-2

1. me va   2. lui va   3. te vont   4. lui vont   5. leur vont

Written Practice 10-3

   A. 1. me   2. te   3. te   4. me   5. nous

   B. 1. l'   2. lui   3. l'   4. lui   5. les   6. lui   7. lui   8. le

Chapter Practice 10

   A. 1. c   2. h   3. f   4. b   5. a   6. i   7. d   8. j   9. g   10. e

   B. 1. Lequel   2. Laquelle   3. Quels   4. Quelle   5. Lequel

Chapter Quiz 10

1. marron   2. pointure   3. C'est   4. vont   5. plaisent   6. en solde   7. Quel
8. vous   9. carte de crédit   10. reçu

Part Two Test

   A. 1. a   2. b   3. b   4. b   5. a   6. a   7. b   8. a   9. b   10. a

   B. 11. F   12. F   13. V   14. V   15. V   16. V   17. F   18. F   19. V   20. F
      21. V   22. F   23. F   24. V   25. V

CHAPTER 11

Written Practice 11-1

1. avait   2. était   3. était   4. faisait   5. préparait   6. donnaient   7. s'amusaient
8. voulait

Chapter Practice 11

A. 1. J'allais à la plage.   2. Nous nagions tous les jours.   3. Mes cousins jouaient au ballon toute la journée.   4. Mon oncle pêchait tout le temps. 5. J'aimais les sardines.   6. Je passais tous les étés chez mes grands-parents.

B. 1. est allée   2. était   3. est arrivée   4. avait   5. a commencé   6. ont prononcé   7. se sont embrassés   8. se sont passées   9. a fait   10. se sont amusés   11. sont partis   12. est né

Chapter Quiz 11

1. était   2. est né   3. a préparé   4. avons donné   5. sont arrivés   6. avait
7. avons joué   8. nous sommes amusés   9. était   10. était

CHAPTER 12

Written Practice 12-1

1. e   2. h   3. a   4. j   5. i   6. b   7. c   8. d   9. f   10. g

Written Practice 12-2

1. y est   2. n'y vais pas   3. y est   4. y reste   5. n'y dîne pas   6. y vais   7. vas-y
8. Allons-y

Written Practice 12-3

1. a pris   2. a surpris   3. a pris   4. prennent   5. comprend   6. surpris
7. y compris   8. compris

Chapter Practice 12

A. 1. est   2. veut   3. s'est inscrite   4. a appris   5. comprend   6. était
7. faisait   8. est

Chapter Quiz 12

1. ce soir   2. y   3. étoiles   4. Allons-y   5. J'espère   6. la réceptionniste
7. Où   8. pourquoi   9. surprise   10. comprends

CHAPTER 13

Written Practice 13-1

1. irons   2. fera   3. sera   4. travaillera   5. deviendrai   6. pourrai
7. continuerons   8. marierons

Written Practice 13-2

1. Ce qui   2. Ce que   3. Ce que   4. Ce qui   5. Ce que   6. Ce qui

Chapter Practice 13

A. 1. irons   2. verra   3. pourrons   4. sera   5. mangerons

B. 1. voudrais   2. aimerait   3. préférerait   4. serions   5. aurions

C. 1. Dès que j'aurai mon passeport.   2. Je voudrais voyager en Afrique.
3. J'espère faire du bénévolat.   4. Ce que je voudrais faire, c'est apprendre
aux enfants à lire.   5. Je souhaite être programmeur mais je pourrais
enseigner aussi.   6. Non, heureux.

Chapter Quiz 13

1. devenir   2. voudrais   3. seras   4. Peut-être   5. Ce qui   6. serai
7. étudierai   8. devrais   9. Ce que   10. aimerions

CHAPTER 14

Written Practice 14-1

1. e   2. a   3. f   4. d   5. c   6. b

Oral Practice 14-1

1. resterons   2. aurez   3. feront   4. va   5. travaillez   6. irait   7. habiterait
8. écriraient

Written Practice 14-2

1. candidature   2. remplir   3. obtenir   4. demande   5. rédiger   6. respecter
7. documents   8. dossier

Written Practice 14-3

1. aimaient, s'inscriraient   2. était, apprendraient   3. avait, participeraient
4. avait, poseraient   5. avait, respecteraient

Written Practice 14-4

1. Il faut   2. Il faudrait   3. Il faudra   4. Il faudra   5. Il faudrait   6. Il faut

Chapter Practice 14

A. 1. e   2. d   3. a   4. f   5. b   6. c

B. 1. c   2. f   3. a   4. e   5. d   6. b

C. 1. Il faut faire   2. Il faut aller   3. Il faudrait appeler   4. Il faudra vivre
5. Il faut poser   6. Il faudra

Chapter Quiz 14

1. faut   2. finissez   3. remplir   4. dossier   5. recommandation   6. date limite
7. pour   8. ferais   9. devrais   10. voulez

CHAPTER 15

Written Practice 15-1

1. J'aurais fait ce voyage.

2. Mon ami serait venu avec moi.

3. Nous aurions acheté les billets d'avion tout de suite.

4. Je n'aurais pas attendu.

5. Mon ami aurait dû poser sa candidature.

6. Il aurait fallu le faire.

Written Practice 15-2

1. d   2. f   3. a   4. b   5. c   6. e

Chapter Practice 15

A. 1. That's too bad!   2. I thought (that) you would arrive soon.   3. The saleslady (whom) he is looking for is on break.   4. We think (that) it is time to leave.   5. They missed the train. Darn! How irritating that is!

B. 1. de partir   2. de décevoir   3. d'être   4. d'avoir fait   5. d'avoir été 6. d'être arrivé

C. 1. avais pu   2. avait fini   3. était parti   4. avions écouté   5. avaient téléphoné

D. 1. aurais répondu   2. aurait/oublié   3. aurions vu(e)   4. serais allé(e) 5. aurait fallu

E. 1. mal   2. déjà   3. sincèrement   4. facilement   5. furieusement

Chapter Quiz 15

1. h   2. f   3. j   4. a   5. i   6. b   7. c   8. d   9. e   10. g

CHAPTER 16

Written Practice 16-1

1. fassions   2. finissent   3. réussisse   4. soient   5. sache   6. je prenne 7. ailles   8. appreniez

Written Practice 16-2

1. d   2. g   3. e   4. a   5. c   6. h   7. b   8. f

Chapter Practice 16

A. 1. faut   2. devons   3. dois   4. faut   5. peux

B. 1. comprenne   2. remplisse   3. finisse   4. respecte   5. sache   6. soit

C. 1. étudier   2. passer   3. permette   4. soit   5. avoir   6. pense

D. 1. et   2. ni   3. Mais   4. En effet   5. Donc   6. Je crois

Chapter Quiz 16
1. c   2. e   3. a   4. d   5. b   6. j   7. h   8. g   9. i   10. f

Part Three Test
A. 1. a   2. b   3. b   4. b   5. b   6. a   7. a   8. b   9. a   10. a

B. 11. a   12. b   13. a   14. a   15. b   16. a   17. b   18. b   19. b   20. a

C. 21. Good day, Sir. Please come in.   22. Good day, Madam. Thank you for granting me this interview.   23. I assure you that your dossier was very impressive!   24. I'm delighted that you are interested, Madame.   25. You're very well liked by your colleagues. I'm sure you are an excellent candidate.

FINAL EXAM
1. b   2. c   3. a   4. c   5. b   6. b   7. a   8. b   9. b   10. c   11. b   12. c   13. a
14. c   15. a   16. c   17. c   18. b   19. a   20. c   21. b   22. a   23. c   24. c
25. a   26. c   27. a   28. b   29. a   30. a   31. b   32. b   33. a   34. b   35. b
36. a   37. b   38. c   39. c   40. b   41. b   42. a   43. c   44. c   45. b   46. b
47. a   48. a   49. c   50. b   51. c   52. b   53. b   54. b   55. c   56. c   57. a
58. c   59. c   60. a   61. b   62. b   63. b   64. b   65. a   66. b   67. a   68. b
69. a   70. b   71. b   72. a   73. b   74. c   75. b   76. a   77. a   78. a   79. b
80. a   81. a   82. c   83. b   84. c   85. a   86. b   87. a   88. b   89. c   90. a
91. a   92. b   93. b   94. a   95. a   96. b   97. a   98. c   99. a   100. b